CIVIL SOCIETY AND DEMOCRATIZATION

NORDIC INSTITUTE OF ASIAN STUDIES
MONOGRAPH SERIES

Civil Society and Democratization
Social Movements in Northeast Thailand

Somchai Phatharathananunth

Nordic Institute of Asian Studies
Monograph series 99
First published in 2006
Reprinted in 2007
by NIAS Press
NIAS – Nordic Institute of Asian Studies
Leifsgade 33, DK–2300 Copenhagen S, Denmark
tel: (+45) 3532 9501 • fax: (+45) 3532 9549
E–mail: books@nias.ku.dk • Website: www.niaspress.dk

British Library Cataloguing in Publication Data

Phatharathananunth, Somchai
  Civil society and democratization : social movements in
  northeast Thailand. - (NIAS monograph ; 99)
  1.Social movements - Thailand 2. Democratization - Thailand
  3. Civil society - Thailand 4.Thailand - Politics and
  government - 1988- 5.Thailand - Social conditions - 1986-
  I.Title
  303.484'09593'09051

  ISBN 978-87-91114-85-4 (pbk)

Typesetting by NIAS Press
Produced by SRM Production Services Sdn Bhd
Printed in Malaysia

Contents

Preface

This book, a study of the role of civil society in the democratization process, focuses on the experience of the Small Scale Farmers' Assembly of Isan (SSFAI), a major grassroots social movement in Thailand. Democratization has undoubtedly been the 'great transformation' of world politics in the twentieth century. It became one of the most pressing issues of academic research. The most influential work on democratization, known as the transition literature, was the collective study edited by O'Donnell, Schmitter and Whitehead (1986). The study, according to Gill, 'stimulated a whole literature on democratization' (Gill 2000: 46). The transition literature was an effort to synthesize the demise of authoritarian rule and the upsurge of democracy in the late twentieth century, which Huntington called the 'third wave' of democratization (Huntington 1991). It 'has conceptualized the course of regime change in terms of three phases: regime breakdown, democratic transition, and democratic consolidation' (Gill 2000: 8).

This school of thought emphasized the importance of political elites to democracy. It believed that democratization would succeed 'if elites can learn the "right" way to proceed' (Grugel 2002: 57). According to Huntington, 'negotiations and compromise among political elites were at the heart of democratization processes'. Elites, argues Huntington, 'bargained with each other, explicitly or implicitly, and worked out acceptable if not satisfying arrangements for the transition to democracy' (Huntington 1991: 165). And 'whether democracy in fact falters or is sustained will depend primarily on the extent to which political leaders wish to maintain it and are willing to pay the costs of doing so' (Huntington 1991: 279).

Because of its elitism discussed above, the 'transition literature' had a very narrow view of democracy. As Grugel has pointed out, democracy for this school of thought was 'visualized as a set of procedures for government negotiated by and between political leaders'. As a result, it 'separates democracy from its essential meaning as rule by the people and conceptualizes it principally as the establishment of a set of governing institutions' (Grugel 2002: 61). Although the transition literature referred to the 'resurrection of civil society'(O'Donnell and Schmitter 1986: 48), it rarely played any significant role in advancing democracy. Civil society was seen as a residual category. It was never seen as 'a concept that was allowed to engage with the elite focus to explore more fully the dynamics of transition' (Gill 2000: 59). On the contrary, it viewed the struggles of the popular masses as activities harmful to democracy, and to be avoided.

> It seems as if an almost docility and patience on the part of organized workers are needed for a democratic transformation to succeed. Here again it may be worth noting that the democratic system was solidified in Belgium, Sweden, France, and Great Britain only after organized workers were badly defeated in mass strikes and adopted a docile posture as a result. (Przeworski 1986: 63)

Przeworski's elite-ascendant view of democratization was echoed by Karl, who asserted that '*no* stable political democracy has resulted from regime transitions in which mass actors have gained control, even momentarily, over traditional ruling classes'. For Karl, 'the most frequently encountered types of transition, and the ones which have most often resulted in the implementation of a political democracy, are "transitions from above"' (Karl 1990: 8–9). Moreover, he also declared that democratic consolidation 'if it is to be successful, should require skills and commitments from leading actors' (Karl 1990: 17).

The top-down model of democratization of the transition literature, which emphasized elite, formal political institutions and the docility of the subordinate classes, was more or less similar to the Asian values argument proposed by conservative political leaders in Asia in the sense that both emphasized the importance of elites in society. According to the Asian values argument, 'the political leadership is ordained to handle the interests of the entire society', and the citizens had to sacrifice their civil and political rights for the sake of stability (Bruun and Jacobsen 2000: 3).

The present book challenges such perspectives. First, the elite-oriented approach, as Grugel has pointed out, ignored 'empirical evidence which points to the role of popular struggles in some transitions as the determining element in unleashing democratization in the first place' (Grugel 2000: 61). Second, even in cases where elites play major roles in democratic transitions, democratic deepening still needs popular participation, because formal political institutions set up by elites are unlikely to continue functioning democratically without popular control. It is popular struggle from below that is crucial for the dynamics of democratic progress in the post-authoritarian period. To illustrate the role of civil society in democratic deepening, this book will examine the struggle of the Small Scale Farmers' Assembly of Isan (SSFAI) from 1993 to 2002. Although civil society was crucial to democratization, it has long been a neglected area of inquiry among students of Thai politics. Most studies of Thai politics have been focused mainly on political history, on electoral politics and on key institutions such as the bureaucracy or the army. Only recently have political scientists begun to become interested in the political role of groups outside key institutions, such as business associations (Anek 1992). However, there are still few major works on Thai civil society organizations in the form of social movements: Prapas (1998) and Missingham (1999) on the Assembly of the Poor, and Callahan (1998) on NGO movements. This is an important gap in the study of Thai politics because from the 1970s onwards, civil society organizations in the form of social movements have played an important role in the country's democratization.

This book tries to fill this gap by examining the struggle of the SSFAI. This case was selected as the focus of research because the SSFAI was a major social movement in Thailand that played an eminent role in protecting and campaigning for the rights of the rural poor in the post authoritarian period. The political campaigns of the SSFAI encouraged farmers and other marginal groups to set up political organizations to defend their rights, which became an important means of ensuring their survival. Moreover, the struggle of the SSFAI represented a new period of political radicalism in Thailand. After the defeat of popular movements in 1976 and the collapse of the Communist Party of Thailand (CPT) in the early 1980s, radical politics in Thailand seemed to come to an end. The emergence of the SSFAI in the early 1990s sparked a new round of political mobilizations which has lasted until the present day.

The investigation of the struggle of the SSFAI will focus on how the group, as a civil society organization, contributes to the democratization process in the key area of citizenship rights, and how, in the course of the struggle, it tries to strengthen itself in order to enhance its effectiveness. The book will also explore the shortcomings of the organization. Such an investigation will help us to understand the strengths and weaknesses of Thai civil society. To undertake this study, this book attempts to apply the concept of civil society, social movement and class agency to the struggle of the SSFAI. In so doing, it also seeks to test, verify and critically engage this body of theory to help deepen understanding of the role of civil society in the process of democratization.

Abbreviations

AIF	Assembly of Isan Farmers
AIFLRINR	Assembly of Isan Farmers for Land Rights and Improvement of Natural Resources
AIFO	Alliance of Isan Farmers' Organization
AIP	Alliance of Isan People
ASSF	Assembly of Small Scale Farmers
AOP	Assembly of the Poor
BAAC	Bank of Agriculture and Agricultural Cooperatives
CP	Chareon Phokapan
CFG	Cassava Farmers' Group
CISP	Cooperatives for Isan Sugarcane Planters
CPT	Communist Party of Thailand
CSD	Crime Suppression Division
DPF	Democratic Patriotic Front
EGAT	Electricity Generating Authority of Thailand
FIC	Federation of Isan Cooperatives
FRF	Farmers' Rehabilitation Fund
FRPT	Federation of Rubber Planters of Thailand
FSF	Farmers' Support Fund
IMF	International Monetary Fund
Kho Jo Ko	Land Redistribution Project for the Poor in Degraded Forest Areas
KKAC	Khon Kaen Agricultural Cooperative
KKF	Komol Keemthong Foundation
MDU	Mobile Development Unit
MIU	Mobile Information Unit
MST	Landless Rural Workers' Movement
NAP	New Aspiration Party
NGO	Non-Governmental Organization
NGO-CORD	Coordinating Committee of Non-Governmental Organization for Rural Development

NSCT	National Student Centre of Thailand
NSMs	New Social Movements
OFCT	Organic Farming Club of Thailand
PFI	Peasants' Federation of Isan
PO	People's Organization
POI	People's Organization of Isan
RFD	Royal Forestry Department
RFSPSP	Readjustment of Farming Structure and Production System Programme
RMT	Resource Mobilization Theory
SFT	Student Federation of Thailand
SMO	Social Movement Organization
SSFAI	Small Scale Farmers' Assembly of Isan
TFF	Thai Farmers' Foundation
TOSC	Teachers' Organizations of Society Council
TRRM	Thailand Rural Reconstruction Movement
UNEP	United Nations Environmental Program

CHAPTER 1

Introduction: Civil Society and the Struggle for the Right to Have Rights

This chapter attempts to examine the context in which the SSFAI operates and to outline the available theoretical resources for its study. To this end, the chapter is organized into seven sections. The first section provides a brief overview of Thai politics. The second section examines the shortcomings of Thai electoral politics. This examination helps to situate the struggle of the SSFAI in the wider national context. The third section criticizes the elite civil society line of thought proposed by leading Thai public intellectuals to overcome the shortcomings of electoral politics, on the grounds that this approach tends to strengthen the status quo instead of transforming the existing power equation. The fourth section proposes an alternative to the concept of elite civil society. Since the case study used is a farmers' movement, the fifth section attempts to situate it in wider debates about farmers' politics by reviewing the literature on farmers' movements. Section six offers an explanation of the research methods used. Section seven provides an outline of the book.

AN OVERVIEW OF POLITICS IN THAILAND

This section provides a brief overview of Thai politics. Until 1932, Thailand was under an absolute monarchy. In June 1932 a group of military officers and civil servants seized power from the monarchy. Since then Thailand has been a constitutional monarchy (McCargo 1997a: 6). According to Riggs, after the overthrow of absolute monarchy, Thailand became a 'bureaucratic polity'. 'Such a polity', argues Riggs, 'was defined in terms of the domination of the official class as a ruling class' (Riggs 1966: 396). During the half-century following 1932, Thailand was ruled mostly by the military. According to Chai-Anan, in that period the country 'had 13 constitutions, 14 elections,

14 coups and 42 cabinets'. Military prime ministers 'were in power altogether for almost 37 years while their civilian counterparts were in office for a total of only 11 years' (Chai-Anan 1982: 1). The bureaucratic polity was also characterized by the weakness of the business sector. According to Riggs, the survival of business people 'has been made possible only by patrons, by influential men in government who can restrain their colleagues from touching this or that individual merchant' (Riggs 1966: 252).

Riggs's conception of the bureaucratic polity was criticized by Hewison. Hewison points out that Riggs portrayed Thai politics between the 1930s and the 1960s in terms which 'indicate that it is relatively unchanging or slowly evolving, emphasizing the continuities in political life while downplaying conflict'. Such an analysis, argues Hewison, obscures the political activism that was evident throughout much of the period. For him, even though civil and military elites dominated the country's politics, other non-bureaucratic forces such as the press, political parties, students, workers and other urban groups also played significant roles (Hewison 1996: 75–80).

In October 1973, the military regime was toppled by a popular uprising (see Chapter 3). After 1973, the military was weaker than before. Between 1973 and 2000, Thailand was ruled by a dictatorial regime for only four years (1976–79, 1991–92). Therefore, this was the first period in history when the country experienced a long spell of parliamentary rule. The decline of military power and the increasing power of the business sector led to the rejection of the concept of bureaucratic polity. Anek Laothamatas (1992) disputed the continuing validity of Riggs's arguments, arguing that since the late 1970s Thailand had ceased to be a bureaucratic polity, at least in the realm of economic affairs. He pointed out that government policy was no longer determined solely by high ranking officials, since businessmen had formed 'politically effective extra-bureaucratic groups' that enabled them to exert influence on public policy-making (Anek 1992: 14). Anek proposed that the new relationship between the bureaucratic elite and businessmen should be described as 'liberal corporatism'. According to Anek, corporatism is a system in which 'interest groups are organized hierarchically and then linked to the government'. For him, there are two kinds of corporatism: authoritarian and liberal. Authoritarian corporatism is marked by 'a high degree of dependence and subordination of groups in relation to the government'. On the other hand, liberal corporatism is characterized by 'a high degree of autonomy and spontaneity' and also by the important role of groups in the 'creation and operation of their representative associations, as well as a system of government interest mediation' (Anek 1992: 13–14).

The decline of the military appeared to reverse when the National Peace Keeping Council led by General Suchinda Kraprayoon staged a coup against the elected government on 23 February 1991. However, the intervention of the military in politics faced strong opposition from the public. In May 1992, Thailand witnessed a popular uprising that finally led to the demise of a military-dominated government .

PROBLEMS OF THAI DEMOCRACY

After the victory of democratic forces over a military clique, some authors commented that '…In Thailand the process of democratic consolidation seems well under way'. The reason for this optimism was that there were no political forces calling for political rule, other than by a parliamentary system (King and LoGerfo 1996: 102). However, such a view ignored the domination of money politics and the exclusionary nature of Thai democracy.

Minimal Democracy

Thailand's democratization process faced similar problems to those of many developing countries, whose post-authoritarian regimes fell short of being fully democratic. Thai representative democracy is a form of 'minimal democracy', under which democracy means 'just a system in which rulers are selected by competitive elections' (Przeworski 1999: 23). Minimal democracy is democracy in form, not in substance. The weakness of this kind of democracy is that it confuses democracy with elections. As Fox points out, electoral politics should not be confused with political democracy (Fox 1994: 151). Democracy is a complex object, variously defined. According to Beetham and Boyle (1995: 31–33), democracy has four main components:

1. *Free and fair elections.* Competitive elections provide the platform for popular control over government, electoral choice between candidates and programmes, and equality between electors.

2. *Open and accountable government.* This kind of government will guarantee the public accountability of officials. The accountability of government to citizens depends on two principles: the rule of law upheld by independent courts and decision making that is responsive to public opinion.

3. *Civil and political rights.* Such rights encompass freedom of expression, association, movement and so on. These rights enable citizens to express divergent or unpopular views, to create an informed public opinion, to associate freely with others and to find their own solution to collective problems.

4. *A democratic or 'civil' society.* In a democratic society, state power needs to be countered by independent social associations of all kinds. In addition, democracy will have a strong basis when such associations (family, school, church, workplace and voluntary associations) are not only independent

from the state but also internally democratic. The democratic experience in these associations will make their members active citizens who feel responsibility for their society at large.

From this point of view, democracy will be deepened only when the population is transformed from subjects to effective citizens who can fully enjoy their socio-economic and political rights beyond simply casting their votes.

THE DOMINATION OF MONEY POLITICS AND THE EXCLUSIONARY NATURE OF THAI DEMOCRACY

Thai electoral politics is dominated by money interests. From the point of view of almost all Thai politicians, becoming involved in politics is a means to wealth. Therefore, for them, competing in elections or 'playing politics' has become a special kind of business activity, which can make one rich quickly. Frequent elections do not necessarily mean democratic progress; as Neher commented on the 1995 elections, 'rather than moves toward more progressive democracy ... elections set back the clock with the re-emergence of old style politicians and money interests' (1995:435). The same holds true for the 1996 and 2001 elections.

To win elections, politicians spend a lot of money on vote-buying. For example, during the July 1995 elections, candidates and parties spent almost US $700 million in election campaigning, much of which went to buy votes (King and Lo Gerfo 1996: 115). According to Pollwatch documents, one MP from central Thailand bought more than 200,000 votes for $2.4 million, including payment to canvassers of about $2 per vote, and $40,000 for travel costs. In the November 1996 election, politicians handed out more than $1 billion for buying votes (Vatikiotis and Fairclough 1996: 16–17). The trend continued in the January 2001 election, despite the fact that this election was held under tougher election laws introduced by political reforms in 1997, which intended to curb vote-buying and other corrupt practices. It was estimated that politicians spent some 25 billion baht (about US$ 625 million) on vote-buying, 5 billion baht more than for the 1996 election (Tasker and Crispin 2001: 23).

Such expensive elections require a lot of money. It has been shown that much political funding, especially in rural areas, comes from illegal and untraceable sources. For example, in Chiangmai, the biggest city in Northern Thailand, one MP reportedly owns a major illegal gambling den. To fund their campaigns, other politicians rely on underground lotteries, drug trafficking and oil smuggling (Vatikiotis and Fairclough 1996: 18).

The domination of money in electoral politics has led to widespread corruption. Politicians use their power to reap rich rewards after winning elections.

When the military seized power in 1991, it set up an Assets Examination Committee to investigate corruption charges against 13 high-ranking politicians. The Committee found that they were 'unusually wealthy', their unexplained wealth ranging from more than $24 million in the case of a former minister of commerce to about $13.24 million for a former communications minister and about $9.04 million for the former prime minister (Neher 1995: 435).

Equally important, the domination of money interests also led to the increasing influence of the business sector in politics. As Pasuk and Baker point out, from the 1980s onwards businessmen not only became a majority group in parliament, but also dominated seats in the Cabinet. In the 1988 election, business people won 243 out of 357 seats, and 70 per cent of the Cabinet members came from the business sector (Pasuk and Baker 1995: 339). The most interesting point is that most of these business people came from the provinces. The increasing power of business people in the Thai political order was recognized by Pasuk and Baker (1995). Economic development in the preceding three decades had led to economic growth in the provinces. As a result, a new class of provincial businessmen arose. Some of them ran semi-legal or criminal businesses, such as logging, smuggling or gambling. This group of businessmen has become known as *jao pho* (godfathers). They used money, friendship and connections in exchange for protection and co-operation from government officials, both civilian and military. According to Pasuk and Baker, elections provided opportunities for provincial business-men to translate their wealth and informal influence into political power at the provincial and national levels. By 1990, 62 per cent of the members of provincial councils and town councils were businessmen. At the national level, over 80 per cent of parliamentary seats were elected from provincial areas. More importantly, in electoral politics the *jao pho* acquired enormous significance. Some of them became leaders of political parties, and their relatives and business associates were elected to parliament (Pasuk and Baker 1995: 332–337).

The political power of the business sector reached new heights in the 2001 election when Thaksin Shinawatra, one of Thailand's richest businessmen, won the election. Thaksin, a former deputy prime minister in the Chavalit government in 1997, is an owner of a communications conglomerate. He formed his political party, Thai Rak Thai (Thai love Thai), in 1998. In the 2001 election, Thai Rak Thai won 248 of the 500 parliamentary seats (McCargo 2002: 248). According to Pasuk and Baker, Thaksin won the election by a combination of old and new politics. While he did all the 'old things' of money politics, he also campaigned on policy platforms such as a revolving fund of one million baht for every village, a thirty baht per visit scheme of health care and a moratorium on farmer debts (Pasuk and Baker 2002: 7). The rise to power of the Thaksin government, according to Crispin and Tasker, was 'more likely represents a full-blown merger between politics and big business… with political and economic power being fused even more closely than in the past' (Crispin and Tasker 2001: 17). In coalition with veteran politicians and bureaucrats, businesspeople dominated electoral politics. In effect, this excluded the popular masses from meaningful participation in the political process. As Surin and McCargo point out, 'this political-bureaucratic-business "iron triangle"…which is essentially conservative in its political orientation…is making the electoral process increasingly exclusionary' (Surin and McCargo 1997: 145). The exclusionary nature of Thai electoral politics made politicians more arrogant. Politicians believed that elections provided them 'a form of absolute legitimacy'. 'This belief', noted Surin and McCargo, 'may lead elected figures to regard all-extra parliamentary political activities as illegitimate' (Surin and McCargo 1997: 148). For them, the democratic rights of the population were confined to only casting their votes (Prapas 1998: 123). As a result, the basic rights of the ordinary citizens were not fully acknowledged and have often been violated by the state (see Chapter 3).

ELITE DEMOCRACY: DEMOCRATIZATION FROM ABOVE

The question of how to overcome money politics and to deepen democracy has become an important issue for Thai democratic movements in recent years. Generally, before the popular uprising against a military clique in May 1992, hopes for any change among Thai social activists and progressive intellectuals rested on popular initiatives from below. However, after the victory in May, political reform became a national issue, and meaningful democratic change carried out by the state seemed possible. In this optimistic atmosphere, some public intellectuals began to propose the concept of democratization from above. The best known element was the concept of elite civil society.

The idea of elite civil society

The idea of elite civil society was proposed by a group of leading Thai public intellectuals, the most prominent being Prawase Wasi. Their idea is more or less a combination of the concepts of 'state-led civil society' (Frolic 1997), 'the third way' (Giddens 1998) and 'social capital' (Putnam 1994).

According to Frolic – whose work looks at China – state-led civil society in China is a form of unequal partnership between the state and social organizations. The state dominates the partnership but allows 'some degree of autonomy to those organizations'. The partnership is 'based on cooperation within specified sectors, usually in tripartite arrangement among business, labor, and the state'. It is a trade-off between them. While 'the state perceives the need for change and regards social organizations as functionally useful, without threatening the state's hegemony', the actors in those organizations 'are more interested in short term economic gains than individual autonomy at the expense of state power' (Frolic 1997: 58).

State-civil society cooperation is also central to the idea of the 'third way' proposed by Giddens. 'The fostering of an active civil society', argues Giddens, 'is a basic part of the politics of the third way' (Giddens 1998: 78). However, the active civil society of the third way plays a different role from the anti-statist model (Arato 1981). Instead of engaging in political mobilizations against the state, civil society, according to the third way scheme, involves building a partnership with the state (Giddens 1998: 79). Giddens proposed state–civil society partnership as a vehicle to 'foster community renewal and development' (Giddens 1998: 69).

In a similar vein, the elite civil society concept emphasizes cooperation between the state and social organizations. For elite civil society theorists, both the state and social organizations are components of 'civil society'. 'Civil society', argues Chai-Anan Samudavanija, is a partnership of the state, the private sector and the popular sector (Chai-Anan 1998: 41). Social organizations, according to the theorists of this line of thought, have to cooperate with the state because the state is very strong; it is impossible to achieve any meaningful change without state cooperation (Prawase 1998: 5). For them, the state must play a key role in efforts to construct '*prachakhom*' or 'civil society' in Thailand. As a result, they rejected the idea of excluding the state from civil society, and believed that building civil society from below had no future in Thailand. According to Prawase, such ideas will lead to conflict, hate and rivalry, which will weaken the efforts for a better life within society. For him, the endeavour to strengthen civil society should be based on 'love' and 'cooperation'. To avoid confrontation, Prawase proposed that the state, business sector, NGOs, local elite and intellectuals should form a 'partnership' and work together to solve the country's social and politico-economic problems. Such a partnership, which includes all parts of society, will create a powerful and sustainable civil society that is able to solve all kind of problems (Prawase 1998: 22–26).

The concept of elite civil society was also influenced by the idea of social capital proposed by Putnam. According to Putnam, the quality of a democracy depends on the quality of its citizens. Such a quality depends on the degree of 'civicness' of community. In other words, democracy is the result of righteous conduct of its citizens. The civicness of community, argues Putnam, depends on the strength of social capital (trust, norms and network of civic engagement) of society (Putnam 1993: 167). Therefore, building social capital is 'the key to making democracy work' (Putnam 1993: 185).

In the early stage, Prawase proposed the idea of partnership to build 'local civil society' in the provinces. The main theme of this plan was to build civic communities by strengthening their social capital. His idea was incorporated into the Eighth National Socio-Economic Plan (1997–2001). However, after the economic crisis in the late 1990s, he developed such ideas into the concept of 'good governance'. According to Prawase, to overcome the crisis, Thailand needed politico-economic and social reforms to achieve 'good governance'. Such reforms would strengthen Thai society in every aspect, intellectually and materially, and create transparency, happiness and new prosperity within the country on a stable basis (Prawase 1998: 22).

His ideas are similar to those of Thirayuth Boonmi, another theorist of 'good governance'. For Thirayuth, 'good governance' is the interactive relation between the state, private sector and society that would lead to a transparent, efficient government and economic sector, and at the same time increase popular participation, reduce state power and strengthen civil society (Thirayuth 1998: 12; Yod 1998: 62–70). To carry out reforms, both of them proposed the setting up of a committee, which would comprise 'good' and 'capable' elites from various groups such as political leaders, army officers, government agency, businessmen, academics, media, religious leaders and the leaders of urban-oriented NGOs, to carry out the reforms (Jai 1998: 169; Prawase 1998: 21, 33–34).

Problems with the elite's view

The concept of elite civil society discussed above suffers from a number of problems. First, the elite civil society line of thought is quite similar to the idea of democratic elitism, which argues that the threat to democracy comes from the masses because 'they are prone either to take direct action against democratic institutions and value, or provoke counter elites to engage in antidemocratic action'. Therefore, the survival of democracy depends upon 'the leadership of "an enlightened elite" to shape and direct policy aimed principally to keep the masses politically quiescent' (Bachrach and Botwinick 1992: 22–23).

Second, the idea of strengthening civil society and democracy through cooperation and good behaviour along lines of Putnam's civic community was misleading. As Foweraker and Landman have shown in their empirical research on the citizen rights–social movement relationship in Latin America, 'the democratic qualities of civil society do not have to do with "civicness" but with the associationalism which supports social mobilization and political contestation'. Therefore, 'democracy is not the comfortable result of righteous conduct but the result of prolonged struggle in often difficult and dangerous circumstances' (Foweraker and Landman 1997: 243).

Third, the reforms proposed by elite civil society theorists are reforms carried out by elites that aim at preserving the existing structure. Such reforms, as Saneh Chamarik has pointed out, assume that '*prachakhom*' and 'good governance' have to be built from above and led by capable elites. Any change in society must confine itself to the improvement of the existing structure without fundamental changes in the status quo. It means that there will be no change in the unequal relationship between the state and economic sector on the one hand, and society on the other. It is reform designed to perpetuate the rule of the elite over the common people. Such reforms will never generate democracy but merely the domination of the elite (Saneh 1998: 8). Since this kind of change does not restructure the existing politico-economic structure in any fundamental way, it may at best be described as 'conservative reform'.

Fourth, it is difficult to find any evidence to support the view that the state is at all interested in democratic development. On the contrary, the state often acts against efforts to strengthen civil society. Elite civil society theorists naively believe that if social organizations give up their activities against state oppression, in return, the state will change its anti-democratic policies into democratic ones. In other words, they treat the state as something that can be manipulated easily. In reality, as Chai-Anan has argued, the Thai state is difficult to change 'because of the longstanding and deeply ingrained authoritarian, centralist, clientelistic and corrupt tradition of its bureaucracy' (Kasian 1996: 47).

Fifth, the argument against the independent struggle of the grassroots movements made by the concept of elite civil society supplied ammunition for the state to de-legitimize the activities of the democratic movements. The Thai state, as mentioned above, frequently accuses those involved in popular movements of being 'troublemakers', whose activities threaten national security. To argue that the struggle against state oppression was improper because it caused conflict within the nation was easily exploited by the state to support the 'troublemaker' accusation, in order to isolate the movements from the rest of society. Such an accusation is a form of what Therborn called 'ideological excommunication'. According to Therborn, the victim of such accusations will be 'excluded from further meaningful discourse as being insane, depraved, traitorous, alien, and so on'. The excommunicated person, argues Therborn, 'is condemned, temporarily or forever, to ideological non-existence: he is not to be listened to' (Therborn 1988: 83).

Sixth, the idea of 'partnership' proposed by the elite civil society theorists also helps to strengthen the state's position vis-a-vis civil society. It invites the state to become involved in a wide range of activities that were formerly carried out independently by social organizations. As a result, instead of reducing the power of the state, the partnership helps it to increase its control over society. In theory, in a partnership all members are equal. But in reality the state is stronger than other groups. The strength of the state is further enhanced by the assumptions of elite civil society theory, which regards conflict with the state as undesirable. Furthermore, since the state is the main source of funding, it can influence, neutralize, de-politicize and manipulate the activities of the partnership. Under such conditions it is not difficult for the state to dominate the partnership, and turn it into state corporatism. This fear is confirmed by the activities of such partnerships in 1998–2000. As a member of *prachakhom* (civil society) in Khon Kaen has pointed out, since it was founded in 1998, *prachakhom* has been 'a tool for the government to co-opt and control civil society' (Crispin 2000: 21).

Seventh, to avoid conflict with the state means that the partnership has to ignore the violation of human rights by the state. As mentioned earlier, many policies of the Thai state have violated the rights of the underprivileged masses, especially in rural areas. In some cases they threaten their survival. However, a partnership is unable to take any action against the state because such actions will lead to conflict with the state. As the chairman of *prachakhom* in Khon Kaen has pointed out, the partnership should refrain from activities that may led to conflict with officials, 'in order to gain credibility, respect, and cooperation from the government' (Ratana 1999: 15). As a result, their activities are confined to 'non-political' issues such as promoting a clean and green city, the preservation of cultural heritage and the creation of children's playgrounds (Ratana 1999: 16).

Finally, elite civil society theorists tend to forget that conflicts have been generated by state policies. To avoid conflict within Thai society means that the state has to stop violating the rights of the population. If the state remains committed to such undemocratic policies, conflict will not only continue to exist, but also intensify.

It is clear that elite democracy fails to provide mechanisms to generate significant democratic change that will lead to democratic deepening. It is the argument of this thesis that if any democratic progress is to materialize, it is necessary to address the problem from a different angle. The following section provides an alternative perspective on the issue of deepening democracy in Thailand.

CIVIL SOCIETY AS A DOMAIN FOR THE STRUGGLE FOR THE RIGHT TO HAVE RIGHTS: A VIEW FROM BELOW

The domination of business interests and the exclusionary nature of Thai democracy make it very difficult to initiate meaningful changes that will lead to democratic deepening from above. This limitation has enhanced the importance of civil society as a domain for the struggle for democratic progress because it provides a space for the popular sector to organize itself independently of the state. As Callahan has pointed out, since electoral politics 'has not responded to the changing needs of the people, informal citizens' organizations have been growing up to articulate and promote the demands of a broader civil society' (Callahan 1998: 151). According to Rueschemyer et al., the spread of civil society organizations 'should facilitate the development of democracy...because it creates favorable conditions for the classes previously excluded from the political arena to organize for collective action' (Rueschemeyer et al. 1992: 50).

The Concept of Civil Society

According to Schecter, 'in a great deal of contemporary usage, civil society is extremely complex and difficult to locate precisely' (Schecter 2000: 2). The concept, as Dickens had pointed out, 'is used very differently by different authors, and this is largely a result of the different political purposes' (Dickens 1996: 132). In general, argues Lummis, civil society 'refers to the sphere of society which organizes itself autonomously, as opposed to the sphere that is established and/or directly controlled by the state' (Lummis 1996: 30). Differences among civil society theorists arise over the issue of what should be included in, or excluded from, civil society. In the current debate, concepts of civil society can be divided into two main approaches: liberal and critical perspectives. The liberal perspective has its origins in the political economists of the Scottish Enlightenment of the eighteenth century, such as Adam Ferguson and Adam Smith. In his famous book, *An Essay on the History of Civil Society*, Ferguson narrates a history of the human species in its transition from a 'rude' form of life to a 'polished or civilized' one (Becker 1994: 6). For Ferguson, civil society was 'seen as one in which urban life and commercial activities flourished'. Ferguson, argues Shils, 'regarded associations for commercial ends, associations which were not primordial, as characteristic of civil society' (Shils 1991: 5). The contemporary liberal perspective of civil society takes up the idea that the market economy as a sphere of social regulation independent of the state was the main component of civil society (for example, Black 1984; Keane 1988; Perez-Diaz 1993; Shils 1991). According to Shils, 'the market economy is the appropriate pattern of the economic life of a civil society' (Shils 1991: 9). However, their conception of civil society does not consist solely of the market economy, but also of voluntary associations, political parties and the sphere of public debate (Keane 1988: 1; Perez-Diaz 1993: 56–57; Shils 1991: 9). These institutions will protect civil society from state suppression, and so preserve it (Shils 1991: 10).

The critical perspective takes up Marx's critical attitude towards 'civil society' as defined by the original 'liberal' theorists. In Marx's view, 'civil society' ('bourgeois society') was 'dominated by considerations of narrow self-interest' (Kukathas and Lovell 1991: 19). It was the realm of alienation, which had to be abolished together with the state (Giner 1985: 250–251). More recent critical theorists do not advocate abolishing 'civil society' as Marx did, but instead they redefine it. However, following Marx, they adopt a negative attitude towards the market economy and the state. They exclude the market economy from their conception of civil society together with political society (for example, political parties and parliament). Cohen and Arato explain the reasons for such exclusion: although the market economy and political society generally arise from civil society, the two realms have their own logic (control and management) which is impossible to subordinate to civil society (Cohen and Arato 1997: ix). For Cohen and Arato, civil society was

> a sphere of social interaction between economy and state, composed above all of social intimate sphere (especially the family), the sphere of associations (especially voluntary associations), social movements, and forms of public communication. (Cohen and Arato 1997: ix)

Although they differed on the above points, most civil society theorists agreed on the positive relationship between civil society and democracy. As Bibic notes, today civil society has become 'a permanent condition and element of democratic theory and democratic socio-political order' (Bibic 1994: 44).

The present book defines civil society broadly as a public sphere, a space for action, which makes it possible for the population to organize itself independently from the state. The argument is that instead of becoming part of the state or helping the state to expand its function as proposed by elite civil society theorists, civil society must, as Lummis suggests, play a role in transforming the state and radically reducing its power, restructuring it by 'eliminating functions that have been made redundant by the autonomous organization of the civil society itself', and 'reforming or establishing new government institutions appropriate to the new situation' (Lummis 1996: 37). However, most of the literature on civil society tends to overemphasize the autonomous nature of civil society and its abilities to influence state policies, and to ignore the complex interrelationship between the state and civil society. Here, we claim that civil society is not totally immune from state influence. Therefore, while it acknowledges the role of civil society as an autonomous actor in counterbalancing state power, it also recognizes the possibility that the state can have some sort of influence in shaping the development of civil society. As Rueschemeyer et al. point out, the state 'can ease or obstruct the organization of different class interests; it can empower or marginalize existing organizations'. The state may also 'succeed in co-optation and, in the extreme, use whole organizational networks as conduits of hegemonic influence'. The interaction between the state and civil society, note Rueschemeyer et al., 'creates a wide variety of possible relations between the state and different social classes and, consequently, of conditions conducive or hostile to democracy' (Rueschmeyer et al. 1996: 67).

SOCIAL MOVEMENTS AND CITIZENSHIP RIGHTS

Civil society organizations are diverse in form (formal and informal) and purpose (political, cultural and economic). They can be local sports clubs, neighbourhood associations, or other kinds of voluntary association. Here, however, the emphasis is on the importance of civil society organizations in the form of social movements because we argue that social movements have played a major role in democratic deepening by broadening popular partici- pation and rights, which was crucial in the efforts to overcome money politics and exclusionary democracy. Social movements, as Cohen and Arato have pointed out, 'constitute the dynamic element in processes that might realize the positive potentials of modern civil societies' (Cohen and Arato 1997: 492).

The most important task of civil society in the democratization process in the Third World, Blaney and Pasha write, is the establishment of a system of citizenship rights (Blaney and Pasha 1993: 6). This involves

> eliminating the arbitrary exclusion of certain members of society as a rights-bearing individuals/citizens, extending participatory structures both within civil society and in relation to the state, reformulating and extending rights, as well as acting in defense of the institutions of civil society against possible threats from abuses of power by the state or from within civil society itself. (Blaney and Pasha 1993: 8)

The establishment of rights is the establishment of effective citizenship (Foweraker and Landman, 1997: 1). However, the realization of effective citizenship requires collective action from below. Effective citizenship, notes Fox, 'requires the capacity to participate autonomously in politics, and to take propositional action which actually shapes state decisions and enforces state accountability' (Fox 1990: 8), while Harvey points out that 'effective citizenship does not inevitably flow from economic development'. Only when the popular sectors 'are able to organize and open spaces for political representation' can it exist (Harvey 1998: 229). The relationship between collective action in the form of social movements and the strengthening of citizenship rights was also addressed by Foweraker and Landman. They point out that 'it is social struggle in the form of collective action which wins the individual rights of citizenship' (Foweraker and Landman 1997: 226). For them, social movements 'often emerge from contexts where rights are not apparently or are plainly denied, and it is through the process of organization and demand-making that a knowledge of rights arises' (Foweraker and Landman 1997: 33). The struggle for citizenship rights, Foweraker and Landman argue, singled out the state as a prime target because, on the one hand, rights are threatened by the state, and on the other, it is only the state that can impose law to protect rights. As a result, rights are won not only against but also through the state (Foweraker and Landman 1997: 226). Foweraker and Landman did not only consider the influence of social movements on rights, but also examined the impact of rights on social movements. They note that the idea of rights can strengthen the struggle of a social movement by 'increasing its scope and catalysing the spread of common demands across a variety of struggles'. In addition, rights as a common language can 'empower the movements by providing a political agenda and creating a more proactive impetus' (Foweraker and Landman 1997: 228).

THE POLITICAL NATURE OF THE STRUGGLE FOR THE RIGHT TO HAVE RIGHTS

The struggle for effective citizenship, which was also known as the struggle for the right to have rights, was an important political invention of social movements. According to Harvey, the demand for the 'right to have rights' is a novel demand of popular movements in developing countries. It is a deepening of the democratization process after the overthrow of dictatorial rule. Such a demand inevitably leads to new political practices. The demand for the 'right to have rights' does not target corrupt individuals, but the operation of the political system itself. Nor does it not seek government favours for short term material benefits, but demands that rights be respected. 'When movements', argues Harvey, 'no longer petition the government for favors but demand respect for rights, the practices inevitably change, even if authorities attempt to reassert vertical lines of clientelistic control' (Harvey 1998: 22–23).

The struggle for citizenship rights, or the struggle for 'the right to have rights', did not always start from making political demands. More often, the demands of social movements initially involved 'immediate, concrete, and material demands of an economic, corporate, or communal kind'. But since the initial demands were often ignored or reversed by the state, they frequently generated further demands, which revolved around the call for the right to have rights (Foweraker and Landman 1997: 29).

It should be noted that although the struggle for the right to have rights challenges traditional forms of representation by singling out extra-parliamentary mobilization as a channel to advance popular demands, it does not aim at the radical transformation of the political system, unlike the revolutionary struggle. On the contrary, the struggle for the right to have rights is the struggle for the 'gradual and piecemeal conquest of reforms that expand the possibilities for democratic struggle'. Therefore, the impact of this struggle on the political system has to be judged on the basis of its limited objectives (Harvey 1998: 20).

SOCIAL CLASS AND DEMOCRACY

The struggle for the right to have rights and issues of social class have a significant correlation. According to Barbalet, the importance of rights and class power are closely related. For him, 'rights are much more significant for those without social and political power than they are for the powerful' (Barbalet 1998: 18). This idea echoes the conclusions of Rueschemeyer et al. on the relationship between social class and democracy. According to Rueschemeyer et al., social class is a central category in the analysis of democratization. For them, class and democracy are interrelated: 'those who have only to gain from democracy will be its most reliable promoters and defenders', while 'those who have the most to lose will resist it and will be most tempted to roll it back when the occasion presents itself' (Rueschemeyer et al. 1996: 57).

Democratization was both resisted and pushed forward by class interest. It was the subordinate classes that fought for democracy. By contrast, the classes that benefited from the status quo nearly without exception resisted democracy. (Rueschemeyer et al. 1996: 46)

Therefore, in the process of democratization, the strength of subordinate classes is critically important for the advancement of democracy. The subordinate classes can strengthen their position by social mobilization and by the development of relatively autonomous groups within civil society. For Rueschemeyer et al., the density of these autonomous groups is important in three different ways:

as a way in which the empowerment of subordinate classes is realized,

as a shield protecting these classes against the hegemonic influence of dominant classes, and...

as a mode of balancing the power of state and civil society. (Rueschemeyer et al. 1996: 49)

Here, the argument is that in the Thai context, the struggle of civil society organizations of the underprivileged classes, if strong enough, has the potential to contribute to the deepening of democracy in at least five different ways. First, it promotes popular participation. The importance of civil society for democratic development in Thailand is more pronounced because of the exclusionary nature of Thai democracy. As discussed above, even though electoral democracy is gaining increased significance as a legitimate form of political rule in Thailand, a large strata of the population remains excluded from meaningful political participation. For Thai political leaders, popular participation has been confined to merely casting votes. To overcome electoralism, it is necessary to open up political space so as to increase democratic participation. However, since there are no channels for increased political engagement within electoral politics, civil society has become the major base of the struggle for popular participation. In this way, the mass of the population can push the democratization process further, and expand the scope of participation beyond elections by organizing themselves into different kinds of social organizations in order to enhance their bargaining power with the state. Linz and Stepan have noted that a robust civil society has 'the capacity to generate political alternatives and to monitor government and state'. It can also help 'transitions get started, help resist reversals, and help deepen democracy' (Linz and Stepan 1996: 9).

Second, participation in civil society organizations provides opportunities for the masses to learn about democracy through their experiences. As noted above, in the context of electoral politics, democratic participation only involves voting on election days. The masses, especially in the countryside, have no chance to engage in other democratic activities. However, when they join grassroots organizations, they are able to learn how the democratic system works, and how to act democratically. Through working within organizations, they learn to work in groups, which are, in one sense, crucial for democratic development in any society. In addition, they have a chance to engage in debate in meetings in which they can express opinions, as well as having to abide by majority rule. The more they are involved in the activities of these organizations, the more they will deepen their understanding of democracy. These are very valuable experiences, impossible for the poor to gain in other ways. More importantly, since the activities of the grassroots organizations are related to their survival, it makes democracy an integral part of their lives.

Third, the empowerment of civil society organizations will undermine patron–client relations. One reason for the existence of patron–client relations is that the underprivileged classes are unable to rely on themselves, and thus have to find someone to help or protect them. The empowerment of grassroots movements changes such a situation. According to Bacharach and Botwinick, the struggle to increase the political participation of the poor will 'nurture and heighten group identity,… sharpening awareness of the individual self', and 'engender a transformation from a sense of powerlessness to power' (Bachrach and Botwinick 1992: 30). As a result, instead of relying on political patrons, they rely on their own strength and their collective action.

Fourth, civil society organizations are the most important mechanisms for protecting the rights of the underprivileged classes in rural areas. In recent years, the rights of the rural poor have been violated in many areas by elected governments. Frequently such violations threaten their survival. The government has sometimes used force to evict farmers from their lands for dam projects and agri-business plantations. The only way available for farmers to protect their lives from disaster is to organize themselves against state intrusion. This is the weapon of the weak in a society in which the violation of human rights has been conducted in the name of the law, development and national interest.

Last but not least, the activities of civil society organizations generate counter-hegemonic ideologies that are crucial for democratic development. Such ideologies are a product of the struggle; they develop among the members of organizations via participation in practical activities. Engaging in collective action, the masses will view their relationship with the state from a new angle. One of the most important features of the Thai dominant ideology derives from the idea of karma. It is believed that one's status in society results from karma accumulated in past lives in the form of merit (*bun*) and demerit (*bap*). According to Chai, 'the degree of "high-ness" or "low-ness" of an individual's status is believed to vary according to his store of *bun* and *bap*: the more *bun*, the higher one's status' (Chai 1998: 40). In other words, those who are rulers become so because of their *bun*. As a result, the differences between the ruler and the ruled are perceived to be natural and appropriate. Such a belief implies that the existing socio-political structure is unchangeable, and therefore the ruled have no choice but to depend on the ruler (Sombat 1998: 72). This is the ideological basis of patron–client relations in Thai society. This idea prevents the subordinate classes from acting in their class interests. It obstructs them from developing into what Marx called 'class for itself' (Kolakowski 1981: 356). As Scott and Kerkvliet note on peasant consciousness, 'as long as peasant sees his relation to agrarian elites as one of legitimate dependent – as long as he feels himself part of a vertical community – peasant "class-consciousness" is unlikely' (Scott and Kerkvliet 1977: 439).

The empowerment of the subordinate classes through collective action undermines such ideas. Subordinate classes realize that if they act together, they have the power to bargain with the state, and may sometimes be able to force the state to comply with their demands. They are increasingly convinced that it is possible to change the relationship between dominant and subordinate. As a result, they stop viewing government officials as 'masters' whom they dare not challenge. Furthermore, they see their struggle as a struggle for better lives, not as troublemaking. In sum, instead of accepting the existing socio-political structure as a natural manifestation of karma, they condemn it as unjust and aim to change it.

This section has reviewed the literature on civil society, social movements, citizenship rights, the struggle for the right to have rights and the idea of social class agency. This literature provides the theoretical framework for the present book. The following section looks at a different set of literature, the debate on farmers' movements, which will help to locate the case study within wider debates about the struggle of farmers.

FARMERS' MOVEMENTS: OLD AND NEW

This section is organized into two parts. The first part reviews the literature on classic peasant unrest by focusing on the moral economy paradigm. The second part considers two types of new farmers' movements.

Classic Peasant Unrest

Here the focus will be on the moral economy paradigm because it addresses the impact of capitalism on the rural community and on the struggle of peasants. This impact was reflected in the struggle of the SSFAI and other farmers' organizations studied presently. Capitalism was singled out by the moral economy paradigm (Moore (1967), Wolf (1969), Migdal (1974), and Scott (1976)), as a factor that contributed to peasant unrest. In *The Moral Economy of the Peasant: Rebellion and Subsistence in Southeast Asia* (1976), Scott points to the impact of capitalism on the 'subsistence economy' as a prime source of peasant rebellions. He argues that 'commercial agriculture and the growth of the state was to steadily reduce the reliability of subsistence guarantees to a point where peasants had hardly any alternative but resistance' (Scott 1976: 40). According to Scott, in peasant societies the relationship between landlords and peasants commonly took the form of patron–client bonds. While landlords received goods and services from peasants, they had an obligation to 'subsidize and assist peasants when their subsistence is in jeopardy'; the landlord's claims to produce or labour 'must not jeopardize the peasant's right to subsistence' (Scott 1976: 178–179). For Scott, the norm of reciprocity provides peasants with the idea of justice and legitimacy. If landlords fail to deliver their obligations, peasants will feel that their basic social rights are being violated and that they have rights to act against landlords (Scott 1976: 189). A 'sudden imposition' on peasant life was another factor that caused rebellion. According to Moore, peasants will generally accept slow economic deterioration as a part of a normal situation, especially when there is no alternative. But actions that break with accepted customs and rules are likely to lead to rebellion (Moore 1967: 474–475).

The moral economy paradigm reviewed above provides valuable insights on the causal link between the violation of peasants' basic social rights (the right to subsistence), or the accepted customs and rules, and peasant rebellion. However, the paradigm suffers from over-generalization. Starn has pointed out that the moral economy paradigm tended to suggest that 'a single answer could be developed to the question of why peasants rebel'. It overlooked 'the fact that every protest emerges from a unique and historically specific set of circumstances ... the reasons for protest vary from case to case' (Starn 1992: 92).

In some cases the survival of rural communities depended on the expansion of the market economy. Based on his field research on peasant protest in China, Thaxton (1997) showed empirically that peasant uprisings in the North China plain were reactions to the efforts of the state to intervene in a salt market that was vital to community well-being. So, in this case, the expansion of capitalism into the countryside did not threaten the survival of peasants; on the contrary, it boosted their prosperity. Peasant rebellions were also sometimes determined by political factors. In her review of the peasant uprising literature, Skocpol questioned the idea that capitalist commercialization is a necessary cause of peasant rebellions. She pointed out the importance of political factors in such rebellions. In China, for example, the Communist Party gained wide support from peasants by 'addressing the issue of tax and security' and by 'transforming long-standing local political and class relations between peasants and landlords' (Skocpol 1995: 233). Skocpol contends that peasant uprisings have not only grown out of agrarian commercialization. For her, 'such revolutions have emerged more invariably out of occasionally favorable political situations shaped in large part by the inter-state dynamics of the modern world-capitalist era' (Skocpol 1995: 235). However, it should be noted that in some cases the state acted as an agent of capitalist development. For example, in the case of the Land Redistribution Project for the Poor in Degraded Forest Areas (*Kho Jo Ko*) (see Chapter 3), the Thai state forced peasants to leave their lands for commercial reforestation, which resulted in widespread peasant protests. In such a case it was impossible to separate economic factors from political ones.

New Farmers' Movements

This section looks at the literature on new farmers' movements in India and Latin America, which typify two important types of new farmers' movements in different parts of the world. The Indian case represents the struggle of commodity-producing farmers on 'income issues', while the Latin American case exemplifies the agitation for land by landless peasants.

The Indian Case

So-called 'new farmers' movements' were a recent form of farmers' mobilization. What are the differences between the 'new' movements and the 'old' ones? In his study of Indian farmers' movements, Lindberg argues that the difference between the two movements 'can be summarized in the replacement of one slogan "Land to the tiller!" by another "Remunerative prices!"'. The shift reflected the structural transformation in the agrarian economy from a pre-capitalist to a capitalist mode of production. 'Land to the tiller', argues Lindberg, is the slogan of an 'old' farmers' movement 'organized around the major contradiction in a pre-industrial, class-divided agrarian society – the contradiction between landed and non-landed groups'. This type of movement has land-hungry peasants (rural workers, small tenants and poor peasants) as its political mass base (Lindberg 1992: 209).

The other slogan, 'remunerative prices', is the slogan of 'new' farmers' movements. Although prices had been the rallying issue of rural agitation long before the 1970s, they had never become the dominant issue among peasants' movements (Byres 1995: 1). The slogan indicated the importance of the commercialization of agriculture to commodity-producing farmers. For Lindberg, 'new' farmers' movements are movements 'based on a peasant economy in which the process of reproduction has to a certain extent been commoditized'. These kinds of farmers are involved in the market economy not only as commodity producers, but also as consumers. They use commodities as inputs in their production. As a result, argues Lindberg, the 'new' movements 'have acted not just on the issue of the price of agriculture produce but also on the price of inputs' such as 'fertilizers, electricity and terms of credit from state-owned or state-sponsored financial institutions'. Such new economic conditions led to a new contradiction.

The peasantry is now linked to a market where to a significant degree price formation is influenced by the state, which in effect regulates the conditions of reproduction of the peasantry. The contradiction on which the 'new' peasant movements act is therefore one *between the state and the peasantry*: it is the state which is seen as the main target of agitation, not the local landlords as in the traditional type of peasant movement. (Lindberg 1995: 101)

Even though 'price and related issues' had come to dominate rural protest, this does not mean that they had replaced the land question. On the contrary, as Lindberg has pointed out, 'the two contradictions are both actively influencing the shape of the peasants' movements', which resulted in diverse forms of peasant activities (Lindberg 1992: 216).

The Latin American Case

The 'newness' of farmers' movements can also be viewed from a different angle. In an article entitled 'Latin America: The Resurgence of the Left', Petras points out the differences between the new peasant movements of the 1990s and the traditional peasant movements of the 1960s in Latin America. For him, the new movements 'are not peasant movements in the traditional sense, nor are the rural cultivators who comprise them divorced from urban life or activities'. Actually, in many cases they are displaced workers or former miners. In other cases, peasant militants had experience with religious institutions but left the church to enter the struggle for land reform. In some instances, they had a chance to attend primary or secondary school before they joined the movements (Petras 1997: 19). The leaders of the 'new peasantry' often traveled to the cities to participate in political debates and seminars, and attend training schools. According to Petras, despite the fact that 'they are rooted in the rural struggle, live in land settlements and engage in agricultural cultivation, they have a cosmopolitan vision'. Another important point about the new peasant movements is that, like new farmers' movements in India, they are independent of political parties. They are 'largely engaged in direct action rather than the election process' (Petras 1997: 20). Furthermore, in differing contexts, the new peasant movements are influenced by a mixture of ideas of class struggle and by ideas related to gender, ecology, ethnicity, nationality and culture. Last but not least, the 'new peasantry' in the region work together on the basis of regional organization and are increasingly involved in international forums, called 'Via Campesino'. 'Through these links and others', argues Petras, 'an emerging "internationalist" consciousness and practice is emerging' (Petras 1997: 21).

While the majority of the members of the new farmers' movements in India come from middle farmers (Lindberg 1995: 102), Latin American peasant movements, especially in Brazil, have landless rural workers and poor peasants as their political base. The new Latin American farmers' movements are the movement of landless rural workers and poor peasants fighting for land. In other words, 'land for the tiller', not 'remunerative prices', is their political slogan. However, it should be noted that even though the objective of the 'new peasantry', the struggle for land, is similar to that of traditional peasant movements, the politico-economic factors behind their emergence in the 1990s originated in the age of globalization. It was, for example, popular discontent with neo-liberal economic policies, which the governments implemented under the instructions of the World Bank and IMF, that facilitated the upsurge of the Landless Rural Workers' Movement (MST) in Brazil (Petras 1997: 21).

It should be noted that, as in India, new peasant movements in Latin America also take on various forms. Although the struggle for land occupies the most important place in Latin America's farmers' struggles, this does mean that other kinds of farmers' movements do not exist in the region. As Starn has pointed out, apart from land rights, farmers in the region have also protested about other issues such as the prices of agricultural products and loan subsidies (Starn 1992: 91).

The focus here – the struggle of the SSFAI – is on the struggle of a new farmers' movement. However, this struggle was not confined only to the issues raised by the Indian or the Brazilian cases. It involved a combination of the two. The SSFAI dealt not only with price issues, but also with land rights. The issues raised by the SSFAI reflected the internal differentiation of Isan farmers that resulted from the transformation of the Isan rural society into a 'post peasant society' (see Chapter 4).

RESEARCH METHODOLOGY

The book is based mainly on fieldwork conducted from July 1997 to August 1998. Information was collected mostly through participation in the SSFAI's activities. During this period, I took part in a month-long major protest and several minor protests organized by the SSFAI. I also had a chance to attend the meetings of the SSFAI committee at all levels (village, district, province and central committee). Participating in these activities provided me valuable insights on strategy and organization. Another source of information came from interviews with leaders and members of the SSFAI. I also attended the SSFAI political school, discussing the strategy and policies of the organization. Moreover, I spent periods of time with SSFAI members in several villages. Those activities provided me both with insights and also with useful background material impossible to obtain from printed sources.

Apart from the participatory research, I had privileged access to internal documents of the SSFAI. These documents included the minutes of the central committee and other documents for internal circulation. Another source of material came from newspapers. Because the SSFAI was at times a main focus of newspaper coverage, its activities were intensively reported and this information was useful in that it recorded events or interviews at the time the activities were carried out. Thus, in some cases, newspaper accounts were more accurate than information obtained through interviews. However, in many cases they were inaccurate due to the political bias of reporters or their sources. Whenever I doubted the accuracy of information either from newspapers or from interviews, I consulted internal documents or cross-checked two different sources. This method proved successful in clarifying conflicting information.

THE STRUCTURE OF THE BOOK

The struggle of the SSFAI is not an isolated phenomenon. Its origins are related to the political history of Isan and the specific political juncture and stage of capitalist development existing in the late 1980s and early 1990s. Following the present chapter, which has provided the context and theoretical justification of the book, Chapter 2 discusses the historical background of political radicalism in Isan by looking at the causes and consequences of political resistance in the region, and the measures implemented by the Thai state to suppress and defuse popular resistance during the period from the seventeenth century to the 1980s. Chapter 3 considers how the political conditions and economic developments in the late 1980s and the early 1990s contributed to the revival of NGO movements, which led to the founding of the SSFAI. Chapter 3 also looks at political activities during the transitional period of the Assembly. After exploring the origins and the transition periods of the SSFAI, the thesis moves on to address the most successful period, the radical period of the SSFAI (1993–95). This is done in Chapter 4 which focuses on the organizational structure, objectives, strategy and tactics, demands and major protests of the SSFAI. It also assesses some achievements and limitations of the SSFAI in this period. The successes of the SSFAI in the radical period were followed by conflicts and splits within the Assembly. The causes of conflict are considered in Chapter 5. Following a discussion on the causes of conflict within the SSFAI, this chapter looks at the founding of the Assembly of the Poor (AOP) and the subsequent split in the SSFAI. The establishment of the AOP led to the implementation of two competing strategies: a compromise strategy adopted by the SSFAI, and a mobilization strategy used by the AOP. Based on the discussion in previous sections, the final section of Chapter 5 analyses differences and similarities between the SSFAI and the AOP, and assesses the strengths and weaknesses of the two competing organizational structures and strategies. The experiment with a compromise strategy led to a new conflict within the SSFAI which resulted in the break up of the organization into two factions. Chapter 6 gives a detailed account of the activities of the two factions. It also considers the reconciliation between the SSFAI and other rival groups. The final section of the chapter addresses the implementation of a land occupation strategy by the SSFAI. Chapter 7 looks at factors that contributed to the rapid growth of the SSFAI during 2000–2002, which saw the organization develop from a regional to a national organization. The chapter also examines a new strategy of the Assembly. Chapter 8, in conclusion, restates the main points of the analysis described in the previous chapters. It also attempts to fit the findings of the thesis within a wider perspective around the following themes: the relationships between civil society, class and democracy, the nature of Thai civil society, the strategy and tactics of the struggle for the right to have rights, and the organizational structure of the struggle for the right to have rights.

CHAPTER 2

Political Radicalism in Isan

The struggle of the SSFAI was not an isolated event: it had its roots in a long tradition of resistance against the Thai state in Isan (Northeast). The Isan region is central to the politics of resistance in Thailand. The struggle against Thai state domination in Isan has lasted from the time of the Siamese kingdom to the present day. This tradition is the result of the discrimination and exploitation that the Thai state has imposed on the region. The resistance of Isan has manifested itself in different forms, using different ideologies at various times. The tasks of this chapter are to explore and analyse the popular resistance in Isan from the seventeenth century to the early 1980s, when Isan farmers gave up their armed struggle against Bangkok, by focusing on the following questions: (1) What were the causes of resistance? (2) What forms did the resistance take? (3) How did the Thai state try to defuse or suppress the resistance? To answer these questions it is necessary to look at the relationship between Isan and the Siamese kingdom.

ISAN AND THE SIAMESE KINGDOM

The relationship between Isan and the Siamese kingdom was full of conflicts, first of all due to ethnic differences. The majority of Isan people were Lao, who had migrated from Laos into Isan from the mid-fourteenth to the beginning of the seventeenth centuries (Srisakkara 1990: 283–284). This migration turned the region into part of the Lao cultural area (Keyes 1967: 7).

Isan was situated between two rival kingdoms, Siam and Laos. Before the eighteenth century, Isan was a buffer zone between the two kingdoms. This status came to an end after the Lao kingdom was defeated by the Siamese. In 1827 the region was brought under the direct control of Bangkok (Keyes 1964: 2). However, the rule of the Siamese kingdom over Isan was rather weak. 'Siamese rule over the region was, … on the whole nominal – so much so that the foreigners who visited the region doubted that it at all existed' (Cohen

1991: 70). At that time the region was ruled under the *huamuang* system. *Huamuang* were principalities consisting of an important town and subordinate villages and they were smaller in size and lower in status than tributary states, but similar to vassals in that their elites belonged to the local nobility and possessed considerable autonomy (Keyes 1967: 15). In the 1880s there were 27 major *huamuang* located in Isan. The Isan *huamuang* had to pay obeisance and bring presents to Bangkok (Elliott 1978: 64). In turn, they were allowed to *kin muang* (eat the city) 'by keeping part of taxes and fees they collected' (Tandrup 1982: 42). Moreover, they also had rights to control and use corvée labour, and mobilize military conscripts (Siffin 1966: 23). This semi-autonomy lasted until the late-nineteenth century.

The *huamuang* system came to an end when King Chulalongkorn (Rama V) introduced his reforms, the Chakri reformation, to turn the 'traditional' Siamese kingdom into a 'modern' nation-state under the absolute power of the monarchy. Under the new centralized administrative structure Isan was divided into three *monthon*: Lao Phuan, Lao Klang and Lao Kao. After 1892, the Ministry of Interior renamed these regions as Udon, Nakhon Ratchasima and Isan respectively (Thaveesilp 1988: 113). Some time later a fourth *monthon*, Roi Et, was instituted (Srisakara 1990: 285), and in 1922 the four *monthon* became known collectively as *Phak Isan* (Isan region) (Kamala 1997: 48).

ABSOLUTIST STATE AND THE MILLENARIAN REVOLTS

The introduction of a centralized political system radically transformed the relationship between Bangkok and the provinces. The Chakri reformation marked an important development of internal colonialism (Tandrup 1982: 14). The over-centralization and over-bureaucratization of the country, especially the increased taxation, aroused widespread discontent among the rural population. This discontent finally led to rebellion in the former Lao tributary states and outer provinces in the North and Isan.

The purpose of this section is to provide an account of the millenarian revolts in Isan. The importance of these rebellions to the struggle of the grassroots movements is that they became a legend with which later Isan farmers' movements identified themselves. The SSFAI, for example, declared that it was the millenarian movement of the modern period (fieldnotes, 23 March 1998). The material below will examine the idea of millennialism in Isan, and then explore the biggest millenarian revolt in the region, the Holy Men rebellion. In exploring the Holy Men uprising, particular attention will be paid to the idea of 'village socialism', which was partly responsible for Isan being receptive to socialism. We shall also look at the defeat of the Holy Men revolt and discuss its effect on the centralization plans of Bangkok.

Millennialism in Isan

In Isan, rebellions took the form of millenarian revolts. The rebellions were the first attempt of Isan farmers to resist the domination of the Thai state. From the late seventeenth to the mid-twentieth centuries, at least eight millenarian revolts broke out in the region (Chatthip 1984: 111). Millenarian revolts, according to Malalgoda, seem curious to some Western scholars, who 'consider millennialism as something characteristically Judeo-Christian' (Malalgoda 1970: 439). For example, Eric Hobsbawm believes that millenarianism is a conception alien to such religions as Hinduism and Buddhism (Hobsbawm 1959: 58). Such a view conformed with Weber's attitude to Buddhism. For him, Buddhism 'lacks virtually any kind of social-revolutionary ethics', because the notion of karma legitimates the idea that an individual's status cannot be changed except in the next rebirth (Weber 1963: 113–114).

There is, in fact, another Buddhist interpretation that provides the basis for millennial actions. According to this interpretation, there are rare individuals who have an abundance of merit accumulated in past lives, which can be translated into the elimination of this-worldly suffering and saving the mankind from catastrophe (Keyes 1977: 287–288). For Ishii and Chattip, this interpretation which formed the basis for millenarianism in Isan, derived from the royal version's of Buddhism, such as *Triphum*, a Buddhist cosmological treatise (Ishii 1975: 68–75; Chattip 1984: 126). It is true that the ideas of the Holy Men movement and *Triphum* share the notion of influential 'men of merit'. Nevertheless, the Isan millenarians did not draw their ideas from royal sources, and this resulted in a quite different political stand. The difference lies in the nature of the political structure of the Siamese state before the Chakri Reformation. As mentioned earlier, under the *huamuang* system Bangkok did not extend its control over various *huamuang* beyond the collecting of taxes from the local elites. As a result, under the Siamese domination these *huamuang* still maintained their political, cultural and religious beliefs and practices. As Kamala points out, because of differences in history, literature, language and religious customs, 'substantially different forms of Buddhism existed among the Siamese in the Central Plains' and other ethnic groups in the provinces, including the Lao in Isan. Actually, the difference was so great that 'even within one principality, religious customs varied from one m(e)uang to the next and from one village to the next' (Kamala 1997: 5). While the Siamese court followed a Buddhist tradition with affinities to that of the Khmer, Isan followed Buddhist traditions linked to the Lan Chang kingdom of Laos and the Lan Na kingdom of Chiang Mai (Kamala 1997: 40). Different Buddhist traditions inevitably led to different concepts of moral authority.

In *Triphum*, the saviour, a man of merit, is the King of Siam who has legitimacy to rule because of the amount of merit he has accumulated from previous lives. The text points out that when the righteous king 'emerges people all over the realm come to revere, pay respect and obey him. Whenever the king commands, it is legitimate because he is righteous' (Somboon 1993: 39). The implication of this interpretation is that any change in the existing system is unnecessary. While this 'elite version' emphasized the status quo, the 'popular version' widely believed in Isan was a blueprint for radical change. The Isan interpretation was based on the idea of 'Holy Men' or *phumibun* (one who has merit). Even though sometimes a *phumibun* claimed to be *Thao Thammikarat* (the king of righteousness), he did not belong to the existing monarchy and his mission was to eliminate the misery of the peasantry by changing the existing social order. It was under the influence of the idea of *phumibun* that the peasant-based millenarian movements broke out in Isan.

The Holy Men Revolt

The first Isan millenarian uprising, the Bun Kwang revolt mentioned in the royal chronicles, occurred in 1699 (Ishii 1975: 67–68). After this revolt there were seven millenarian movements in Isan. The biggest revolt, the Holy Men revolt, covered most parts of Isan and occurred during the Chakri Reformation. The scope and extent of the revolt reflected the economic difficulty that arose from the centralized control in the region. In 1890 and 1891, Isan experienced two years of bad harvests from either 'too little rain' or 'too much flooding'. The difficulties from natural disasters were exacerbated by the new economic policies. As a part of the reforms, new tax systems were introduced into the regions all over the country. Bangkok increased its tax demands in the provinces sharply. According to London, the government's revenue rose from 15,378,144.91 baht in 1892 to 28,496,029.33 in 1898, and to approximately 40 million baht by 1902 (London 1980: 76). These figures were the evidence of wealth transfer from the peripheries to the capital, which caused considerable pressure on the countryside. As Tandrup points out, although in the Central Plain the burden of taxation was balanced by the commercialization of rice farming, which offered new economic opportunities to peasants, in Isan and the North 'the increased taxation must have been a considerably heavier burden to the villagers ... who hardly witnessed any economic development' (Tandrup 1982: 47).

It was under such circumstances that anti-government activities took place. The revolts occurred because the state tried to strengthen its grip over the region. This situation was quite different from what Skocpol describes in her theory of peasant rebellion. For Skocpol, a peasant uprising 'had to coincide with and take advantage of the hiatus of governmental supervision and sanction' (Skocpol 1995: 146). This kind of argument, which 'amounts to saying that more acts of defiance will occur if the danger they entail is reduced', was branded 'hydraulic structuralism' by Scott (1990: 220). The rebellion of 1902 broke out because of 'too much' state interference. Not only did the new tax burdens and economic restrictions cause trouble to the peasant communities, but, more importantly, they also violated the traditional state-peasant relationship that peasants used to define their rights and justice. The violation of their customary rights, either by lords or the state, was unacceptable to the peasantry (Mullett 1987: 5).

In the initial stage, peasants reacted to the worsening conditions by turning to banditry (Tandrup 1982: 52). However, by the end of nineteenth century their dissatisfaction took the form of collective action. In 1899 there was a circulation of palm-leaf manuscripts (*lai thaeng*) predicting an imminent holocaust and urging people to prepare for a promised emancipation from the danger. Furthermore, Isan folk singers (*molam*) who traveled around the region also spread the message about the emergence of *phumibun* (Chattip 1984: 116; Ishii, 1975: 68; Keyes 1977: 296–297). Furthermore, the message also pointed out that things would be turned upside down: for example, rice, which was usually chicken food, would eat chickens. The implication of this message was that the weak would defeat the strong (Isan folk singers who believed in *phumibun*, interviews 25 December 1997, 4 January 1998).

While Bangkok officials viewed the Holy Men movement as illuminating the 'stupidity' and 'ignorance' of Isan peasants who blindly followed super-stitious prophecies (Keyes 1977: 300), the movement gained widespread support from Isan peasants. The peasant support for the Holy Men movement arose not only from the appeals of messianic predictions, but also their opposition to the reforms. Prince Sanphasit, the high commissioner at Ubon, accepted that the Holy Men were a movement of Isan people, peasants and members of the petty nobility, against the centralization of state power that destroyed their means of livelihood (Tej 1977: 151). Therefore, it is not sur-prising to find that one of the main activities of the Holy Men revolt involved resistance against the collection of taxes, which were imposed on the region by the central authorities.

THE IDEA OF 'VILLAGE SOCIALISM'

The struggle of the Holy Men was not just an uprising against particular policies of the state; it also sought to negate state power. For the Holy Men, the state was repressive and exploitative in nature. They regarded it as a demon, the most vicious thing in Buddhist beliefs. According to Chattip, the objective of the revolt was liberation from state power. After liberation from the state, the Phra Si Ariya era (the millennium of Buddhist millenarian movements) would begin. The village would be 'the centre of a new society' and the villagers would be united through 'socialist' principles (Chattip 1984: 124–125). In addition, the establishment of 'village socialism' would not only get rid of exploitation, but also of poverty. The new society would be a society of 'true egalitarianism and abundance' (Chattip 1984: 125). This kind of 'utopian socialism', which has deep roots in Isan culture, is still popular among Isan peasants, though not as strong as before. It is the persistence of this ideology that is partly responsible for the region being receptive to socialism from the late 1940s to the late 1970s. How can the 'village socialism' of the *phumibun* be explained?

'VILLAGE SOCIALISM' AND THE PECULIARITY OF THE *SAKDINA* SOCIETY

According to Chattip, 'village socialism' has 'its origins in primitive communal society when villages were autonomous, pre-existing the state', and then persisted throughout the *sakdina* period (from mid-fourteenth to mid-nineteenth centuries). For him, the reasons for the persistence of primitive communal society can be found in the distinctiveness of Thai *sakdina* society and the geographical location of Isan. The *sakdina* society 'had several characteristics similar to the so-called Asiatic Mode of Production', which included 'the absence of landed fiefs owned by feudal lords, the union of agriculture and craft manufacturers in village communities' (Chattip 1984: 127–128). Furthermore, Isan was located on the periphery of the kingdom, which made it difficult for capitalist penetration. The combination of these conditions, according to Chattip, was the main reason for the persistence of a primitive communal form of society and the 'village socialist' consciousness that negated the state among Isan peasants (Chattip 1984: 129).

Chattip's analysis was inadequate because it failed to take the wider picture into account. It is true that the rejection of state power in Isan villages had its origins in the social formation of the *sakdina* state and the geography of the region itself. However, it would be more reasonable to think that such ideas also reflected the political status of Isan in relation to the two rival kingdoms, Siam and Laos. It has already been shown that the Siamese state regarded Isan people as Lao, and the region was never fully integrated into the kingdom until the Chakri reformation. Therefore, the rejection of the Siamese state among Isan peasants is not difficult to understand. But why did they not want to join up with their brother kingdom on the opposite bank of the Mekong River? To answer this puzzle requires an examination of the nature of the Lao Kingdom.

'Village Socialism' and the Lack of National Identity among Lao People

The concept of nationhood is alien to the Lao state because the Lao nation never achieved unity. Power was divided among various ruling groups, influential families or tribal leaders (Zasloff 1973: 1). The obstacles to national unity were ethnic diversity and physical environment. Over the centuries successive waves of people, under pressure from other ethnic groups, migrated into the region that later became Laos. These people comprised different ethnic groups. Because the country is rugged and has only narrow valleys, 'the pattern of settlement has favored tight linguistic and ethnic communities and discouraged notions of larger national unity' (Brown and Zasloff 1986: 4). Furthermore, the diversity of tribal groups within the linguistic families is considerable, so that the idea of Lao nationhood has been quite tenuous, only barely derivable from the history of several semi-independent localized dynasties exercising sovereignty in the area as recently as the nineteenth century. (Brown and Zasloff 1986: 5)

Within this context, the people who moved across the Mekong River to settle in Isan did not identify themselves with a single political unit, which would enable them to define their national identity. Instead, they tended to identify themselves with their ethnic groups. For example, there are three main groups, Phuthai, So and the lowland Lao, who inhabit Mukdahan. Even though all of them know that they have migrated from 'Laos', they do not think that they belong to the same nation (field notes, 7 August 1998). This phenomenon did not only reflect the nature of the Lao state, but also the political structure of Isan. Unlike other regions, the Isan local elite failed to unify the region into a single political centre under the *huamuang* system. While other regions identified themselves with a major political-cultural centre – the Central region with Bangkok, the North with Chiangmai and the South with Nakhon Sithammarat (Keyes 1967: 3) – the people who lived in the Isan region 'though generally members of the Lao cultural area, were, if at all, narrowly identified with various *huamuang* to which they happened to belong, but not with any wider entity' (Cohen 1991: 69, 71). It is not surprising that even in the present day, factionalism is more pronounced in Isan than in any other region. This tendency also exists within Isan grassroots movements, including the SSFAI.

The alienation of Isan from the Siamese and Lao kingdoms naturally led to the idea of independence from both kingdoms. Since they did not have a 'nation' of their own, Isan villages became their politico-economic reference points. The idea of an independent Isan, though not strong, still persisted at least until the 1940s. It surfaced in the debate about the future of Isan when Fong Sititham, an MP from Ubon Ratchathani, called for complete autonomy for the region (Pasuk and Baker 1995: 265). However, subjected to continuous politico-economic and cultural integration from the Thai state (see below), the idea of an independent Isan finally succumbed to the idea of a 'unified' Thailand. As a result, Isan regionalism at the present time does not manifest itself as a separatist movement.

The Defeat of the Holy Men Revolt

The activities of the Holy Men mostly involved peaceful resistance and turned to violence only when the state tried to suppress them. In the early stages of the revolt *phumibun* blessed Siamese officials when they visited (Chattip 1984: 118). However, in late February 1902 royal troops attacked the Holy Men in Sisaket and killed Bun Chan, the leader of the largest group of six thousand people. Meanwhile, two lesser groups of the Holy Men led 2,500 villagers to storm *muang* Khemmarat (in today's Amnat Chareon province), captured the provincial governor and destroyed the town. In April they planed to attack Ubon, the major city in the region, and clashed with the troops of the Commissioner of *monthon* Isan. Armed with modern weapons such as rifles and artillery, the Siamese army assaulted the Holy Men's forces who were equipped only with spears, knives, swords and old flintlock rifles. The battle lasted for four hours, 200–300 rebels died, more than 500 were injured and the rest were captured or dispersed. Nine major leaders who were arrested, except one who was a monk, were executed in their villages as a warning to peasants of the consequence of anti-government activities. Villagers were ordered to drink the water oath of allegiance and swear never to betray the Siamese monarchy (Chattip 1984: 117; Keyes 1977: 227–229; Tandrup 1982: 53–54).

The Effect of the Holy Men Revolt on Bangkok's Centralization Plans

The Holy Men revolt, according to Tej, had 'badly shaken' the confidence of the government and forced Bangkok to 'immediately decide to relax the pace of the centralization' (Tej 1977: 154,155). A number of measures were implemented to assure Siamese control over, in the king's word, 'the *Lao* provinces'. One among such measures was co-opting the local elite under Bangkok hegemony. In fact, among outer provinces, only in Isan were almost all of the provincial noblemen excluded from high office. This contrasted sharply with Bangkok's policy towards the South and the North. According to Girling, those regions 'were permitted for the time being to retain their ruling families, local customs, and traditional powers'. The policy reflected 'the strong prejudice of the minister of interior … with regard to "Lao" nationalism' and the resentment of Bangkok over the 'uncertain loyalty' of Isan (Girling 1981: 53–54). In 1908 the Interior Minister told King Chulalongkorn that the centralization of Isan would take more than a decade to complete. The reasons for such delays were the lack of 'energetic, qualified and trustworthy officials' and 'the resistance from unspecified groups of people' (Tej 1977: 164). Although only a few members of the petty nobility joined the revolts, it was necessary for Bangkok to co-opt the traditional leaders into the new bureaucracy to prevent further disobedience. To win over these elites, the officials from Bangkok were told 'to be kind' to local leaders and in some cases the government returned power in the provinces back to them (Tej 1977: 155). This measure proved effective in preventing the provincial nobility from involvement in any regional movement. It meant that mass mobilization in Isan could occur only at the village level. This is why there have not been any strong town-based movements in Isan history comparable with the vigorous peasant movements.

The general picture that emerges from the discussion in this section is that the millenarian rebellions in Isan were a reaction to the implementation of a centralized political system, which upset the traditional state-peasant relationship. The growing intrusion of state power into peasant communities finally led to peasant uprisings. Although the Siamese state was able to defeat these, it had to revise its plans for centralization, and adopted a more compromising stance towards Isan in order to maintain its domination. However, the most far-reaching measure that Bangkok introduced to consolidate its rule in Isan was in the realm of ideology – the implanting of the Siamese world view among the Isan populace through the reform of Buddhism and the creation of Thai identity.

CREATION OF A DOMINANT IDEOLOGY

The aim of this section is to examine the measures that the Siamese state employed to establish ideological hegemony in Isan. The first part of the section gives a brief review on the role of the state in creating the dominant ideology. The second part provides a factual account of the reform of Buddhism that resulted in the establishment of new spiritual authority over local communities. This is followed by a discussion of the efforts to implant Thai identity into Isan.

The State and the Creation of a Dominant Ideology

According to Poulantzas, the state has two important functions to play: organizing physical repression and ideological domination.

The state cannot enshrine and reproduce political domination exclusively through repression...but directly calls upon ideology to legitimize violence and contribute to the consensus of those classes and fractions which are dominated from the point of view of political power (Poluntzas 1978: 28).

For him, 'the ruling ideology constitutes an essential power of the ruling class'. Such ideology 'is embodied in the state apparatuses. One of their functions is to elaborate, inculcate and reproduce that ideology' (Poluntzas 1978: 28). Based upon the necessity of dual functions, the state formed two kinds of apparatuses – repressive and ideological. According to Althusser, while the repressive state apparatuses comprise the government, courts, police, army and prisons, the ideological state apparatuses comprise elements such as church, school, and official communication networks (press, radio and television) (Althusser 1971: 136–137). The main objective of ideological domination was to make sure that the ruled obeyed the rulers. Such a situation would occur, according to Therborn, when the ruled believed that (a) the rulers were ruling on their behalf, (b) there were no alternatives to the existing regime, (c) the rulers alone possessed those superior qualities that were necessary for ruling (Therborn 1980: 93–97). This Althusserian theory of ideology provides a useful framework for studying the process of creation of Bangkok's hegemony in Isan.

The Reform of Buddhism and the Establishment of New Spiritual Authority over Local Community

In 1902, King Chulalongkorn passed the Sangha Act 'in order to integrate monks of all traditions into a national sangha hierarchy. Under this law a standard Buddhist practice, based on the Bangkok court system, was enforced throughout Siam. This new sangha bureaucracy was organized along vertical lines parallel to state hierarchies' (Kamala, 1997: 40). This can be seen as a direct response of the state to Isan Buddhism, which had lent support to political activity that challenged Bangkok's authority. Such measures were introduced to prevent any dissent. According to Kamala, before the Act was introduced, spiritual authority and community culture were interwoven and hence no one could claim supreme authority (Kamala 1997: 43). The new rules were implemented to eliminate provincial Buddhist traditions. Before 1902 'honors and positions were decided by local elites or villagers' in Isan. Under the new Act, rewards were only offered to monks who complied with central controls (Kamala 1997: 40).

Another important measure implemented to destroy regional Buddhist traditions was the modern education system. Under this system 'knowledge came to be transmitted in the form of textbooks written in Bangkok Thai by individuals who had little direct contact with those for whom the books were intended'. Traditionally, monks in the provinces acquired their knowledge through 'palm-leaf texts, medical work, astrology, music, ritual, chants, and meditation'. Such sources of knowledge were considered inferior to new curricula introduced by the central government. Local monks and ordinary people were repeatedly told about the superiority of Bangkok court culture

(Kamala 1997: 42). Furthermore, before the reforms, Wachirayan, the Supreme Patriarch, had recruited some of the most popular monks in Isan into Thammayut, the royal Buddhist sect, on the grounds that both of them shared a 'common interest in combating the superstitious local practices muddled into Buddhism'. After the implementation of the 1902 Act, these monks were appointed to important posts in the new Sangha bureaucracy and helped Bangkok to set up the new administrative framework and the Thammayut order in Isan. In their home area, and under royal patronage, they built 'impressive monasteries and went on to build a wide network of followers through the north-east' (Pasuk and Baker 1995: 232). The Siamese state, therefore, used the Act of 1902 to establish new spiritual authority over local communities, and at the same time to undermine the social and ideological base of local Buddhism. In other words, Buddhism under the domination of a centralized state functioned as 'state ideological apparatus', to create and consolidate state hegemony.

THE CREATION OF THAI IDENTITY

Another important move in the realm of ideology was the creation of Thai identity by Chulalongkorn's successor, King Vajiravudh. His invention of Thai identity meant the completion of his father's reforms. When Chulalongkorn launched his reforms, he concentrated on reorganizing or setting up new administrative systems. His son Vajiravudh consolidated the reform process by providing an ideological justification for the new nation state. However, this move was not only the completion of one particular reform; more importantly, it was the construction of the ideological foundations of the Thai state, which are still in place. In an effort to maintain the rule of the absolute monarchy, Vajiravudh proposed that 'nation, religion, and king' form an integral part of the Thai state. In the late nineteenth century, when Bangkok tried to consolidate its rule over the provinces, the concept of 'Thai-ness' had been given a new meaning. The 'nation' was no longer confined to the Thai in the Central Plains, but also included various non-Thai ethnic groups living in the Siamese territory. These ethnic groups formed the same 'nation' under the Siamese king. The notion was made official in 1911, when the Nationality Act, which classified anyone born within the national boundaries as a 'Thai', was enacted. For Vajiravudh, the Thai language, Buddhism and loyalty to the Thai monarch were the three main characteristics of Thai nationality. Furthermore, he pointed out that nation was an important entity in the modern world, and only through allegiance to a nation could man function as a political being (Pasuk and Baker 1995: 233–234). Vajiravudh, under the influence of the Hobbesian theory of the state, asserted that within the nation the people needed a leader who could protect his followers from danger and settle conflicts among them, and the only leader who possessed this capability was the king. Therefore, the people entrusted him to be their leader and in return the king used his power for the happiness of the whole nation. Such an argument led to the idea that the king was the embodiment of the Thai nation. As Vella points out, Vajiravudh 'saw kingship as natural to Siam, essential to Siam's progress' and argued that 'anyone who would harm the king could only be considered as someone who was exceedingly evil and would do harm to the nation, would destroy the peace and welfare of the group' (Vella 1978: 60, 61).

For Vajiravudh, another vital institution for the survival of the nation was Buddhism. It was true that the relationship between king and religion had been close since the earliest history, and religion had long been used to justify the monarch's rule. According to Vella, what Vajiravudh introduced 'was his use of Buddhism to buttress nationalism' (Vella 1978: 216). The king contended that Buddhism was central to national prosperity. If a nation lost its moral principles it would definitely be unable to survive. However, he also argued that the vitality of Buddhism depended on national security. A lack of stability would lead to the destruction of Buddhism and consequently the Thai nation. Henceforth, to avoid such a disaster everyone must perform the duties that derived from his origins. For Vajiravudh, there were two groups of people in Thai society. The upper classes, the *phuyai* (the big people), which comprised royalty, noble officials and leading businessmen, had a duty to direct and supervise the lower classes, the *phunoi* (the little people), while the lower classes, who came from the rest of the population, had to obey the instructions and orders of their superiors. Barme points out that, from the king's point of view, 'those individuals who understood their place and who carried out their duties were deemed to be good citizens, that is, they were civilized' (Barme 1993: 30–31).

Vajiravudh's ideological formulation of Nation, Religion and King had great influence on the development of Thai identity. His idea was used for co-opting non-Thai ethnic groups in the peripheries into the Thai state, and it was the most powerful ideology that the military used to justify their authoritarian rule. Today, his concept of Nation, Religion and King remains the ideological foundation of Thailand. Nonetheless, before it could attain such a high status, the idea had to be implanted in the minds of the 'uncivilized' population in the provinces.

The process of 'Thai-ization' was carried out by elements of the ideological state apparatus such as schools and temples. Actually, in the past schools and temples were closely linked because schooling in the regions was conducted at temples, and almost all of the teachers were monks. Therefore, Buddhist reforms and the creation of Thai identity were part of the same process. It is not surprising that when Chulalongkorn decided to centralize the education system in 1898, he authorized Wachirayan to draw up a 'Plan for the Organization of Provincial Education'. The aim of the plan was to replace the traditional local educational system, which used a variety of local languages, scripts and styles, with a uniform national educational system. Under the new system, schools had to use the official syllabus and textbooks. Furthermore, only the Thai language could be used as a medium of school instruction, and the spread of the Thai language was deemed the most important aspect of the new system. It meant that in Isan local languages such as Lao, Khmer, Khmu, and local dialects, which had been taught in schools before the reforms, were now banned. In 1910, just before Chulalongkorn died, the responsibility for provincial education was transferred to the Minister of Interior. A decade later, Vajiravudh passed a law that made primary education compulsory (Pasuk and Baker 1995: 232–233). However, in practice the law was not introduced into Isan until the early 1930s (Keyes 1967: 20). Therefore, in the time of the absolute monarchy only a small proportion of the Isan population had a chance to attend school. It is reasonable to assume that education in that period was confined mainly to children from the upper and middle classes. Nevertheless, under the new school system Isan children were required to attend four years of primary education. At the school they were 'taught to respect and honour country, king, and religion' (Keyes 1967: 20). Although inadequate at that time, the introduction of elementary education and the subjugation of local Buddhism marked the beginning of a long process of ideological domination in Isan, which intensified in the later period.

This section has explored the creation of a dominant ideology in order to establish the hegemony of the Thai state in Isan during the reigns of Chulalongkorn and Vajiravudh. The process was carried out through the reform of Buddhism and the creation of Thai identity. It laid the basis for the subsequent 'Thai-ization' of Isan. However, after the reign of Vajiravudh, political issues replaced ideological issues as the focal point of contest in the period from the 1930s to the 1950s. In 1932, the absolute monarchy came to an end. The end of autocratic rule provided an opportunity for new forms of political activities. The next section will examine the political struggle of 'Isanists' after the end of the absolute monarchy.

ISAN REGIONALISM IN THE EARLY PERIOD OF PARLIAMENTARY RULE

The first questions discussed here are; Who were the protagonists of Isan regionalism? From what class did they come? The second question concerns the nature of Isan regionalism. Did it arise from personal interests or socio-economic interests?

During the 1930s, political dissent in Isan took on new dimensions. This new development was the result of the end of the absolute monarchy. In June 1932 a group of army and civilian officers, who called themselves the People's Party, seized power from King Prajadhipok, the seventh king of the Chakri Dynasty (Riggs 1966: 148). The opening of new political space after the end of the absolute monarchy provided an opportunity for Isan political activists to pursue their plans aimed at regional improvement. So far, the only work to provide a useful overview of Isan regionalism from the 1930s to the 1960s is Keyes's *Isan: Regionalism in Northeastern Thailand.* However, Keyes's account covers only parliamentary politics; what was missing from his account is the Isan grassroots movements outside the parliament. This omission bars us from a fuller understanding of the dynamics of Isan regionalism, since extra-parliamentary politics played an important role in the formation of much more radical revolt in the region.

The social origins of Isan oppositionists

In terms of parliamentary politics, Keyes points out that there were two kinds of Isan MPs in the 1930s–1940s period, whose social origins were quite different. The first group came from former local elite families and the second from relatively humble backgrounds. Regarding their political ideology, the former local elite MPs 'tended to be conservative, since their own way of life was rooted in the traditional past' (Keyes 1967:26). However, Keyes also points out that the involvement of the traditional northeastern aristocracies in electoral politics manifested their political discontent over the interference of the central Thai in the region (Keyes 1967: 17). At the same time, he also argues that Isan MPs who voiced their defence of regional interests came from lower origins, and had risen to national politics through access to education. He and Brown (1994: 188) believe that these Isan MPs committed themselves to such political stands because they wanted to 'increase their popularity in the countryside and bring them to the attention of the national leadership' (Keyes 1967: 27). By contrast, Pasuk and Baker contend that it was the provincial upper classes that spearheaded the resentment over Bangkok domination (Pasuk and Baker 1995: 263). There is some truth in all of these arguments, since Isan politicians did hold different political attitudes in dealing with centralization. Many of them reacted furiously, while others supported the government because they believed that the central leadership 'could get things done and steer the country to prosperity and safety' (Kobkua 1995: 214). Therefore, it is not difficult to find members of the provincial upper and lower strata on both sides. It will be more fruitful if the question is asked from a different perspective: What was the nature of regionalism in Isan? Was it about the restoration of the old elite, or progressive struggle on behalf of the underprivileged masses?

On the question of the political motivation of Isan MPs from humble origins raised by Keyes and Brown, while there is some truth in their analysis, it clearly fails to acknowledge the different shades of political ideology among Isan oppositionists. Undoubtedly, there were opportunists among Isan politicians who opposed the government's policies just to gain popularity. But other kinds of politicians were sincerely committed to ameliorating the region's plight and tried to organize Isan peasants' struggle for social justice. Many of them were jailed, and some sacrificed their lives in political struggle.

The Nature of Isan Regionalism

The conflict between Bangkok and Isan can only be properly understood if it is viewed in relation to the government's socio-economic policy. As Kobkua points out, Isan MPs criticized the government because they disagreed with the government over the country's budget allocation. While the government, supported by the military and conservatives who emphasized national security, wanted to expand and modernize the army on a grand scale, Isan MPs demanded more government spending on rural socio-economic development. They believed that the government's investment in the military build-up was at the expense of improving the living standards of the whole country. Henceforth, it was time for the countryside to fight for better living standards. As a consequence, Isan MPs always singled out the military budget as their main target, while relentlessly demanding rural development. Such a political stand inevitably put Isan MPs at the forefront of the forces opposed to military dictatorship (Kobkua 1995: 184, 213). From this point of view, the Isan–government conflict did not arise from personal interests, but from structural ones. Kobkua aptly sums up this conflict as 'an outcome of their conflicting socio-economic interests' (Kobkua 1995: 213). It must be noted that so far, students of Thai politics have not properly understood the contribution of Isan regionalism to democratization in the country. They tend to view Isan regionalism and democracy separately, even though in the Thai politico-economic order, the struggles for better living standards in Isan and for democracy were inseparable, since fighting for regional betterment involved direct confrontation with dictatorial power. The end of authoritarian rule and the rise of democracy were central demands of Isan political leaders. The last words of Krong Chandawong, one of these leaders, before being shot by his executioner, were 'Dictatorship must fall. Long live popular democracy' (Plaeo 1995b: 13).

Prominent Isan MPs in 1933–47 were Tiang Sirikhan (Sakhon Nakon), Thong-in Puripat (Ubon), Chamlong Daoruang (Mahasarakham) and Thawin Udol (Roi Et). They were the first generation of 'Isanists' in the parliament. In the National Assembly they supported the left wing of the People's Party under the leadership of Pridi (Keyes 1967: 26). According to Kobkua, the Isan political leaders supported Pridi because they were attracted by his socio-economic and political policies (Kobkua 1995: 214). In 1933, Pridi submitted to the National Assembly a national economic plan 'inspired partly by the French and partly by the Russian Revolution in reaction to the widespread distress caused by the great slump'. In that plan Pridi proposed 'nationalization of all farm land, with farmers working for the government as paid employees and receiving pensions'. Moreover, 'the government would also take over the production and sale of rice, thus eliminating middlemen' (Girling 1981: 105). The plan also called for the setting up of cooperatives and the introduction of mechanized methods of agriculture. Pridi concluded his plan with a utopian prophecy similar to that of the Isan millenarian movement by stating that the implementation of his plan would be the beginning of the Sri Ariya Mettraya age, in which prosperity and happiness would be realized by all members of society (Stowe 1991: 36–37). The plan produced hostile reaction from the royalists and the right wing of the People's Party. Under pressure from both sides, Pridi was sent abroad to 'study' agricultural economics (Batson 1986: 245). However, after a failed royalist coup in October 1933, he managed to return to Siam and became successively the minister of interior, foreign minister and finance minister (Girling 1981: 106).

From 1933 to 1938, Isan MPs ceaselessly criticized the military budget and opposed the economic and financial policies that ignored the urgent needs of the rural population. Thong-in, the spokesman of the group, questioned the massive government spending on defence and security. 'Where should we begin our development of the country? Should we begin with the construction of a house or of the fence?' (cited in Kobkua 1995: 184). The government's slogan was 'the country was a house, the military was a fence'. Furthermore, the Isan MPs challenged the power of the armed forces by revealing the corruption of high military officials, and criticized the secret budget of the military. They opposed judicial controls on the press under the Printing Acts, the authoritarian power of the prime minister under the Special Courts Acts and the ten-year extension of the tenure of appointed members of the National Assembly. They also protested against misuse of government funds, demanded more detailed budget statements, and tried to defeat the government over the budget (Pasuk and Baker 1995: 246). The Isan oppositionists, according to Kobkua, branded Phibun Songkram, who became the prime minister and army commander in 1938, 'a dictator in the mould of Hitler, Mussolini, and the Japanese militarists' (Kobkua 1995: 214). They called for a lifting of the ban on political parties and for parties to be allowed to have branches all over the country (Keyes 1967: 27). In addition, they attacked the government's discrimination against the countryside in general, and Isan in particular (Pasuk and Baker 1995: 264).

In the 1930s, the political activities of Isan oppositionists concentrated on parliamentary struggle. However, the changing political situation in the early 1940s led to a new type of political opposition in Isan.

THE FREE THAI MOVEMENT AND THE GRASSROOTS MOVEMENT IN ISAN

The expansion of imperialist power into Southeast Asia intensified the conflict between Isan political leaders and the military. The Japanese army landed in southern Thailand in 1941, leading to a conflict within the Thai government. While Phibun aligned himself with Japan, Pridi resigned from the government and founded the Free Thai Movement, an anti-Japanese underground organization. The founding of the Free Thai Movement opened a new chapter of political opposition in Isan. This time the site of struggle moved from parliamentary politics to grassroots activism. This section traces the activities of Isan political leaders in organizing farmers for the Free Thai Movement, and its future impact on political radicalism in the region.

In Isan, the Free Thai Movement operated under the leadership of Tiang. Their main tasks were setting up armed forces, building secret runways and cooperating with the Independent Lao. In Northern Isan Tiang recruited peasants from villages near Phu Phan mountain for arms training in the jungle, and later such a practice was introduced into various provinces all over the region. The movement expanded rapidly and the number of its members in Isan reached 3,000 at the end of the World War II. Secret runways for the Allied forces were built in Sakhon Nakon, Kalasin, Loei and Ubon Ratchatani. Furthermore, Tiang arranged meetings with the Independent Lao and agreed to cooperate with them in anti-Japanese activity. Because of his prominent role in that period, Tiang was later called 'The General of Phu Phan' (Plaeo 1995a: 13; Udon 1995: 9).

Most of the literature on Thai politics (for example, Keyes 1967) has failed to explain the importance of Tiang's political activities in the Phu Phan period for mass politics in Isan. The Free Thai Movement in Isan was not only an anti-Japanese force, but also a political school for the peasant masses. It was the first time since the Holy Men revolt that Isan peasants had a chance to engage in politics in the form of collective action. This time they organized under a modern political ideology. Tiang, according to a former activist of the 1950s generation, was a 'social democrat' who believed in democracy and the social control of the means of production (Plaeo 1995b: 12). He was the leader of the Cooperative Party, which, according to Pasuk and Baker, 'contested the elections in August 1946 on a platform of Owenite socialism' (Pasuk and

Baker 1995: 266). At the same time, he was a 'son of Isan' who relentlessly fought for regional justice. The combination of these two political trends resulted in progressive, anti-Bangkok dictatorial government networks. After the death of Tiang in the early 1950s, most of his followers joined the *Samakkhitham* [solidarity] Movement under the leadership of Krong Chandawong, one of Tiang's closest friends.

Krong was born to a peasant family at Sakon Nakhon. He started his career as a provincial primary school teacher. During the war he worked closely with Tiang in the Free Thai Movement. Like Tiang, Krong committed himself to working for the poor peasants of Isan, but he was more radical than Tiang. He was a member of the Socialist Front and the Peace Committee of Thailand. Although involved in electoral politics, winning elections was not his priority in organizing peasants. More important for him was raising the political consciousness of the peasants. Krong founded the *Samakkhitham* Movement as a self-help public organization to encourage peasants to help pool their labour in doing farm work, and through economic activity they learned about politics. With his sincerity, courage and hard work, Krong won deep trust and respect not only among villagers but also village headmen and sub-district chiefs around *Dong Phra Chao* (Jungle of God) in Sakon Nakhon. As a result, the *Samakkhitham* Movement became one of the strongest peasant organizations in Isan, if not in the whole country, with thousands of members. The government reacted to the popularity of the movement among peasants by arresting Krong and his family. He was charged with being a separatist, traitor and communist instigator and jailed for almost five years before he was sentenced to death after his third arrest in May 1961 (Naowarat 1995: 4; Plaeo 1995b: 12).

After his death, thousands of peasants around *Dong Phra Chao* 'went into the jungle' to escape from being arrested or killed, and prepared to engage in an armed struggle. They and Krong's family later joined the Communist Party of Thailand (CPT), and also built up its mass bases for rebellion around that area (Tandrup 1982: 114). The *Samakkhitham* Movement members formed the backbone of CPT organisation in the early period of revolutionary struggle in northern Isan. *Dong Phra Chao* became the strongest base of the CPT, and in the 1960s the general-secretary of the party led the revolutionary war from there (former CPT member in Sakon Nakon, interview, 3 May 1998).

ISAN AND PARLIAMENTARY SOCIALISM

The focus of this section turns away from grassroots politics and back to parliamentary politics. However, the parliamentary politics in which Isan MPs become involved this time differed from the previous period in terms of political platform. This time they were not confined only to campaigning for regional improvements, but also embraced an alternative socio-political system, socialism. Their radical political platform was a reaction to the intensification of authoritarian rule and to American interference in the kingdom's internal affairs.

After World War II, the military lost some influence because they had supported Japan. As a result, the period 1944–47 was the best for the anti-military group and Isan MPs. However, in November 1947 the military staged a coup that finally led to the return of Phibun in 1948. After the 1947 coup, hundreds of dissidents were arrested or brutally killed by government agents (Thak 1979: 13–14, 84–90). The radical MPs from Isan were accused of being communists and separatists (Kobkua 1995: 215). Thong-In Chamlong and Thawin were killed in 1949, and three years later Tiang was brutally killed by the police chief (Keyes 1967: 34). Such actions radicalized Isan oppositionists. Furthermore, it is not surprising to find that hostility to the Thai government inevitably led to action against American imperialism, since the US was the main supporter of the ruling regime. With US help, the government 'expanded the Thai armed forces from 50,000 to 100,000 men' and 'strengthened the Thai police forces', and, more importantly, urged Bangkok to use 'stringent suppressive measures against opponents of the government' (Darling 1967: 217). When fighting for the underprivileged classes was opposed by an alliance of authoritarianism and imperialism, the attraction of socialism among Isan regionalists increased.

When a number of parties with a socialist orientation were formed, Isan was their strongest political base. In the February 1957 elections, the socialist parties won 21 seats, and only one outside Isan (Keyes 1967: 44). This trend also manifested itself in the January 1975 elections, when the Socialist Party of Thailand and the United Socialist Front Party won 25 seats, 21 of them in Isan (Turton 1978: 131). The Isan socialist MPs campaigned on both regional improvements and other political issues. Among their demands was the election of village headmen and sub-district chiefs. They contended that these elections would help to strengthen democracy at the grassroots level (Kaen 1995: 8). Furthermore, they planned to set up an Isan Party, arguing that conditions in Isan would improve only through socialism (Keyes 1967: 49). However, their plan was thwarted by a military coup led by Field Marshal Sarit Thanarat in late 1958.

ISAN UNDER DESPOTIC PATERNALISM

Sarit's rule, known as one of 'despotic paternalism' (Thak 1979), had far-reaching effects on both ideological and political development in the country in general and Isan in particular. The Sarit political system marked a new stage of intensive government intervention in the region. From the late 1950s onwards, the 'Isan problem' was central to Bangkok's security strategy. Regional dissent, according to Keyes, was redefined by the ruling elite 'from having been one of minor provincial complaints to one of the potential dangers to the continued existence of the government and of Thailand itself' (Keyes 1967: 51). Such fears arose from the escalation of conflict in Indo-China, which had resulted in the renewal of civil war in Vietnam and Laos. Bangkok was suspicious that because Isan was located on the Laotian border, regional dissent might turn into a separatist movement and seek support from the communist parties in China, North Vietnam and Laos (Keyes 1967: 51–52). In 1965, the government allowed the Americans to build four major military bases in Nakhon Phanom, Udon Thani, Ubon Ratchathani and Nakhon Ratchasima, and a smaller base in Khon Kaen (Viksnins 1973: 443–444). The bases in Isan were the biggest US air bases outside Vietnam (Luther 1978: 86). Apart from such policies, the government responded by intensifying the national integration project, while simultaneously increasing political suppression in the region.

This section is divided into four parts. The first part, the Thai-ization of Isan, looks at the efforts to strengthen Thai identity in Isan by the Sarit government. The second part considers the impact of economic development on Isan identity. The third part examines the split identity of Isan and the final part considers the impact of political suppression on political opposition in Isan.

The Thai-ization of Isan

In terms of ideology, the government deployed the monarchy and religion to promote national integration. In the early 1940s, Phibun attempted to play the role of supreme leader; he was, for some critics, 'elevating himself into a presidential or even royal role'. He promoted himself as *phu nam* (the Leader) with the slogan 'Our Nation's Security Depends on Believing in Our Leader' (Pasuk and Baker 1995: 260). This slogan downplayed the importance of the royalist concept of 'Nation, Religion and King'. After the overthrow of the Phibun government, the role of the king in the Thai political order changed dramatically. Under Phibun's rule, the king performed only the role of titular head of state. Sarit, by contrast, vigorously boosted the importance of the royal family. Royal ceremonies and traditional festivals were revived. He also tried to increase the popularity of the king by helping him gain more exposure to the population. Another important move by the government was the strengthening of the relationship between the monarchy and Buddhism. The regime encouraged the king to preside over Buddhist ceremonies to enhance his prestige as a patron, as protector of the Buddhist communities and to create his image as a future Buddha (Thak 1979: 323).

Sarit used such moves to strengthen his rule and also to underpin the 'Thai-ization' of Isan. Under the Sarit regime, according to Thak, 'the throne played the vital function of legitimizer, not only of the seizer of power, but a wide range of regime policies' (Thak 1979: 311). Along with the legitimization of the Sarit political regime, the monarchy and Buddhism played a significant, if not decisive, role in the national integration process. The connection between the king and Buddhism was crucial for co-opting Isan into the Thai state, since most of the Isan population was Buddhist. Therefore, the strategy was designed to foster the kingBuddha connection. As Keyes has pointed out, 'symbols of the king and the Buddha are linked – centers around the idea that the only "person-who-has-merit" who has the power to share the benefits of this merit with others is the King of Siam' (Keyes 1977: 300). The worship of the king would result in allegiance to the Thai state, because the king was identified with the nation. During the late 1950s and 1970s, Sarit and his successor, Thanom Kittikachorn, implanted this idea continuously into Isan through various types of programmes.

According to Keyes, the identification of Isan with the Thai king and Thai state 'has been brought about more through the impact of national education than through the impact of any other type of national program' (Keyes 1967: 20). This may be true in urban areas, but in the countryside where the majority of adults had no chance to go to school, the influence of the king was exerted through other channels such as royal tours, propaganda programmes and other development projects. Royal tours in the region were an important opportunity for the king to communicate directly with his subjects about their national identity. For example, in 1962 he told the Isan sub-district and village leaders that 'being Thai does not necessarily depend on the religion one follows, nor the customs and language used. There may be variations, but we are all Thai' (cited in Thak 1979: 318). Another type of national integration effort which operated throughout Isan villages, was the propaganda project of the Mobile Information Units (MIU). The activities of MIU concentrated on 'reinforcing the allegiance of the population to the Thai nation and, even more, its loyalty to the monarchy' (Cohen 1991: 78). Alongside propaganda efforts, Bangkok set up the Mobile Development Units (MDU) to accelerate the construction of road, dams, village schools and to provide free medical care to farmers in remote areas. The aim of such activities was 'to establish the authority of the government … and to support official propaganda' (Luther 1978: 93–94).

The Impact of Economic Development on Isan Identity

However, the integration of Isan was also affected by the government campaigning to promote the idea of '*kanpatthana*' (development). This idea emerged after 1957 'as the key element in the politico-economic philosophy' of Sarit's economic development plan (Demaine 1986: 95). To implement the plan, government officials were ordered to campaign among the people. For them, 'development' meant economic growth and urbanization, and the traditional way of life was a form of 'underdevelopment' that should be eliminated. Meanwhile, development also has 'ideological power' of its own. Therborn has pointed out that 'the co-optation by economic growth has constituted an original and increasingly important process'; it performed a clear function 'which is to rally all classes behind policies and institutions of quantitative economic expansion' (Therborn 1978: 229). The kingdom's economic growth from the 1960s onwards made the idea attractive to sections of Isan's population. As a consequence of these two combined factors, they had begun to renounce their own culture and look to Bangkok as a model. Moreover, the worship of 'development' did not only lead some Isan people to reject their 'Isan-ness', but also to distance themselves from Laos because of her 'underdevelopment'.

The Split Identity of Isan

The intensive national integration programme carried out by ideological state apparatuses, coupled with economic growth throughout the 1960s and 1970s, had a significant impact on Isan consciousness. Even though Isan people still referred to themselves as Lao, they insisted that they were Thai citizens (Keyes 1966: 367). The split identity caused confusion as to the meaning of the word '*isan*'. For example, when Keyes suggested that an increasing number of people in the region referred to themselves as 'Isan people' (*khon isan*), who spoke 'Isan language' (*phasa isan*), and lived in 'Isan region' (*phak isan*) to show 'their growing sense of regional/ethnic identity' (Keyes 1967: 3), his argument was only partly true. Actually, the word '*isan*' has two different meanings. The first meaning, the government usage, indicate the 'Thai-ness' of the region. It argues that although the people who live in Isan are different from the people in the Central Plain, they are Thai ('*thai isan*'), not Lao. This meaning is now commonly use by educated people and is very popular among the young generation, especially in urban areas, who do not want to identify themselves with the Lao of the underdeveloped region. Another meaning of 'isan' employed by many social activists and progressive farmers not only implies an ethnic difference between the region and Bangkok, but also the struggle of underprivileged masses.

This ambiguous identity, however, partly reflects the influence of the historical past of the region (see above) and the conflicting nature of government policies towards the region. While trying to establish a dominant ideology in Isan, Bangkok still discriminated against the region, and, more importantly, the state brutally suppressed those movements that voiced regional interests.

The Impact of Political Suppression on Political Opposition in Isan

The Sarit dictatorial regime not only closed political space for peaceful opposition, but also forced the political activists in Isan to engage in other forms of resistance. After the 1958 coup, Sarit organized series of raids in both cities and countryside. Between 1958 and 1962, the government arrested 1,080 alleged communist agents and supporters (Tandrup 1982: 113). In 1961, government forces raided several towns and villages in Isan and arrested hundreds of alleged communist agents and supporters. They were imprisoned without trial for many years, and military courts were later unable to prove their guilt (Thongbai 1974). In May of that year, two of Isan's political leaders, Krong Chandawong and his colleague, Thongpan Sudthimas, were executed by the government in Sakhon Nakhon. The killings and other arrests had a great impact on political development in the region; they generated the idea among political leaders and peasants that non-violent resistance to state repression was impossible. The only political channel through which they could express their regional grievances was the armed uprising of the Communist Party.

ISAN AND THE ARMED STRUGGLE OF THE COMMUNIST PARTY OF THAILAND (CPT)

This section studies the most radical period of political dissent in Isan, the period of armed struggle. In 1965, under the leadership of the CPT, Isan farmers engaged in armed struggle against the Thai state. From the 1960s to the 1980s, Isan was the strongest base of the armed struggle of the CPT. The purpose is now to examine the relationship between Isan farmers and the CPT. The main question raised here is: What were the factors behind the decision of Isan farmers to support the armed struggle?

The CPT and the Armed Struggle in Isan

The CPT was founded on 1 December 1942. During the war, some CPT members worked with the Free Thai Movement in their anti-Japanese effort. Most observers tend to minimize the benefits the party gained from that period, though some believe that the CPT made substantial progress from participating in the Free Thai Movement (de Beer 1978: 144–145; Tandrup 1982: 101–103). How much the party gained from its anti-Japanese activities is very difficult to prove. However, co-ordination with various anti-Japanese organs in different areas, especially in Isan (Tandrup 1982: 103), provided opportunities for the party to contact political leaders in rural areas, which became crucial for the party's armed uprising in the 1960s.

Isan was the first region in which the CPT tried to implement its armed struggle strategy. According to Brown, the party chose Isan as the head-quarters of its armed uprising because the region was 'particularly attractive with its tradition of mass-based opposition to the central governments, and its strategic location and porous boundary with Laos' (Brown 1994: 193). For the CPT, in practical terms, a rebellion was more likely possible in Isan than in any other region because, as mentioned above, the party had established a close relationship with other mass-based groups in the region since the anti-Japanese period. In 1961 the CPT founded the Democratic Patriotic Front (DPF) to organize peasants for armed struggle. Between 1961 and 1964, the centre of the DPF organization's work was in remote villages of Isan. On 7 August 1965, CPT armed forces skirmished with government troops in Nakhon Phanom. The incident marked the beginning of the insurgency, which later spread throughout the country (Prizzia 1986: 12–13).

The Underlying Causes of the Rebellion

The causes of the armed struggle will be analysed under the following sub-headings: poverty, ethno-regional factors, end of the armed struggle in Isan, and the Central Thai composition of the party leadership.

Poverty

Why did Isan farmers support the CPT? Luther (1978) and Brown (1994) argued that poverty was the main reason for rebellion in the region. According to Luther,

> an ethno-linguistic approach alone is not sufficient to analyse the cultural, social and political allegiances of these people, more important is the degree of their political, i.e. regional consciousness, and their attitude towards the government which is very closely linked to prevailing economic con-ditions and the regional 'welfare' in general. (Luther 1978: 55)

Nevertheless, for a fuller understanding of the problem, it is necessary first of all to introduce political factors into the analysis. The relationship between Isan political opposition and the armed struggle of the CPT must be viewed through the long history of regional political development as well as regional poverty. As shown above, the Isan political leaders and farmers decided to undertake armed struggle when peaceful resistance was suppressed by the authoritarian regime; the rebellion was a reaction to state brutality. The suppression of the state was also the main source of farmers' resentment after the August 1965 incident. In 1966 the government forces 'tortured suspects, raped women, and carried out summary executions of supposed communists' in various villages in Isan (Pasuk and Baker 1995: 294). They also burned down three villages (Nasai, Nahinkong and Longpabun) in northern Isan in 1974.

Under such circumstances villagers had no choice but to join the insurgency: some feared further government suppression, while some, whose parents or relatives had been killed by the government forces, became 'jungle soldiers' because they wanted revenge (former CPT members in Mukdahan, interview, 18 March 1998).

There is, however, no doubt that the underlying cause of the rebellion was the poverty in the region. The economic disparities between Isan and other parts of the country had existed since the region was incorporated into the Siamese state and the gap increased after World War II. Even though, according to London, the 'threat of insurgency led to the implementation of a number of "social overhead" programs which were designed to accelerate regional economic development' (London 1980: 92), Isan's economic progress still lagged far behind the rest of the country. 73.2 per cent of Isan rural households lived below the poverty line in 1969, and this increased to 74.7 per cent in 1971/ 72, while the percentages of poor households in the Central Plains were 25.1 and 34.9 respectively (Luther 1978: 64–65). In the 1990s, Isan was still the poorest region in Thailand. In 1994, the top ten poorest provinces were in Isan (*Thailand in Figures* 1997: 275). One reason behind the continued under-development of the region was that although Bangkok increased government expenditure in the region, the priorities were 'political and strategic benefits' (London 1980: 93).

Ethno-Regional Factors

Regional poverty has both economic and ethno-regional implications. According to Cohen, before the 1960s 'the region was of no particular interest' to either Bangkok or to foreign investors; as a result 'its position in the country changed little in the period following the death of King Chulalongkorn'. The region 'suffered from neglect and became the forgotten region of the country' (Cohen 1991: 74). Such discrimination inevitably led to 'we–they' sentiments; underdevelopment in Isan and ethno-regional consciousness were closely linked. For Isan social activists, Isan, poverty and underprivileged masses are identical. Furthermore, the 'we–they' sentiment was compounded by the attitude of the Bangkokians towards the region. Although Isan people were well known 'for their outstanding ability to endure physical hardship and turn out a heavy day's work' (Textor 1961: 15), the people in the capital city held a different opinion. For them, the Isan were lazy, dirty, lying, ignorant, uncultivated, and stupid. They called them by the pejorative term '*Siao*' to look down upon them. In Isan the word means 'close friend', in Bangkok the word means 'fool' (Cohen, 1991: 74). Even in the 1990s they still called the people from Isan 'Lao' (Pasuk et al. 1996: 19).

Since this consciousness was inseparable from regional poverty, it is reasonable to assume that it also had an impact on the rebellion. The problem lies in evaluating how strong an effect this ethno-regional consciousness had on the insurgency. According to Brown, there is no evidence to support the idea that the CPT used such ethnic consciousness to rally support among the Isan villagers, or that such identities played an important role in motivating Isan farmers, despite what has been claimed by various authors. For him, two main factors influenced 'the CPT decision to rely on class identities rather than on ethno-regional identities in the Northeast'. The rivalry between the Vietnamese and Lao Communist parties and the CPT was the first factor. Brown believed that the CPT were afraid demands for Isan regional autonomy would help the Vietnamese and Lao in their efforts to incorporate Isan into the Indochinese Federation. Therefore, they refrained from such an attractive stance (Brown 1994: 195–196). To support his claim, Brown relied on a 'stolen' North Vietnamese document and a story told by a former Laotian communist defector. Since there is no evidence from the CPT, and such sources are often manipulated by the government, his argument seems unconvincing. The conflict between the two sides came rather from the Sino–Vietnamese rivalry. When Vietnam invaded Cambodia in December 1979, the CPT joined Beijing in criticism of Vietnam. Hanoi retaliated by telling Vientiane, her close ally, to close all CPT bases in Laos, and then the long fraternal relationship came to an end (Yuangrat 1983: 19–20).

According to Brown, another factor that prevented the CPT from taking advantage of the Isan autonomy issue was 'the Central Thai composition of the party leadership'. He argues that the Central Thai party leaders did not accept the autonomy of Isan because their 'claim to ethnic distinctiveness was based on the argument that they were a sub-group of the Thai family who had been treated by the Central Thais as … second-class Thai'. The solution to the problem, therefore, 'lay in the recognition of the Northeasterner as fully equal and integrated Thai' (Brown 1994: 196–197).

However, did this kind of solution reflect Central Thai preferences? From the late 1950s, demands for regional autonomy were rare among Isan radical leaders. Instead, they asserted that only socialism could solve Isan's problems. Such a tendency reflected the risks of advocating regional autonomy. Since there was no clear-cut understanding about the difference between regional autonomy and separatism in Thailand and among Isan peasants, the demand for any kind of autonomy in Isan was confused with pan-Laoism. The government exploited this confusion by repeatedly accusing Isan oppositionists of being 'separatists advocating the secession of the Northeast from Thailand and its unification with Laos' (Brown 1994: 189). Although the Isan peasantry thought that 'the Laotian people are our brothers' (Luther 1978: 59), they did not want to join them because they also believed that they were Thai citizens. Luther was wrong when he suggested that a 'Pan-Laotian State' was popular in Isan (Luther 1978: 60). Therefore, advocating autonomy for Isan was a weak point, not a strong point, for any political movement. According to a former CPT member, a question peasants kept asking was 'Did the party support unification with Laos?, and they were happy when the answer was 'No' (former CPT member in Udon Thani, interview, 10 December 1997). Under such circumstances Isan regionalism could express itself only in terms of regional improvements within a unified Thai socialist state.

The End of the Armed Struggle in Isan and the Central Thai Composition of the Party Leadership

From 'the Day Gunfire Erupted' in 1965, the CPT armed forces expanded steadily. The number of clashes between insurgent and government forces increased from 154 in 1965 to 680 in 1972 (Bowie 1997: 65). In 1973 officials estimated that there were 3,500 guerrillas; the number increased to 5,000 in 1974, and to 8,000 in 1975 (Prizzia 1986: 20). In 1978, when the insurgency reached its peak, there were about 14,000 insurgents operating in 52 of the 72 provinces (Brown 1994: 193). Only one of Isan's 19 provinces had no guerrilla base. According to official figures, half of the insurgents were in Isan (de Beer 1978: 148).

However, after the peak followed a rapid decline of the numbers of the insurgents in Isan. According to Brown, 'one more specific reason for the decline … was an influx of the Central Thai students and intellectuals into the ranks of CPT cadres in the Northeast.' Such an influx meant that the cadre positions, either in leadership or at village level, were 'manned by recently arrived Central Thai youths who did not recognize the legitimacy of Isan identity or aspirations.' As a result, Isan farmers withdrew their support for the CPT (Brown 1994: 198). In fact, after the influx of students, the cadre positions at all levels in Isan were still dominated by farmers. The decline of the party was caused by other factors. After the CPT was expelled from Laos, the party line was severely criticized by the students. They attacked the CPT leadership for their psychological and ideological connection with China. In 1980 the students, disillusioned with the CPT, began to return home (Pasuk and Baker 1995: 312). Their defections shook the confidence of farmers. In addition, the conflict with Laos and Vietnam led to major setbacks for the CPT: its supply routes from China, which went through Laos were cut, and hospitals, political schools and military training camps were closed. At the same time the conflict caused dissatisfaction within some sections of party members in Isan, since they had close relationships with the Lao and Vietnamese cadres (Yuangrat 1983: 20–21). At the Fourth Party Congress, held in 1982, the Isan leadership challenged the party's political line and demanded a new strategy and tactics. However, the Politburo made only minor changes to their Maoist approach. The party's intransigence resulted in mass defections, which finally led to the end of insurgency in Isan.

SUMMARY

This chapter has attempted to provide the historical background of political radicalism in Isan, a region central to the politics of resistance in Thailand. Political radicalism was focused on the struggle against the domination, discrimination and exploitation of the Thai state. The first major uprising against the Thai state, the millenarian revolts, took place in 1902. The rebellion was not only against heavy taxes and Bangkok's interference, but also against the existence of the state itself. It proposed 'village socialism', an egalitarian communal life, as an alternative to the state. The idea of 'village socialism' arose from the peculiarity of *sakdina* society and derived from the lack of coherent national identity among Lao people. Although the Siamese state was able to defeat the uprising, it had to revise its plans for centralization, and adopted a more compromising stand towards Isan in order to maintain its domination in the region. The most far reaching measures that Bangkok introduced to consolidate its rule in Isan were in the realm of ideology, through the reform of Buddhism and the creation of Thai identity.

A new form of political opposition in Isan emerged after the overthrow of the absolute monarchy 1932. During the 1930s, Isan MPs pressed for the improvement of the region. They opposed the government's budget allocation and demanded more government spending on rural socio-economic development. Such a political stand inevitably put Isan MPs at the forefront of the forces opposed to military dictatorship. As a result, their struggles for regional improvement and for democracy were inseparable.

The political activities of Isan oppositionists shifted from parliamentary politics to grassroots activism after the Japanese army invaded Thailand in 1941. They organized farmers in rural Isan and set up farmers' networks all over the region. After World War II, many of them joined the *samakkitham* movement, one of the strongest farmers' organizations in Isan during the 1950s. When Kong Chandawong, the leader of the movement, was arrested and executed by the government, thousands of its members decided to engage in armed struggle and became the backbone of the CPT organization in northern Isan in the early period of revolutionary struggle.

After World War II, an important change in political orientation among Isan oppositionists took place. After a brief period of political freedom (1945–1947), Thailand experienced another coup in 1947. This time the military singled out regional representatives, including radical Isan MPs, as one of their main targets for suppression. The military's repressive policy was supported by the US. Radical Isan MPs reacted to the military and US alliance by advocating socialist political platforms. However, the 1958 military coup led by Sarit ended the experiment with parliamentary socialism. Since peaceful channels for airing their grievances were closed, the Isan activists turned to the armed struggle of the CPT. From 1965 to the early 1980s, Isan was the major base of the party's armed struggle.

The radicalism of the Isan political opposition has been questioned by some authors such as Wilson (1960: 81). The political history of the region discussed above clearly answers those doubts. Experienced in long political dissent, radicalism now had deep roots in the region. Although the insurgency in the region ended in the early 1980s, this did not mean the end of the struggle for justice within the region. The defeat of the CPT only led to a new chapter of the struggle of Isan farmers.

CHAPTER 3

Origin and the Transitional Period of the Small-Scale Farmers' Assembly of Isan

To understand the origins of the SSFAI, it is necessary to look at the development of Thai NGOs in the 1980s, since the SSFAI grew out of an NGO movement. The expansion of NGOs in this period was influenced by two factors. The first was the re-opening of the political space by the government in order to cope with the deteriorating political situation and to regain the political initiative in the struggle against the CPT. The second was the intensification of conflicts over the use of natural resources in the countryside. Under such conditions, movements began to resume their activities based on small, issue-based organizations, and later developed into different types of organizations, among them the important Small Scale Farmers' Assembly of Isan (SSFAI). The purpose of this chapter is to examine the origins of the SSFAI and its activities in the transitional period. To this purpose, the chapter reviews ideas concerning the political opportunity structure of social movements. Then it traces political developments and environmental conflicts during the period of the 1970s, the 1980s and the early 1990s. It also explores the conflict within Isan grassroots movements, which had a significant impact on the development of the SSFAI.

POLITICAL OPPORTUNITY STRUCTURE OF SOCIAL MOVEMENTS

Political opportunity structure was recognized by some social movement theorists as an important factor that had great influence on the course of struggle of social movements. They believed that 'the timing and fate of movements' were 'largely dependent upon the opportunities afforded insurgents by the shifting institutional structure and ideological disposition of those in power' (McAdam 1996a: 23).

According to Tarrow, 'political opportunity structure' means 'consistent … dimensions of the political environment which either encourage or discourage people from using collective action'. This concept, argues Tarrow, 'emphasizes resources *external* to the group – unlike money or power – that can be taken advantage of even by weak or disorganized challengers' (Tarrow 1994: 18).

For Tarrow, there are four important aspects of political opportunities:

a. *Increasing access to participation.* This opportunity may occur when the elites decide to partially open the political system.

b. *Shifts in ruling coalitions.* The instability of political alignments creates uncertainty and induces elites to compete for support from the masses. Alternatively, a change in ruling coalitions encourages people to engage in political actions.

c. *The availability of influential allies.* The presence of influential allies has a strong correlation with movement success. Such allies include not only distinguished persons, but also other anti-government organizations.

d. *Cleavages within and among elites.* Conflicts within elites will provide incentives to ordinary citizens to risk collective action, and sometimes encourage some factions of ruling groups that are out of power to side with social movements. (1994: 86–89)

Although 'most political movements … are set in motion by social changes that render the established political order more vulnerable or receptive to challenge' (McAdam at al. 1996: 8), it is important to understand the dialectical relationship between social movements and political opportunities. We need to recognize the agency elements of social movements because their success does not depend upon outside forces alone. As Gamson and Meyer pointed out, 'opportunities open the way for political action, but movements also make opportunities'. They are 'active in structuring and creating political opportunity'. Furthermore, present movements 'often benefit from opportunities created by predecessors or other contemporary movements' (Gamson and Meyer 1996: 276).

Piven and Cloward also pointed out that while political opportunities generate favourable environments for social movements, social movements themselves also 'make an important contribution to elite fragmentation and electoral dealignment'. They emphasized that 'the role of disruptive protest helping to create political crises is the main source of political influence by lower-stratum groups' (Piven and Cloward 1992: 321).

This chapter will apply the idea of dialectical relationship between social movements and political opportunity structure to examine political conflict in Thailand during the 1970s and the 1980s, which will help us to understand the political context of the origins of the SSFAI. My argument is that political opportunity that favoured the founding of the SSFAI was the outcome of the contention between the state and social movement in the 1970s. The strength of popular resistance forced the state to compromise with social movements by opening political space and starting democratization process in the late 1970s, which made it possible for the underprivileged class, among them the small scale farmers of Isan, to organize themselves within civil society.

REFORM OR REVOLUTION?

This section explores the political conflicts in the 1970s, which finally led the state to implement some kind of reform in order to prevent a successful social revolution. The section is organized into three parts. The first looks at the popular uprising in 1973 that ended the period of authoritarian rule and led to the expansion of civil society organizations. The second focuses on the repressive policies of the state, which were implemented to counter the political radicalism of popular movements. The third examines the reaction of the movements to state oppression.

The Popular Offensive

In 1973, Thailand witnessed the first democratic uprising from below, which finally overthrew the authoritarian regime begun by Sarit 15 years earlier. The anti-dictatorial movement of the 1970s was led by the National Student Center of Thailand (NSCT). In October 1973, the NSCT organized a demonstration in Bangkok in which some 400,000 people participated; they came under attack by riot police and troops equipped with tanks and helicopters, and the students fought back bravely. The student-led revolt forced the Thanom government to resign, though it should be noted that the resulting victory was facilitated by a deep split within the military, and the intervention of the king (Prudhisan 1992: 65). The 1973 student-led revolt marked a turning point in Thai democratic development. As Zimmerman points out, it changed the balance of political forces in Thailand. It was the first time in Thai history that a government had been changed by the popular masses, outside the established power cliques (Zimmerman 1974: 514). According to Anderson, during the 'democratic period' of 1973–76 'Thailand had the most open, democratic political system it has experienced, before and since' (Anderson 1998a: 289). After the junta was overthrown, Thai people had a chance to experience freedoms they had never enjoyed before. Different kinds of civil society organizations were formed to express grievances and make demands. Most active among them were students, labour unions and farmers' organizations. They protested against the US military bases in Thailand, corruption by political business interests, abuses by government officials and general social injustice. In 1973 and 1974 the number of strikes increased fourfold compared with the 1968–72 period. In the countryside, the Farmers' Federation of Thailand, an independent peasants' organization, demanded land reform and rent regulation. Apart from political activities, the students challenged the ruling ideology. They denounced traditional values (such as seniority) and proposed replacing them with radical or socialist ideas (Girling 1981: 200–206; Wedel and Wedel 1987: 138–149).

The Elite Response

The activities of the grassroots movements and their radicalization undoubtedly frightened the ruling elite. The victory of the communists in Vietnam in 1975 and the American military withdrawal from Thailand in 1976 intensified their fears (Mallet, 1978: 83). Right-wing terrorist groups, such as the Red Gaurs and the Village Scouts, were set up to counter the growth of popular movements (Anderson, 1998b: 157–160). The groups, according to Girling, were supported by the 'traditional establishment' and businessmen, who were afraid of alternative changes (Girling 1981: 210).

The right wing launched an attack on the movements by accusing them of being 'Chinese', 'Vietnamese', 'un-Thai', and 'anti-monarchists' (Anderson 1998b: 162). In addition to a psychological warfare campaign, they used physical violence to intimidate the left. Eighty farmers, students and workers died as a result of right-wing terror (Mallet 1978: 85, 91). The violence against the left culminated in the military coup of October 1976. More than 100 were killed, 145 wounded, and 3,059 political activists arrested (Bowie 1997: 28). After the coup, Thanin Kraivichien, the new prime minister, imposed martial law on the country, universities and schools were subjected to greater supervision, meetings of more than four people were made illegal and strikes were banned. Some 8,000 people were arrested on charges of being a 'danger to society' in the first few months after the coup (Girling 1981: 216; Mallet 1978: 91). In this situation, 'from the countryside to the cities, from rural to urban activists, the right seemed to be in complete control' (Bowie 1997: 115).

The Left Revolt

The apparent strength of the right after the 6 October coup proved to be an illusion. The violence ended hopes for peaceful change. After the coup, many intellectuals went into exile abroad, and some 3,000 activists joined the CPT (Wedel and Wedel 1987: 150). The new recruits not only strengthened the insurrectionary forces, but more importantly, they legitimized the party's armed struggle. More and more Thais viewed 'the CPT as the only credible alternative to the status quo' (Bowie 1997: 137).

After 6 October 1976, the insurgency grew rapidly. In 1975, according to the CPT figures, the 'liberation soldiers' launched 75 attacks and killed 450 'enemies'. Between 6 October 1976 and 6 October 1977, this number increased greatly. In that period there were 717 engagements in which 1,475 government soldiers were killed, 1,802 wounded and more than 50 bases burnt down (de Beer 1978: 149). In 1979, it was estimated that the number of insurgents was about 10,000 (Bowie 1997: 137).

While the CPT was growing rapidly, the government faced a legitimacy crisis. Thanin's ultra-rightist policies alienated the regime from the rest of society. Under martial law, officials exercised power arbitrarily. Thousands of people designated 'elements dangerous to society' were detained and arrested. Several government officials, including senior figures, were dismissed. Moreover, the anti-communist campaign worried business circles and discouraged foreign investment, which resulted in an unprecedented flight of capital to Singapore and Hong Kong (Bowie 1997: 138–139). The growth of the CPT and the legitimacy crisis of the Thanin regime led a senior CIA officer to predict that the guerrillas would be able to seize Bangkok within five years (Pasuk and Baker 1995: 296). In retrospect, such a view over-stated the threat. However, this was understandable since the political crisis in Thailand occurred only about one year after the communist victory in Indochina.

The Politics of Compromise

To prevent predictions of imminent revolution from coming true, Bangkok had to introduce new policies to win over the left, and so isolate the CPT. This section argues that compromise with the students and other democratic forces by offering them new political space was the key to government efforts.

On 20 October 1977, the military staged a coup against Thanin, the first step in the implementation of a new strategy. After the coup, the new government under Kriangsak Chomanan's leadership declared that communism could be defeated only through 'democracy', although it did not fail to emphasize the 'Thai' characteristics of 'democracy'. Kriangsak promised socio-economic and political reforms (Mallet 1978: 98). His major initiative was a rapprochement with the students. In November 1978, he announced an amnesty for 18 student leaders, who had been tried by a military tribunal, and some 3,000 students who had fled to join the CPT after the 6 October incident. The amnesty was later extended to all of those who had joined the CPT (Wedel 1983: 47). Furthermore, Kriangsak eased the censorship of the press, increased the minimum wage and held elections in 1979 (Girling 1981: 220–223). Political activities were allowed both inside and outside universities (Prizzia 1986: 80–83). This was the beginning of a new form of political rule that Chai-anan (1989) called 'semi-democracy'. Semi-democracy, or 'democracy with Thai characteristics', was a form of parliamentary rule dominated by the military. It was a kind of political transition from dictatorial rule to parliamentary democracy, under which the military gradually lost political power to other actors.

In 1980, the army commander Prem Tinsulanonda, Kriangsak's successor as PM, and Chavalit Yongchaiyudth, a staff officer, drafted a counter-insurgency policy that later become known as Prime Ministerial Decree 66/23, to strengthen the policy implemented under the Kriangsak government. The decree was based on the view that to prevent the students and other democratic organizations from joining the armed struggle, the government would have to allow them to engage in 'peaceful' political activities outside the jungle (Chalermkiat 1990: 117).

The struggle of social movements within civil society played a key role in the transition from authoritarian rule to democracy in Thailand in 1973. The contention between them and the state after the 6 October coup in 1976 resulted in a new political arrangement that led to a renewal of the democratization process in Thailand. This renewal offered opportunity for NGOs to recommence their activities.

RISE OF THE NGO MOVEMENT IN THAILAND

The NGO movement played an important role in the formation of the SSFAI. To understand the origins of the organization, it is necessary to look at the development of the NGO movement in Thailand in some detail. After a brief literature review concerning the political role of NGOs, this section explores the history of Thai NGOs and the activities of Isan NGOs. The section ends with a discussion on the debate within Isan NGOs and grassroots activists, known as the debate between the 'community culture' and 'political economy' approaches. This debate had significant implications for the development of the SSFAI.

The Political Role of NGOs

There are three broad claims made by those who support a major role for NGOs. First, NGOs and POs (people's organizations) are viewed as important agents for 'democratization' and vital components of a 'thriving civil society'. According to Edwards and Hulme, NGOs are supposed to 'act as a counter-weight to state power – protecting human rights, opening up channels of communication and participation, providing training grounds for activists and promoting pluralism' (Edwards and Hulme 1995: 4). NGOs, according to Clarke, 'play a significant role in the politics of many developing countries and they have become significant political actors in civil society in Asia, Africa and Latin America' (Clarke 1998: 23). According to Fowler, NGOs can countervail state power by 'strengthening and linking' POs and other community-based organizations into 'people's movements' (Fowler 1991: 61). Second, NGOs are increasingly seen as a mechanism for promoting economic and social development. Since they have a strong commitment to poverty alleviation in rural areas, they therefore actively support the establishment of grassroots organizations through which peasants can express views on their needs (Farrington et al. 1993: 6). Third, compared with private companies and the government, NGOs are more efficient in service delivery. They can do it 'cheaper, better, and faster' (Stewart 1997: 12).

Such claims have been challenged by a number of authors. Stewart points out that many of the case studies contradict pro-NGO claims (Stewart 1997: 13). For instance, Fowler asserts that in the eastern and southern region of Africa, NGOs are not strong enough to pressure governments for significant democratic development. 'There is', argues Fowler, 'little evidence to indicate a coalescence of community-level bodies into politically significant networks and broader independent associations.' In addition, states 'are taking control of mass membership organizations' and make sure that the 'growing number of grass-roots organizations remain fragmented and do not ... form large movements independent of the ruling party.' (Fowler 1991: 72–73). A more devastating critique came from Petras, who viewed NGOs as 'the "radical wing" ... of the neo-liberal establishment' (Petras 1999: 404). NGOs, Petras argues, co-opt the language of the left but 'this language is linked to a framework of collaboration with donors and government agencies' that never goes beyond 'the conditions permitted by the neo-liberal state and macro-economy' (Petras 1999: 434). The different attitudes towards NGOs among authors reviewed in this section partly reflect the diversification of NGO movements. This diversification also existed among Thai NGOs.

The Development of Thai NGOs

The first non-governmental development organization, the Thailand Rural Reconstruction Movement (TRRM), was founded in 1969. The central idea of the TRRM was that 'rural reconstruction is human reconstruction' (Suthy 1995: 99). The TRRM rejected government development policies that emphasized economic growth at the expense of equity and developing the cities at the expense of the countryside. Another important NGO was the Komol Keemthong Foundation (KKF). Based on Buddhist values, the KKF advocated improving the quality of life through self-reliance (Pasuk and Baker 1995: 384–385). From the 1970s to the 1990s, the NGO movement experienced changes in terms of ideology, organizational structure and strategy. The material below will focus on the differences between the NGOs in the 1970s and in the post-1970s period. The picture that arises from this examination will provide a background for understanding the dynamics of NGO movements, and the debate within Isan NGOs.

According to Banthorn Ondam, a veteran NGO leader, the majority of NGOs were large organizations, in the early period run by academics, bureaucrats, members of the upper classes or foreigners. Their work focused on rural poverty and social welfare, while their outlooks were borrowed from the West. During the 1970s, there was no cooperation among them. As a consequence, they did not turn into a movement; they were mere non-profit groups (Wasant 1993: 20).

During the 'democratic period' of 1973–76, NGOs represented a middle force, which advocated gradual improvement within the existing system. As a result, they faced hostility from the left and right. According to Rosana Tositrakul, a veteran NGO leader, NGOs were unpopular among social activists, who were committed to socialist revolution. For them, NGOs were unable to bring about meaningful changes because the scope of their activities was too narrow, and they did not address the causes of social problems. Therefore, NGOs were not considered agents of change; they were, instead, branded 'reactionary' organizations that obstructed the wheel of history (*Bangkok Post*, 10 October 1993: 20). Despite being cold-shouldered by the left, NGOs were mistrusted by the right. Before the 1980s, NGOs, like other social movements, were viewed by the right as communist agents who had set up legal organizations to operate on behalf of the CPT. After the 6 October coup, their activities were suppressed by the ultra-right government (Amara and Nitaya 1994: 27, 56).

The Revival of NGOs after the 6 October Coup

As we have seen above, the contention between social movements and the state after the 6 October coup ended up in the renewal of democratization in Thailand. From the early 1980s onwards, NGOs were able to expand their activities again. According to Kasian Tejapira, a political scientist at Thammasat University, 'the government tried to encourage NGOs to grow as alternatives for idealistic people who were disillusioned with socialism and yet were distrustful of the government' (Wasant 1993: 20). By the mid-1980s, some 50 new NGOs had been set up all over the country (Suthy 1995: 102). In 1985, the Coordinating Committee of Non-Governmental Organization for Rural Development (NGO-CORD) was set up both at national and regional levels, with a total membership of 220 organizations (Amara and Nitaya 1994: 46).

The development of NGOs in the 1980s was not just a response to new opportunities by old NGOs when political space opened to them, without any meaningful change in their scope of work or political orientation. Actually, the NGOs of this period differed from those in the previous decade in several respects. The political composition of NGO members in the 1980s was more diverse than in the 1970s. While most NGO workers in the 1970s were moderate activists, NGO workers in the 1980s included both moderate and radical activists. The radical elements came from the ranks of former left-leaning social activists, who were disillusioned with socialism, but still held on to their desire for social justice. These groups of radical activists included not only those who had returned from the jungles after the collapse of the CPT, but also idealistic youths, searching for a better society (*Bangkok Post*, 10 October 1993: 20). The influx of these radicals into the ranks of NGOs had significant impact on the development of NGOs in the 1980s and 1990s. Some veteran NGO leaders such as Rosana, tended to believe that the presence of the radicals produced no meaningful changes within NGOs, since the newcomers worked under the existing NGO philosophy (Wasant 1993: 20). Yet in reality, when radicals joined NGOs, they transformed themselves and the old NGOs at the same time. This transformation resulted in more radical and more diverse NGO movements. While the radicals-turned-NGO activists rejected the centralized organization and confrontation strategy of the social movements of the 1970s, and searched for a new strategy (Callahan 1998: 99–106), some still appreciated the value of political mobilization as a means to defend the interests of the poor, and they were willing to adopt such a strategy when the political situation required. In the early 1980s, they followed the non-political involvement strategy of the NGOs of the 1970s, concentrating their work on micro-issues, such as alternative livelihoods, health, education and so on. However, from the late 1980s, when conflicts over natural resources and environment in the countryside had escalated, they turned to radical tactics of mass mobilization. In urban areas, they engaged in a variety of political activities, such as campaigning for human rights and greater democracy. They assumed the role of the democratic movements of the 1970s, even though they were less radical than these earlier movements. As a result, from the late 1980s onwards, NGOs divided into two main factions. The first faction comprised NGO workers who followed the 'old' strategy of the NGOs in the 1970s. The second was made up of NGO workers who engaged in political mobilization. Because of the nature of their work, the former were known as the 'cool' faction and the latter as the 'hot' faction. The 'hot' faction had its main base in rural Isan (Sanitsuda 1994: 33). The relationship between these two factions was not static. They both accepted and rejected the ideas of each other in the course of continued debates and practices (see below).

The NGOs of the 1980s differed from those of the 1970s in other respects as well. According to Banthorn, large organizations were replaced by small, issue-based groups. Their activities were not concentrated in Bangkok. They spread into every region of the country. Moreover, they set up networks to coordinate their work all over the country. As a result, they did not function as separate groups, but as a broad social movement (Wasant 1993: 20).

DEVELOPMENT OF NGOS IN ISAN

In 1980, NGOs began expanding their work into Isan (Isan NGO-CORD, 1998: 11). In the early period they concentrated on so-called 'cool issues', involving non-political activities, such as community development. Their activities focused on 'fertilizer, jute, wells, toilets, meetings, training, seminars, visiting, rice and buffalo banks, revolving funds, cooperative stores' and then developed into alternative agriculture, handicrafts and community businesses (Isan NGO-CORD, 1998: 19). According to Bamrung Boonpanya, a prominent figure among Isan NGOs, the early NGO activities were similar to those of the state except that they emphasized people's participation (Bamrung (nd): 5). In 1987 there were 49 NGOs working in Isan and all of them were involved in rural development projects (Chattip 1991: 131). These activities were completely different from the activities of the popular movements of the 1970s. Such differences did not arise from tactical moves, but reflected the strategic shift of the new movements. The activities of NGOs in the 1980s, according to one of their leaders, contrasted with the activities of the popular movements in the 1970s, 'which had adopted a single confrontational strategy for social transformation that *had proved unrealistic in the context of Thailand*' (Srisuwan 1995: 69–70, emphasis added). During the 1970s, according to Pornpirom, popular movements believed that 'social transformations and creation of a just society could only be the result of a revolution', and the revolution would be achieved only under the leadership of a centralized political organization of the working class (Pornpirom 1987: 14). The new strategy, by contrast, emphasized long and gradual progress based on 'consciousness-raising', rather than political mobilization or any kind of political organization. Such a strategy derived from the idea of community culture.

The Debate within Isan NGOs: the Community Culture versus the Political Economy Approach

During the 1980s, there was a fierce debate among Isan NGOs over the strategy and tactics of the movement. The debate, later known as the debate between the 'community culture' and 'political economy' approach, significantly affected the development of the SSFAI and is worth discussing in some detail.

The Idea of Community Culture

The idea of community culture is a variant of populism. According to Brass, populism, in different forms and guises, 'has emerged and re-emerged periodically as a reaction by … farmers to industrialization, urbanization and capitalist crisis' (Brass 1996: 154). Central to populist ideology is an advocacy of a return to a traditional community. Populism, argues Brass, shares the anti-capitalism stand of Marxism. It criticizes 'big business, political injustice, and the effects of capitalism generally'. However, populism 'does this not in the name of the common ownership of the means of production (as does Marxism) but rather in the name of individual, small-scale private property'. Moreover, while Marxism emphasizes the importance of class differentiation, populism 'denies the existence of class and accordingly essentialises the peasantry'. It 'casts them all into the role of "victims", uniformly oppressed by large-scale institutions/monopolies located in the urban sector (the state, big business and "foreign capital")' (Brass 1996: 155).

The community culture approach emerged in Thai society in the 1980s after the failure of the CPT's socialist revolution. The idea was elaborated by NGO leaders from their experiences, and developed by academics in Bangkok and the outlying regions. It has now become an important approach in examining development issues (Yukti 1995: 75–78). The community culture approach argues that Thailand's form of economic development, which was imported from Western countries by the state, destroyed the economy of the village community. According to Bamrung Boonpanya, a prominent Isan NGO leader, such capitalist economic development benefited only the rich and Westerners, and made the poor poorer (Chattip 1991: 121).

Kitahara labeled this argument 'anti-modernism' (Kitahara 1996: 78). 'At the economic level', Kitahara argues, the community culture theorists criticized the commercialization of agriculture by modern technology, such as the use of 'chemicals and machines, limited kinds of marketable crops, and large scale management', on the grounds that it 'often results in total bankruptcy, in particular for farmers who work at it hardest'. The community culture theorists, according to Kitahara, also pointed out the negative aspects of commercialized farming at the social level. For them, the introduction of the market system 'broken down the traditional mutual help and fraternity of the community'; it 'substituted the egoistic competition and resultant rivalry among fellow villagers'. Furthermore, at the cultural level, they bitterly attacked capitalism for having 'stimulated materialist values and caused mental dissatisfaction and instability associated with anomie, by stirring up greed' in order to 'make more profit and to get more consumer goods'. At the political level, they rejected state-led rural development schemes implemented under the hierarchical orders of the central government (Kitahara 1996: 78–79).

According to Bamrung Boonpanya, to avoid the negative effects of the market economy mentioned above, farmers should withdraw from the market economy and rely on subsistence economy as they had done in the past. He believed that they were able to return to self-reliance because the village community had its own culture and way of development. As Chattip has pointed out, Bamrung believed that

[n]o matter what outside circumstances have been and how they have changed, the essence of a village or a community, its economic, social and cultural independence, has remained for hundreds of years. The village community thus has its own independent belief systems and way of development. (Chatthip 1991: 121)

For Niphot, another community culture theorist, if community culture is strong, it is easy for farmers to organize themselves into groups to carry out various tasks. In addition, strong community culture 'also makes it possible to resist external exploitation' (Chatthip 1991: 119).

Since the strength of the farmers lies in their community, their history and their way of life, new form of organization or any progressive ideas are unnecessary. Farmers, community culture theorists argue, can rely on local wisdom, indigenous culture, traditional technologies and Buddhist values (Pasuk and Baker 1995: 387–388). In other words, for community culture theorists, 'the answer is in the village' (Isan NGO-CORD 1998: 18).

Nevertheless, there is a contradiction in the argument of the community culture school of thought. While community culturalists believed that farmers were able to solve their problems by relying on their own culture, they also proposed that to achieve strong communal culture, the villagers needed help from outsiders ('development workers') to recover forgotten cultural consciousness (Chatthip 1991: 139). Such a contradiction reflected the incompatibility between theory and reality. As Bamrung admitted, farmers had succumbed to the influence of 'the cultural domination of the money culture'. They have given up their 'cultural roots' and turned to Western culture (Sanitsuda 1992: 31). Under such a situation, it was clear that villagers were unable to regain their roots, their own culture, without outside help. NGO workers were introduced to perform that role; this helped to solve the theoretical difficulties and justified the presence of NGOs in the villages. The role of outsider in 'consciousness-raising' in the community culture school of thought is quite similar to that of the Leninist theory of organization, which also argued that workers had an inherent class consciousness, but were unable to achieve such consciousness by themselves. To raise their consciousness, they need help from intellectuals (Lenin 1969). However, there was also a big difference between the two schools of thought on this issue. While Leninists believed that intellectuals could help workers gain their class consciousness by introducing them to the revolutionary ideas of Marxism, which had developed outside their everyday lives, the community culturalists, on the contrary, believed that the knowledge necessary for villagers' self-consciousness was generated within the community itself. The task of intellectuals was to discover it, and then help farmers to regain the folk wisdom that was part of their communal lives.

The Political Economy Approach

The community culture line of thought, according to Nakon Sriwipat, present secretary general of the Small-Scale Farmers' Assembly of Isan, was contested by another group of NGOs and school teacher activists, who called themselves the 'political economists'. Although they agreed with the community culture theorists that Western-style development had devastated the rural economy, they rejected the solutions proposed by the community culture approach. For them, the self-reliant economy was a kind of 'utopia' that was impractical in real life. Since capitalism now penetrated deeply into rural areas, it was impossible to return to a subsistence economy. Moreover, many kinds of problems within villages are caused by outside factors rooted in politico-economic structures beyond the control of villagers. The solution to the problems, therefore, is not to escape from capitalism but to live with it, using greater bargaining power. The bargaining power of farmers lies in political organization, not in local wisdom, as the community culture theorists believe. Efforts to solve farmers' problems within the villages based on communal culture without engaging in 'hot issues' or political struggle outside the villages is hopeless (Nakon Sriwipat, interview, 14 December 1997).

Political economists held different views about the nature of the political organizations they wanted to found. The majority, according to Son Rubsung, a leading figure among Isan political economists, proposed that they should set up a farmers' organization and then develop it into a strong political organization with a wide mass-base for bargaining with the state. This group of political economists rejected the idea that farmers should have a political party of their own. For them, to set up a political party was impractical and undesirable for a number of reasons. First, running a political party needed a huge sum of money, which farmers were unable to afford. Second, it was very difficult to supervise or control party members in the parliament. It was highly likely that after being elected they would seek to advance their own interests rather than working for the masses. Nevertheless, a minority disagreed with this view. They contended that only a political party could assert influence on policy-makers effectively. The idea of becoming involved in electoral politics was bitterly criticized by the community culturalists. For them, all politicians were corrupt and insincere. They offered help to the poor only to serve their political interests. In addition, the community culturalists branded the idea of building a strong mass-based organization as an 'out of date political strategy that failed to understand the new political environment' (Son Rubsoong, interview, July 10 1998). For them, as Bamrung Kayota had pointed out, organizing protests was alien to the culture of community. Such activities belonged to workers, or to Western culture (Naruemon and Nitirat 1999: 101).

To strengthen their organizations, political economists suggested that farmers should have a high level of political consciousness, learn to think scientifically, and apply modern knowledge to their work and production. Although believing that some communal traditions were useful for farmers, they insisted that superstition prevented farmers from developing their ability to cope with the modern world (Nakon Sriwipat, interview, 14 December 1997). The community culture theorists, on the contrary, ferociously attacked efforts to convince villagers to give up their superstitious practices as 'brain washing'. For them, local tradition, including superstition, was useful for strengthening the village community (Volunteer for Society Project 1984: 241–42).

According to the Isan NGO-CORD, 'no one won' the debate (Isan NGO-CORD 1998: 18). However, during the 1980s the NGO movement in Isan operated under the influence of the community culture school of thought. The popularity of this approach reflected the ideological atmosphere at that time. Disappointed with socialist ideas, most activists were searching for a new orientation and strategy. While the political economy approach shared many assumptions with popular movements in the 1970s, the community culture perspective offered them a new and experimental perspective. Even though the community culture school of thought prevailed in the 1980s, the changing situation in Isan rural areas in the early 1990s undermined its validity.

ENVIRONMENTAL CONFLICT AND THE RADICALIZATION OF ISAN NGOS

The non-political involvement strategy of the community culture approach was put to the test by the intensification of the penetration of capitalism into the countryside and associated changes in state policy. The aims of this section are to show how industrialization led to environmental conflict in the Isan countryside, and the impact of this conflict on the strategy of the community culture approach.

Unequal Development and Environment Conflict

In the late 1980s, Thailand was experiencing rapid economic growth. Between 1987 and 1991, the country's GDP increased by 10.5 per cent annually. According to Hunsaker, the sources of economic dynamism came from the ability to access foreign markets, foreign direct investment, and 'the conversion of Thai natural resources into exportable goods' (Hunsaker 1996: 1). The country's modernization drive was based on the exploitation of the countryside. The wealth created by the agricultural sector was channeled to finance industrialization and growth in Bangkok (Missingham 1996: 193).

According to Medhi, the agricultural sector has been the source of cheap labour, cheap food supply and revenues since the first Economic and Development Plan (1961–66). However, the most important role of agriculture in industrialization has been foreign-exchange earnings. It helps to earn the foreign exchange necessary to purchase technology and industrial inputs (Medhi 1995: 43–50). It is not surprising to find that after more than three decades of development, the income of the agricultural sector lags far behind that of the non-agricultural sector. In 1990, the income ratio of the non-agricultural sector to the agricultural sector was 11:2. Moreover, in 1992 Thailand had the sixth worst income distribution in the world (Pasuk et al. 1996: 12–14).

Unequal development resulted both in extreme economic disparities between urban and rural areas and environmental degradation and conflict. Economic growth led to conflicts over natural resources in the countryside between farmers and the economic sector and the state. According to Ubonrat, disputes over the rights to control the use of land, forest, river, and waterways have become the focal point of conflicts (Ubonrat 1991: 299). In the early 1980s, only two protests concerned environmental issues. However, after the economic boom in 1987, the number of such protests increased dramatically. In 1990 the number of conflicts over natural resources rose to 58 cases. Between 1994–95, there were 1,742 protests in Thailand, in which 610 cases concerned the use of natural resources. In Isan alone, there were 187 conflicts over natural resources in the period mentioned (Prapas 1998: 30, 39–40). Politicians, bureaucrats, police and businessmen tried to suppress popular protests by using force or intimidation (Fairclough 1996: 20).

The Radicalization of Isan NGOs

The changing situation invalidated the basic assumption of the community culture approach. In many cases, conflicts in their areas forced NGOs to join protests. According to Sompan, a committee member of Isan NGO-CORD, 'NGOs do not want to get involved in "hot issues" but they had to become involved because they happened in the areas where they worked. Sometime villagers and students asked NGOs to help them bargain with the government. Sympathetic to the villagers, NGOs decided to get involved' (Sompan 1990: 107). The three important cases discussed below illustrate the departure of NGOs from the non-political approach of the community culture school of thought.

The Anti-Salt Mining Protest

The major resistance to capital intrusion in rural Isan broke out in Mahasarakham province. In April 1990, about 1,000 villagers from Mahasarakham, Roi Et and Srisaket provinces protested against rock salt

mining in Mahasarakham. The protest was led by social activists outside the
Isan NGO-CORD, mainly from the Thongbai Thongpao Foundation, a
group of human rights lawyers, and students from Mahasarakham, Khon
Kaen and Ramkhamkhaeng Universities (*The Nation*, 11 April 1990: 2). In
the course of the protest, NGO workers in the areas who normally refrained
from involvement in political conflict decided to join in (Sompan 1990: 108).
The protestors demanded that the government close down salt farms that
had discharged salty water into the Siew river, which ran through the three
provinces (*Bangkok Post*, 8 April 1990). It was estimated that the salination of
the river affected 125,000 acres of farmland in which 300,000 farmers in 500
villages grew rice for their subsistence (Tasker 1990: 28). The business was
alleged to belong to local businessmen, politicians and officials (*Matichon*, 19
April 1990: 3).

The protest faced a strong reaction from the authorities; some 500 police
armed with batons and rifles brutally attacked the protestors, arrested 20
villagers and 19 students, injured dozens of them and burned all the food and
kitchen utensils of the villagers. The arrested demonstrators were charged
with causing public disorder, incitement to riot, assaulting police and other
related charges (*Matichon*, 19 April 1990: 3; *Bangkok Post*, 16 April 1990: 1).
The violence was widely condemned by the general public (*The Nation*, 20
April 1990: 20). Supported by the Student Federation of Thailand, farmers
from Nam Siew continued their protest in Bangkok outside the Interior
Ministry. On 20 April, the government complied with their demands and salt
mining was banned (*The Nation*, 18 April 1990: 4; *Bangkok Post*, 22 April
1990: 3). During the protest, villagers from 500 villages formed a committee
to appraise the impact of salt mining on rice fields, and try to find ways to
desalinate the river and restore farmland (Tasker 1990: 28). This committee
became later known as the 'Network of monitoring groups on salinated lands'.
Under the influence of anti-salt mining movements, farmers and NGOs
formed the Peasants' Federation of Isan (PFI) on 25 November 1990. Karawa
Noiyota, a farmer from Roi Et province, was elected as the general secretary
and later he was elected as the general secretary of the SSFAI (*Matichon*, 10
January 1993: 2).

The Anti-Pak Moon Dam Protest

During the same period, in Ubon Ratchathani, students and NGOs from
Bangkok, especially the Project for Ecological Recovery, organized a protest
against the construction of Pak Moon Dam, which is part of Thailand's
development projects (Kanokrat 2002: 134). The country's dam
construction, according to Hirsch, 'has largely been in response to the rapidly
growing demand for energy that is part and parcel of the country's capitalist
growth and industrialization strategy' (Hirsch 1998: 57).

The protest arose from various reasons. The dam would flood 5,700 rai (1 rai = 1,600 sq. metres) of farmland, affecting 903 families. In addition, according to research, the dam would cause health problems along the river. It 'will create new habitats for certain species of disease-carrying snails' (*Bangkok Post*, 23 September 1991: 3). Another negative effect was that the dam would cut the reproduction routes of fresh water species, which would result in a sharp decrease in or even extinction of some species (Atiya 1991: 21). When the cabinet finally authorized EGAT to build the dam in May 1990, the dam opponents reacted to this decision by organizing the most active Thai anti-dam movement ever, with a strong mass base to continue their protests. The anti-Pak Moon Dam movement later cooperated with other groups that faced similar problems in forming a network of environmental groups. The Pak Moon group, like the Nam Siew group, later became a founding member of the SSFAI.

The Anti-National Farm Council Bill Campaign

Another important event crucial to the development of the grassroots movement in Isan was the protest against the National Farm Council Bill. In April 1991, after the military coup, the Anand Panyarachun government planned to pass a bill that called for the establishment of an agricultural council. According to the government, the council was to promote the well-being of the farmers by coordinating and solving the problems of the agricultural sector in production, processing and marketing (*The Voice of Community*, September–October 1993: 3–4). In addition, the council would help farmers to voice their problems through their own representatives (*Bangkok Post*, 13 July 1990: 3).

However, NGOs and farmers, mainly in Isan, disagreed with this idea. According to Bamrung Boonpanya, the council represented the interests of agribusiness, instead of farmers. The objective of the bill was to subjugate small-scale farmers to big corporations. Such a policy, he argued, would push small-scale farmers into bankruptcy (Bamrung 1991: 15). The bill was sponsored by Ajav Taulananda, Deputy Agriculture Minister, a former senior executive of Charoen Pokphan, the biggest agro-industry group in Thailand.

Under the proposed bill, according to NGOs, the council was to be dominated by bureaucrats and agribusiness representatives who constituted two-thirds of the council, while farmers' representatives accounted for only one-third. In addition, they were not elected by farmers themselves, but chosen by the government. Therefore, the farmers had no real representatives at all. They also criticized the bill on the grounds that it gave excessive power to the council, which violated the freedom of the farmers. Under the crop zoning system, the council was to determine where and in what amounts each crop was to be planted. Farmers who defied its decisions were to be penalized.

Opposed to the government proposal, NGOs and farmers called for the establishment of an agriculturalists' council, which would comprise only farmers (*Bangkok Post*, 7 August 1991: 7; 18 April, 1993: 19).

This section has shown that industrialization in Thailand was based on the exploitation of the countryside. Such a process led to economic disparities between the agricultural sector and the non-agricultural sector, and to environmental degradation and conflict within rural areas. The intensification of environmental conflicts in the early 1990s challenged the validity of the non-political stance of the community culture approach. In some areas, conflicts over natural resources forced Isan NGOs to engage in political mobilization. To deal with the new situation, the Isan NGOs proposed a new plan for strengthening the grassroots movements. The following section will look at the implementation of this plan, which finally led to the founding of the SSFAI.

FOUNDING OF THE SMALL SCALE FARMERS' ASSEMBLY OF ISAN

In response to recent events, on 19–20 June 1991 Isan NGO-CORD and several people's networks organized a workshop in Mahasarakham province. After two days of debates and discussions, they put forward a development strategy for Isan, which asserted the rights of the community over the management of natural resources, and urged the state to refrain from imposing on farmers integrated agriculture dominated by agro-industry. According to this strategy, farmers should rely on alternative agriculture. Furthermore, they also called for building a people's organization based on the 'three legs' principles, that is: self-reliance in funding and production, and capability in marketing. They also proposed a strategy to strengthen the bargaining power of the grassroots movements in Isan. This strategy had five stages:

1) building up networks of Isan farmers.

2) strengthening unity among networks both in ideology and concrete demands, and by setting up coordination organs.

3) periodic pressure on the government by making various demands.

4) bargaining with the government and forcing it to agree to a 'social contract' with grassroots movements.

5) setting up organizations to follow up the implementation of the agreements that the government signed with the farmers' representatives.

According to this strategy, NGOs and other organizations would act as allies of the farmers. More important, at the end of the workshop they set up the

Coordinating Committee of Isan Farmers comprising farmers, NGOs and school-teacher activists to prepare for the founding of a small scale farmers' organization (Thong 1993a: 22–23; 1993b: 24). The content of the meeting reflected the increased influence of the political economy approach. Political mobilization was seen as an indispensable tactic for the grassroots movements. Nonetheless, the meeting still followed the community culture approach in terms of organization. Networks, not centralized organizations, were singled out as the preferred form for organizing farmers.

After several meetings, the plan to set up a small-scale farmers' organization was implemented in March 1992. Supported by the Isan NGO-CORD, on 4–5 March some 100 delegates from seven networks of Isan farmers held a meeting in Khon Kaen province. The seven networks were

1) the network of monitoring groups on salinated lands (represented by Suchat Srisung),

2) the network of anti-Pak Moon Dam groups (represented by Wanida Tantiwithayapitak),

3) the network of handicrafts projects (represented by Suntari Sengking),

4) the network of rice farmers' groups (represented by Bamrung Kayotha and Werapon Sopa),

5) the network of households affected by the Land Redistribution Project for the Poor in Degraded Forests Areas, known by its Thai initials as *Kho Jo Ko* (represented by Kam Butsri and Prajak Kutajitto, a forest monk from Dongyai forest),

6) the network of cattle-raising groups (represented by Son Rubsoong)

7) the network of alternative agriculture groups (represented by Arun Waikam). The meeting opposed the National Farm Bill and elected the committee to draft an alternative bill, the Agriculturalists' Council Bill. They also agreed to found the Small Scale Farmers' Assembly of Isan (SSFAI) as a network for campaigning against the government's National Farm Council Bill.

In the early period, the SSFAI was controlled by the community culturalists under the leadership of Bamrung Boonpanya, who acted as chairman of the founding committee of the SSFAI. According to Son, a member of the founding committee of the SSFAI, the name of the organization partly reflected the influence of the community culture school of thought and partly reflected the objectives of the organization. Because the community culture theorists rejected any kind of centralized organization, they chose the word 'assembly' to indicate that the SSFAI was only the meeting of the various networks, not a highly developed organization. And since the main objective of SSFAI was to campaign against the National Farm Council

Bill, the term 'small scale farmers' was included to demonstrate opposition to large-scale agribusiness.

The first congress of the SSFAI was convened on 6 March. Sompop Boonnak was elected as the coordinator of the organization, and later Karawa Noiyota from the Peasants' Federation of Isan was elected as general-secretary. The activities of the SSFAI in this period concentrated on educating farmers through meetings and seminars. They refrained from involvement in political mobilization (Son Robsung, interview, 10 July 1998). According to Kong Thawiworn, a founding member of the SSFAI from Chiayaphum province, the SSFAI emphasized 'consciousness-raising' among its members in the early period. It was not strong enough to organize protests against the government (Kong Thawiworn, interview, 4 October 1997). Therefore, in the initial period the SSFAI played no significant political role in mass politics in Isan. However, the intensification of forced eviction under the *Kho Jo Ko* programme in 1992 forced the SSFAI to turn to radical tactics.

KHO JO KO AND FARMERS' RESISTANCE IN ISAN

The *Kho Jo Ko* programme was a bid by the Thai state to evict farmers from their lands in the so-called 'degraded forest reserves' for commercial reforestation. The logic behind the implementation of *Kho Jo Ko* was that farmers were primarily responsible for deforestation in Thailand. Their presence in forest reserve areas was illegal, and therefore they had to be evicted from the areas prior to reforestation. The effort to drive farmers out of their lands began a new chapter of the state–farmer conflict over land rights in rural Isan, which has lasted until the present day. Farmers, who believed that they had a right to their land, waged strong resistance to *Kho Jo Ko*. The anti-*Kho Jo Ko* movement, an important episode in Isan rural activism, was the first major farmers' movement in the region after the collapse of the CPT. It marked a new phase of radical grassroots movements in Thailand. In addition, it was the first major political mobilization in which the SSFAI got involved. More importantly, the state–farmer conflicts over land rights, which arose from *Kho Jo Ko*, did not end after the abolition of the project. These conflicts became a major point of campaign of the SSFAI. Because of its importance, this section will deal with the causes and consequences of the *Kho Jo Ko* programme in some detail. The section is organized into four parts. The first part examines the cause of deforestation in Thailand. The second part looks at the state-business partnership behind the reforestation plan. The third discusses the role of the military in the implementation of the *Kho Jo Ko*. These three parts provide materials for understanding farmers' resistance to the *Kho Jo Ko*, as discussed in the fourth part.

THE POLITICAL ECONOMY OF DEFORESTATION

In recent years forestation in Thailand has decreased rapidly. In 1968, it was reported that 53 per cent of Thailand was forested. In 1985, according to official figures, the proportion had reduced to 29 per cent (Ross and Suwattana 1995: 270). However, the United Nations Environmental Program (UNEP) believed that in 1986 forests covered only 16 per cent of the national area (Hunsaker 1996: 2), a figure indicating one of the highest degrees of deforestation in Southeast Asia (Hafner 1990: 69).

There are, according to Rigg, two opposite views concerning the relationship between development and environment. For the World Bank, 'environmental problems are the manifestation of poverty and under-development', whereas environmentalists contend that 'such problems are ... an inevitable outcome of modernization and rapid economic growth' (Rigg 1995: 4). In Thailand, as Hirsch has pointed out, deforestation and development are closely linked. 'Both are processes of important changes in the Thai political economy over the past century, and in particular since 1960' (Hirsch 1993: 34). During the 1960s and 1970s, when the country experienced high economic growth, it also experienced a high rate of deforestation (Pasuk et al. 1996: 41). As mentioned above, agricultural exports were the main source of financing the kingdom's industrialization (Hafner 1990: 79). However, the country's agricultural growth rose mostly through extensive rather than intensive expansion (Hunsaker 1996: 10). Hence, even though the government passed the Protection and Reservation Forest Act in 1964 (Kamon and Thomas 1990: 171), in practice it allowed people to clear forests for cash crops (Hafner 1990: 79). It was no coincidence that Thailand experienced a high rate of deforestation during the so-called 'golden era' of Thai agriculture in the 1970s (Medhi 1995: 43). In addition, deforestation also arose from timber-related industries. In 1968 the Royal Forestry Department (RFD) decided to give 30-year logging concessions to companies throughout the country. The decision resulted in more than 500 areas covering 50 per cent of the kingdom's land area being assigned as concession areas (Kamon and Thomas 1990: 172).

Nevertheless, deforestation did not result from development alone, but also occurred for security reasons. To deny areas to the CPT, the military built roads into the jungle. In addition, they encouraged farmers to set up new villages to secure certain areas for the state (Taylor, 1993: 6). Such a policy led to large-scale deforestation. For example, between 1967 and 1988 in Nong Khai, a province of Isan, 1,777,244 rai of forest were destroyed as a result of building strategic roads through the reserve forests where the CPT were active (Chai-Anan and Kusuma 1992: 43). The political rationale for such a policy came to an end with the defeat of insurgency in the early 1980s. However, the state did not immediately end deforestation under the guise of security. In

1987, loggers with close military connections successfully pressured the government to open forest reserves and wildlife sanctuaries to logging companies. Only in 1989, after disastrous deforestation-related floods in the South, did the government, under pressure from environmental groups, impose a total ban on logging (Pasuk and Baker 1995: 81–82). During the period from 1961 to 1988, a combination of the factors mentioned above resulted in massive deforestation; 81 million rai of forest was destroyed in that period. The figure was almost the same as the expanded areas of cash crops (Pasuk and Baker 1995: 61). The problem in Isan was more acute than in the rest of the country. In 1961, according to government reports, forest covered 44.3 per cent of the region, yet by 1991 the figure had dwindled to 13.6 per cent (Medhi 1995: 42).

The Political Economy of Reforestation

As environmental concerns gained momentum, in 1985 the RFD proposed a plan for reforestation. Under the plan, forests should cover at least 40 per cent of the country's land area, of which 15 per cent would be reserve forest and 25 per cent commercial forest. While the former would help to protect the environment, the latter would be used for economic purposes. For commercial forests, the RDF decided to grant concessions to private companies to turn 'degraded forests' into corporate eucalyptus plantations (Handley 1991a: 15). Eucalyptus, a fast growing tree from Australia, was promoted by the RDF as a raw material for the pulp industry (Handley 1991b: 16).

The pulp industry was central to the RDF's reforestation plan for various reasons. The rapid increase in domestic demand for pulp caused strong pressure for an alternative supply of raw materials. Meanwhile, the growing demand for pulp and wood chip in East Asia provided the opportunity for a huge export market (Apichai et al. 1992: 188; Lohmann 1991: 10). Furthermore, the RDF enthusiasm for commercial plantations also derived from the close relationships between bureaucrats, politicians, business interests and transnational corporations. There was evidence to indicate that eucalyptus was chosen for reforestation because high ranking officials in the RDF had close connections with private eucalyptus nurseries (Apichai et al. 1992: 189–190).

The Military and Kho Jo Ko

Most of the land in degraded forest reserves which the RDF chose for reforestation was occupied by farmers before or during the 1960s and 1970s. To make way for large-scale agri-business, the state first had to 'reclaim' the lands from farmers. They justified their actions by claiming that farmers had encroached on the state's land. The farmers, on the contrary, believed that they were entitled to live in these areas because they had settled there with the encouragement of officials, and in many cases they had settled before the areas were classified as forest reserves. Moreover, officials had also regularly collected land taxes from the villages, which in their view signified government acceptance (Pasuk et al. 1996: 44). They therefore moved against the RDF's plan from the outset.

Between 1985 to 1988, there was a series of protests in various provinces of Isan. One of the fiercest protests occurred in Buriram where more than 2,000 farmers burned down the eucalyptus nurseries and 64 hectares of eucalyptus grown by the RDF (Aphichai et al. 1992: 202). Faced with resistance from farmers, the RDF made little progress throughout the 1980s. The reforestation, however, entered a new period when the military intervened in 1990. The National Security Council, which in the past had encouraged farmers to settle in reserve forest areas, proposed a plan to move farmers to make way for pulp plantations (Pasuk et al. 1996: 45, 46). The plan, which was later known as *Kho Jo Ko*, was implemented after the military coup in 1991. It was estimated that more than 10 million farmers lived in degraded forest reserves (Handley 1991a: 15). Under the project, the military was to relocate 970,000 families (9,700 villages) from 1,253 forests all over the country (Pasuk et al. 1996: 45). Isan was chosen as the first region in which to implement the project. For environmentalist NGOs, this decision was made because Isan was the poorest region, and also a region considered inferior by Bangkok (Pasuk et al. 1996: 46). Between 1991 to 1995 the military planned to move more than one million farmers (250,000 families from 2,500 villages) living in degraded forests in various parts of the region and resettle them in other selected degraded lands (Hirsch 1993: 21).

According to Pasuk et al., *Kho Jo Ko* signified the changing relationship between the state and farmers. The change reflected the transformation of the country's economy. Since the 1970s, the importance of agriculture which used to be the backbone of the economy, had decreased dramatically. The economy was now driven by the non-agricultural sector based in the cities. As a result, 'whereas the state once played an active role in promoting peasant expansion, it is now indifferent or positively antagonistic'. The antagonism between the state and farmers mainly involved the access to land and natural resources in the countryside (Pasuk et al. 1996: 37–38). However, intensifying competition over the rural resource base was also facilitated by the changing political equation in Thailand. The collapse of the CPT removed the obstacle that prevented the state from expressing hostility towards farmers. The *Kho Jo Ko* would surely have been unthinkable if the CPT had still been active in the countryside. The defeat of the insurgency, however, meant that farmers had lost their bargaining power because now the military had no reason to fear that their moves would push farmers into the ranks of the insurgents. The ruthlessness of the military in handling the project clearly showed their confidence in their ability to control the rural dwellers.

THE FARMERS' RESISTANCE TO KHO JO KO

In March 1991, the military began to evict farmers from various villages in Isan (*Bangkok Post*, 16 October, 1991: 29). As mentioned above, during the 1980s reforestation made a little progress because the RDF faced resistance from the farmers. To prevent a recurrence of this situation, the military was determined this time to break any resistance with force. In adopting this kind of policy, the military failed to appreciate the attachment of farmers to their land. As a result, the policy created new forms of conflict within rural areas of Isan. By threatening to use force against any resistance, the military succeeded in evicting farmers from their land during the early period of the project. However, when farmers were able to organize themselves, they began to resist the *Kho Jo Ko* programme. As mentioned above, farmers who were affected by the *Kho Jo Ko* formed a network to campaign against the project, and later this network became a founding member of the SSFAI.

To pressure the government to abandon *Kho Jo Ko*, affected farmers from all over Isan held a meeting in Khon Kaen on 25 June 1992 and decided to march on foot from Nakhon Ratchasima to Bangkok (about 160 kilometers). Some 4,500 farmers moved from Nakhon Ratchasima Provincial Hall along the Friendship Highway to Pak Chong district, the border between Isan and the central region (Pasuk et al. 1996: 74). They demanded to meet the Prime Minister or his representative. When the government refused to negotiate, they blocked the highway for three days. This measure proved effective; after the road blockade, a government negotiation team flew from Bangkok to meet them on 5 July (*Bangkok Post*, 30 June 1992: 2; 3 July 1992: 3; 5 July 1992: 1, 3).

The campaign against *Kho Jo Ko* discussed above had a profound impact on the Isan grassroots movements. According to Bamrung Kayotha, a leading figure among the Isan political economists, the anti-*Kho Jo Ko* activities not only helped to strengthen unity among farmers, but also healed the rift between the community culturalists and the political economists. Both sides worked together against *Kho Jo Ko* (Naruemon and Nitirat 1999: 101). However, it was the community culturalists that led the movement. The following section discusses the reasons behind the decision of the community culturalists to engage in protests against *Kho Jo Ko*, and the tactics they adopted during the campaign.

COMMUNITY CULTURALISTS AND *KHO JO KO*

The anti-*Kho Jo Ko* movement was coordinated by the Isan NGO-CORD under the leadership of community culturalist Bamrung Boonpanya. As a part of the Isan NGO-CORD, members of the SSFAI also joined the protest. After the campaign, the Isan NGO-CORD set up the Assembly of Isan Farmers for Land Rights and Improvement of Natural Resources (AIFLRINR) to follow the implementation of the agreement between the government and NGO. The move reflected the anti-centralist tendency within the Isan NGO-CORD, which emphasized issue-based organization. The SSFAI was designed to protest against the National Farm Council Bill, while the AIFLRINR was set up to tackle the land rights problem. It is paradoxical that the first major farmers' protest that reached the regional level in the post-CPT period was led by the very same community culture theorist who had tried to refrain from involvement in political mobilization. What were the reasons behind such a decision?

For the community culturalists, the relocation of farmers from their lands and their villages meant the destruction of what they believed crucial for rural self-reliant development, the farmers' cultural roots. Such a policy would resulted in 'the death of community culture'. According to Bamrung Boonpanya, he decided to rise against *Kho Jo Ko* because it destroyed the social fabric of traditional human settlement which formed the basis of the Isan folk culture. However, the struggle against *Kho Jo Ko* also arose from practical concerns. As Sanitsuda has pointed out,

[f]or the Isan NGOs, *Khor Jor Kor* is a do-or-die issue. They feel that all the NGO's work in ecological farming, community forestry, self-reliant development, human rights, or effort to strengthen the villagers' cultural confidence to fight the tidal wave of consumerism would all be meaningless if local communities were torn apart by the massive resettlement programme. (Sanitsuda 1992a: 4)

In their negotiations with government representatives, the protesters tried to achieve what they thought the grassroots movements in the past failed to achieve. First, they had to avoid former mistakes made by mass protests, which usually ended up with empty verbal promises. Second, at the negotiation table they had to challenge the traditional hierarchy of power. If the farmers let the bureaucrats dominate the negotiations, they would get nothing. Therefore, the agenda and procedures of the meeting must be dictated by farmers, not bureaucrats. With such a political attitude in mind, the farmers took an uncompromising stand in the negotiation. Most NGO activists, who came from urban backgrounds, disliked Bamrung Boonpanya's tactics and felt that they were too aggressive. However, the protesting farmers were mostly impressed (Sanitsuda 1992b: 29).

Such 'aggressive' tactics worked very well. After eight hours of negotiation, the officials complied with the farmers' demands. They agreed to sign a document to end the *Kho Jo Ko* and allow affected farmers to return to their land. According to Sanitsuda, it was the first time that the farmers' movement 'succeeded in setting the agenda as well as obtaining a written commitment from government officials'. In the Thai cultural context, such a move was unusual since 'it is considered "inappropriate" to ask the "*phuyai*" to put [an] agreement down in writing' (Sanitsuda 1992a: 4; *Bangkok Post*, 7 July 1992: 2).

However, apart from the determination of farmers to fight against the *Kho Jo Ko*, the Isan grassroots movement was able to manipulate the negotiations because of the instability of the government at that time. In May 1992 there was a popular uprising against the military-linked government in Bangkok, which forced the ex-army commander to resign as Prime Minister. When the farmers organized the protest in June, the political situation was still uncertain. The interim government was not ready for further political turmoil. It therefore had no choice but to compromise with the farmers.

ANARCHY OR GRASSROOTS DEMOCRACY?

According to Sanitsuda, despite the Isan NGOs success in defeating the *Kho Jo Ko*, their uncompromising tactics were criticized by 'many pro-democracy academics' in Bangkok (Sanitsuda, 1992b: 4). Why did they criticize these tactics? Because they felt that the farmers' protests were 'unreasonable' and 'untimely'. In their eyes, the Isan NGOs based their tactics on 'emotion' rather than 'rational' calculation. They were afraid that the rural protest would led to 'chaos' and would give the army a chance to intervene, which would disrupt the country's democratic transition process (Sanitsuda1992a: 4).

This urban-centred approach to democracy was bitterly criticized by the Isan NGOs. For them, the attitude of the city activists, first of all, reflected the urban cultural domination in the Thai democratic discourse. 'This goes to show', argued Bamrung Boonpanya, 'the power of urban/rural cultural domination at work'. It was 'the result of the cultural superiority which gives the value to the struggles by rich urban residents more than those by the peasants'. Urban activists, according to Bamrung, thought that the rural dwellers did not understand democracy and needed a proper education. Such an idea, for Bamrung, was 'ridiculous and sad', because it failed to understand that the struggle of the farmers to voice their real needs was a form of democracy: grassroots democracy (Sanitsuda 1992b: 29).

IMPACT OF THE ANTI-*KHO JO KO* MOVEMENT ON THE DEVELOPMENT OF THE SSFAI

The anti-*Kho Jo Ko* movement had significant impacts on the development of the SSFAI in many ways. First, the idea of grassroots democracy provided ideological and political justification for their activities. Second, uncompromising tactics based on the assumption that only strong political pressure from below could force the state to comply with popular demands had become the political strategy of the SSFAI, especially in the radical period (1993–95). Third, the form of protest – marching on foot along the Friendship Highway from Pakchong district – was also adopted by the SSFAI in all subsequent major campaigns. Fourth, apart from tactical implications, the anti-*Kho Jo Ko* movement also created a network of farmers' movements in the region, which later formed an important part of the SSFAI. Fifth, the success of the anti-*Kho Jo Ko* movement boosted confidence in their bargaining power among farmers.

The End of Kho Jo Ko and the Conflict within Isan Grassroots Movements

After the anti-*Kho Jo Ko* campaign, cooperation between the 'political economists' and 'community culturalists' came to an end. The two sides engaged in a new conflict over political strategy and the scope of activities.

Political Strategy

According to a former veteran Isan NGO worker, after the anti-*Kho Jo Ko* campaign, the Isan NGOs were under pressure from foreign donors to withdraw from political activities, and funds of some organizations were cut as a result of their involvement in the anti-*Kho Jo Ko* campaign. Moreover, it was more likely that organizations that remained involved in political campaigns would receive no future funds. To avoid conflict with foreign donors many NGOs, including the AIFLRINR, changed their tactics. They refrained from involvement in political campaigns and concentrated on non-political issues (Somdej Panmuang, interview, 4 February 1998). In other words, after a period of deviation, they followed the principles of the community culture approach again.

Such changes led to conflict within the Isan grassroots movement. The 'political economist' faction within the SSFAI, which comprised NGO workers outside the Isan NGO-CORD, school-teacher activists and farmers, challenged the tactics of the Isan NGO-CORD. They insisted that political mobilization was vital for the efforts to solve farmers' problems. Without strong pressure from below, the government would ignore the demands of farmers (Somdej Panmuang, interview, 4 February 1998). The differences between the 'political economists' and the Isan NGO-CORD lay not only in the tactics of the grassroots movement, but also in the scope of their activities.

Scope of activities

Isan activists all agreed that they should fight for the land rights of the rural poor. But the question of whether grassroots movements should help better-off farmers on market-related issues, such as the declining prices of farm products, credit and debt, aroused controversy among Isan activists. For the Isan NGO-CORD, the answer was negative. According to Jarin Boonmathya, the withdrawal strategy of the community culture approach was one reason behind the lack of enthusiasm towards 'price and related issues' within NGO circles (Jarin 1995: 42). Furthermore, NGOs wanted to help only poor farmers. Their attitudes towards some farmers' groups were rather cold. According to Bamrung Kayotha, the Isan NGO-CORD refused to support pig farmers of the Isan Pig Raisers' Co-operative because NGOs believed that the cooperative belonged to rich and middle-income farmers (Boonlers 1995: 32). But Bamrung, as a pig farmers' leader, argued that pig farmers were small-scale farmers, and their problems were just as important as the problems of poor farmers who lacked land rights. He contended that problems in pig pricing and marketing caused damage to small-scale farmers comparable with the *Kho Jo Ko* scheme (Atiya, 1992: 29). Such different attitudes led to differences concerning scope of activities. While the AIFLRINR limited their work only to land rights, Bamrung believed that other problems, such as the declining prices of agricultural products, were also important to small scale farmers and needed to be tackled (Boonlert 1995: 33).

Dissatisfied with the Isan NGO-CORD and the AIFIRINR about tactics and scope of activities, Bamrung criticized these groups as 'powerless' organizations. He proposed to turn the SSFAI into a People's Organization (PO), which operated independently from NGOs (Son Rubsung, interview, 10 July 1998). According to Bamrung, POs differed from NGOs in two respects. First, POs were more active in political mobilization than NGOs. Second, PO activities, unlike those of NGOs, would never be motivated by outside forces (donors), but simply the real problems that existed within their orbit (Supawadee 1995b: 4). Despite such conflicts, Bamrung still considered NGOs as an ally. He did not refuse to cooperate with NGOs, yet he did not want to 'work under the dictation of NGOs' (Pravit 1993: c1). As a result, the conflict between both sides did not develop into a conflict between enemies. In the future, they managed to coordinate their activities on different occasions. When Bamrung resigned from the SSFAI, he joined an NGO-dominated organization, the Assembly of the Poor (see Chapter 5).

The conflict between the community culturalists and the political economists over political strategy and the appropriate scope of activities amounted to a second split between them. This split led to a new phase of the SSFAI, which paved the way for the transformation of the organization into a radical farmers' organization.

The SSFAI in the Transitional Period

This section looks at the transition period of the SSFAI (March–June 1993). The importance of this period lay in the fact that the political activities during this three month period eventually turned the SSFAI from a network to oppose the National Farm Bill into a radical organization independent from the Isan NGO-CORD. The transition period is distinct from both the previous and later periods in terms of the scope of activities and organizational structure. In the early period, the SSFAI addressed only one specific problem, the National Farm Bill. During March–June 1993, the SSFAI tackled prices, credit and related issues, while in the later radical period (1993–95), it raised not only market-related issues, but also land rights and the environment. In terms of organizational structure, in the early and the transition periods the SSFAI was a loose network, but in the radical period it adopted a centralized organizational structure.

The Protests during the Transitional Period

There were three demonstrations in the transition period between March to June 1993. In the efforts to build up a PO, the 'political economists' under the leadership of Bamrung Kayotha left the AIFLRINR and went out to organize farmers outside the SSFAI. The rally was mainly concerned with prices, debt and related issues. Most of the farmers who joined the protests were concerned only with income issues. However, in the case of cassava farmers, some of the protesters were farmers who lacked land rights (The Cassava Farmers' Group (n.d.): 5).

The Protest of Cassava Farmers

The first protest in the period was a demonstration by cassava farmers. In the early 1990s, the price of tapioca in Thailand reached a new low of about 3,500 baht per ton (1 English pound = 60–63 baht [1990s]). One reason for this depreciation was the EC-imposed quota on the import of Thai cassava. On 18 January 1993, some 50 cassava farmers gathered in Buri Ram province to discuss the problem, and decided to set up the Cassava Farmers' Group (CFG) (The Cassava Farmers' Group, n.d.). Verapon Sopa, a leader of the SSFAI, was an important advisor of the CFG (*Phujatkan*, 30 January 1995: 1).

On 4–5 February, the CFG sent their representatives to meet the minister of commerce. The government, however, did not respond to their demands. On 1 March, some 3,000 farmers from 7 sub-districts of Buri Ram and Nakhon Ratchasima provinces gathered in Nong Kie district, Buri Ram province, to stage a protest. In addition to a better price, they also demanded a debt moratorium and asked the government to help farmers who wanted to shift from growing cassava to other crops. In addition, they also raised the issue of land rights of cassava farmers who lived in 'reserve forest land' (The Cassava Farmers' Group, n.d.). After 4 days of protest, the minister of commerce finally complied with farmers' demands. However, in practice farmers were able to sell their products at a guaranteed price only in the 1992–93 season, and the government did not help them with their other demands (SSFAI 1994a: 3).

The Protest of Pig Farmers

The second protest was the demonstration of the Isan Pig Raisers' Cooperatives in Mahasarakham in March 1993. The protest was in reaction to a new law, which allowed large-scale agribusiness to compete with the cooperatives. From 1978 onwards, the cooperatives had been crucial to the survival of poor pig farmers in Isan. Under the law, only the cooperatives had the right to apply for slaughter permits (*Matichon*, March 28, 1993: 3). In late 1990, however, the Chatichai government proposed to open up trade in pigs to free competition. Such a measure was viewed by small pig farmers as a threat to their survival.

In response to government policy, Bamrung, as the leader of the Isan Pig Raisers' Cooperatives, organized a protest in Kalasin province in January 1991. Some 4,000–5,000 pig farmers joined the protest. The government finally complied with their demands after they blocked the Bangkok–Kalasin road for five hours. However, in 1992 the new prime minister, Anand Panyarachun, adopted the 'free trade policy' of the Chatichai government towards the pig trade once again. The result was the collapse of cooperatives for pig farmers (Atiya 1992: 29).

In late March 1993, about two weeks after the protest of cassava farmers, Bamrung led a new protest of pig farmers in Mahasarakham province. Some 4,000 pig farmers from 12 cooperatives joined the rally to show their dissatisfaction in the slump in pig prices and the law on slaughter of pigs and selling of pork, which they believed would lead to a monopoly by agribusinesses, such as the CP (Chareon Phokapan), in pig raising. They gathered at the front of the provincial governor's office for three days demanding the government send a minister to negotiate with them. After waiting for three days without response, they burned an effigy of Anand's successor as Prime Minister, Chuan Leekpai, before blocking the Mahasarakham–Bangkok road (*Bangkok Post*, 25 March 1993: 6). As with previous protests, such tactics forced Bangkok to consider their demands. The government agreed to provide loans with no interest to cooperatives and promised to revise the law on the slaughter of pigs and selling of pork. However, after the protest, no concrete measures were taken (SSFAI 1994a: 3).

The Protest of Cashew Nut Growers

Bamrung organized the third protest of the period from 20–25 June 1993. He led some 3,000 cashew nut growers from 23 districts of 8 provinces in Isan in staging a protest in Roi Et province, demanding that the government clear their debts with the Bank of Agriculture and Agricultural Cooperatives (BAAC) (Thong 1993b: 24; Jittima, 1996: 58). Five years earlier, these farmers had joined a quadripartite project to grow cashew nuts. Their participation in the project had caused disaster for the farmers. According to Jarin, on average, every cashew nut farmer owed the BAAC about 100,000 baht (Jarin 1995: 43). The farmers protested for five days before the government responded to their demands. Nevertheless, as with the first two protests of the period, government promises turned out simply to be rhetoric with no real commitment (SSFAI 1994a: 4).

The protests in the March–June period had a significant impact on the development of the SSFAI because they were seen by farmers as a channel to express grievances and bargain with the government. After the cashew nut farmers' protest, more and more farmers contacted Bamrung's group. During March and June only three groups joined the protests. Three months later, five more groups joined Bamrung's group. The first two groups were farmers who had joined the government's quadripartite projects to raise Brahman cows and to rear silkworms. They faced the same problems as cashew nut growers. The third group consisted of rice farmers who faced low paddy prices, the fourth of farmers who were in dispute with the state over land rights, and the last group of villagers who were under threat of eviction because of dam construction projects. All of these groups agreed to rally together in the name of the SSFAI. According to Bamrung, they reached such a consensus because they realised that if they did not fight together it would be impossible for them to pressure the government to comply with their demands (Bamrung 1993: 22). On 5 November 1993, they elected Bamrung as the new secretary general of the SSFAI (*Thansettakit Kanmuang*, 23–25 December 1993: 13). Such a development meant that the 'political economists' were now in control of the SSFAI. Under the leadership of the 'political economists', the SSFAI turned into a radical farmers' movement. It propounded a new strategy and new objectives, developed a new organizational structure and put forward new demands.

SUMMARY

The struggle of the SSFAI emerged in a different politico-economic context than the previous political resistance in Isan. The SSFAI was founded under distinctive political circumstances, and made possible by compromises between the state and the radical activists forged in the late 1970s. These compromises were designed to defuse the dissatisfaction of those on the left, who had joined the armed struggle of the CPT, by opening political space for them. Political freedom under the politics of compromise, although limited, offered activists opportunities, among which were NGOs, to resume their activities. They set up various kinds of grassroots groups, including the SSFAI.

However, the SSFAI was not only founded in a specific political situation, but also at a specific stage of capitalist development. Thailand's rapid economic growth in the 1980s led to conflicts over natural resources in the countryside between farmers and the economic sector and the state. The SSFAI was founded to oppose the efforts of the government to pass the National Farm Council Bill, which aimed at subjugating farmers to agribusiness.

In the early period, the SSFAI operated under the influence of the community culture school of thought, which rejected the revolutionary strategy of the 1970s. It argued that farmers' problems could be solved through a subsistence economy. To achieve self-sufficiency, farmers had to rediscover their 'cultural roots', folk wisdom and use local knowledge to cope with difficulties that arose from the market economy. For the community culturalists, the process of rediscovering community culture involved gradual 'consciousness-raising' among villagers. They therefore refrained from any kind of political mobilization and organization. The 'non-political' tactics of the community cultural approach, however, were criticized by the political economists, a group of Isan activists who believed that political engagement was crucial in solving farmers' problems.

The intensification of forced eviction under the *Kho Jo Ko* Programme in 1992 forced the SSFAI to adopt more radical tactics. In 1991, the military used force to evict farmers who lived in the so-called 'degraded forest reserves' from their land, to make way for commercial reforestation under the *Kho Jo Ko* project. The project was based on the assumption that farmers were primarily responsible for deforestation. Actually, the underlying cause of deforestation in Thailand was the country's economic development. Although the military succeeded in evicting farmers in the early period of the project, it faced region-wide resistance in June 1992. Farmers affected by the *Kho Jo Ko* staged a protest by marching on foot along the Friendship Highway from Nakon Ratchasima towards Bangkok. Strong pressure from farmers and political instability after the 1992 May events in Bangkok forced the government to abolish the project in July 1992.

The struggle against the *Kho Jo Ko* had significant impacts on the SSFAI's development on a number of points. In strategic and tactical terms, uncompromising stands, based on the assumption that only strong political pressure from below could force the state to comply with the demands of the poor, and the use of protests involving marching on foot, were adopted by the SSFAI during the radical period (see Chapter 4). In ideological terms, the idea of grassroots democracy provided ideological and political justification for their activities. The campaign against the *Kho Jo Ko* also created a network of farmers' movements in the region, which later formed an important part of the SSFAI. Moreover, this victory boosted confidence among Isan farmers in their struggle to protect their rights.

After the campaign against the *Kho Jo Ko* a new conflict emerged between the political economists and the community culturalists. Conflict between the two sides centered around differences over political strategy and the scope of activities. While the political economists insisted that political mobilization was necessary for solving farmers' problems, the community culturalists decided to return to a 'non-political' approach. The political economists also disagreed with the community culturalists concerning the scope of activities engaged by farmers' movements. They criticized the community culturalists for being concerned only with land rights problems, while neglecting other important problems such as declining prices of agricultural products. For them, both problems were of equal importance to farmers.

Because of these differences the political economists, led by Bamrung Kayotha, split with the Isan NGO-CORD and went out to organize protests on price, debt and related issues, which they considered vital to small-scale farmers. These protests influenced the development of the SSFAI because they were seen by farmers as channels to express their grievances and to bargain with the government. As a result, more groups of farmers joined Bamrung's group. They agreed to rally together in the name of the SSFAI. Apart from prices and debt issues, they addressed problems caused by state policies, land and forestry conflicts. These moves signalled the beginning of a new and more radical phase of the SSFAI. This phase will be examined in Chapter 4.

CHAPTER 4

The Small Scale Farmers' Assembly of Isan during the Radical Period (1993–1995)

After the protests of cassava farmers, pig farmers and cashew nut growers, five more groups of farmers joined the SSFAI in September 1993. This development marked the beginning of a new, 'radical period' of the SSFAI. Within three years (1993–95), the SSFAI had developed from a small organization into the most powerful farmers' movement in Thailand. The SSFAI built up its strength through mass mobilizations. To pursue its demands, the SSFAI organized more than 50 protests during this three-year period (Prapas 1998: 64). As a new farmers' movement, the SSFAI addressed not only the prototypical problem of earlier farmers' movements, land rights. In addition to price and related issues raised in the transition period, the SSFAI campaigned on problems caused by government policies, and land rights. Later, it raised new issues, such as debt and the environment.

This chapter analyses the development of the SSFAI in this period by focusing on the following issues: organizational structure, objectives, strategy and tactics, demands, major demonstrations and achievements and limitations. But before exploring the development of the SSFAI, it is necessary to locate the SSFAI within wider debates about farmers' politics and situate it within its economic context. This is the task of the first two sections of this chapter. The first section reviews the concept of the 'postpeasant society'. The second section attempts to situate the politics of the SSFAI within its economic background by examining the transformation of Isan peasant society. The material from the first two sections provides the framework and context for discussing the political development of the SSFAI in the following sections.

RECONCEPTUALIZING THE PEASANTRY

The two main forms of peasant agitation discussed in Chapter 1, campaigns for 'land to the tiller' and 'remunerative prices', reflect the profound changes that rural communities have undergone in developing countries around the world in the late twentieth century. The result of such changes was the transformation of peasant society from 'traditional-subsistence-isolated' communities into a rural society with unique socio-economic forms, a hybrid of modern and non-modern elements that was integrated into the global order. For Kearney, the global transformation in the late twentieth century had significant impacts on peasants in two respects. First, it transformed most peasant societies from traditional communities into what can be characterized as 'nonmodern and nontraditional' communities (Kearney 1996: 116). This transformation is evidenced by the demise of peasants and peasant societies. Kearney argues that although peasants may still exist in some parts of Asia, Latin America and elsewhere, global conditions do not favour their continuing existence (Kearney 1996: 3). The changing nature of rural societies inevitably affected the identity of its members and their politics.

According to Kearney, the nature of rural dwellers in the age of globalization is fundamentally different from that of traditional peasants. For example, in the Mixteca region of Mexico, the members of rural communities are not only involved in farming activities for subsistence, which is typical of the peasantry, but also appear in other contexts. First, they work in agribusiness as farm workers (both inside and outside the country). Second, they appear in shantytowns as 'peasants in cities'. Third, they operate as small vendors around the Mexico–US border. Fourth, a small number of them are small merchants, civil servants, entrepreneurs or politicians. 'Numerous persons from the Mixteca', argues Kearney, 'move in and move out of these various contexts repeatedly from year to year or at major transition points in their lives' (Kearney 1996: 174). Within such contexts, the members of rural communities are not peasants in a conventional sense anymore; rather, they are 'postpeasants'. Kearney called postpeasants 'polybians', whose personal identity embraces diverse kinds of subjectivity (Kearney 1996: 141). 'Postpeasants' comprise a new class with a distinctive class identity. Because of the complex nature of their class identity, 'postpeasants' engage in various forms of political struggle. While prototypical peasant politics mainly revolved around land tenure, 'postpeasants' engage in various issues ranging from other agrarian issues, such as crop insurance, irrigation and agricultural extension services, to non-agrarian issues, such as wages (Kearney 1996: 175–177).

The second effect of the global transformation in the late twentieth century on peasants was that it opened new political spaces for the rural poor, which enabled them to capitalize on global issues for their struggles. After the end of the Cold War, ideological conflicts between communism and capitalism gradually gave way to new issues concerned with socio-economic and cultural rights. Furthermore, the obsession with economic production of developmentalism was countered by a concern with global resources and the environment. Conflict over these issues has now largely replaced the old political ideology conflicts (Kearney 1996: 131–132). Such changes encouraged the growth of international human rights and environmental movements, which organized themselves mainly as NGOs, operating in various parts of the world. The international NGOs 'constitute a vast reticulated sociopolitical field that exists largely outside of the confines of nation-states and has political goals that are in part beyond the economic, political, and cultural hegemony of nation-states' (Kearney 1996: 183). Since communities in a globalized world are socially unbounded and composed of various kinds of social and communication networks, electronic and other media (Kearney 1996: 118, 181), the ideas of eco-politics and human rights have been disseminated into different parts of the world through these channels. The globalization of eco-politics and human rights provided space for the underprivileged class in developing countries to construct new discourses and strategies. Unlike classic peasant struggles, which operated in the political space of specific localities, the struggles of postpeasants operated in a global space. As a consequence, even though they live in the remote areas of underdeveloped countries, the rural poor can appropriate some global issues, such as ethnicity, ecology and human rights, as part of their own struggles (Kearney 1996: 177–178). Kearney's postpeasant thesis reviewed in this section provides a framework to analyse the internal differentiation of Isan farmers and their politics.

THE TRANSFORMATION OF ISAN PEASANT SOCIETY

As mentioned above, the activities of the SSFAI in the radical period covered both types of rural protests: the struggle for land and campaigns for better prices and credit arrangements. Later, the environment became an important issue during this period. The diversification of the SSFAI's activities reflected the transformation of Isan peasant society into a society that Kearney describes as a 'postpeasant' society. To understand the political economy of the SSFAI protest, it is necessary to study the transformation of Isan peasant society.

The Commercialization of Agriculture

Capitalism has been penetrating into the Thai countryside over the last century and a half. This may be seen in the diversification of the agricultural sector. Before the 1950s, rice was the main crop of Thailand. New roads opened up new areas and led to the rapid expansion of upland crops such as maize, kenaf, cassava and sugar cane. While farmers grow rice partly for consumption and partly for sale in the market, most of these upland crops are sold in the market, especially in the world market (Ammar et al. 1993: 82). In 1990 cash crops accounted for 53.9 per cent of Thailand's agricultural export (Medhi 1995: 40, 49). In Isan, according to Hafner, from 1950 to 1984, the share of planted areas under paddy 'declined from 96 per cent to 73 per cent, the number of total holdings increased by over 36 per cent, and the total area in holding rose by 53 per cent'. In 1983, the region had become the major source of the nation's cassava output (supplying 62 per cent) (Hafner 1990: 77).

Agribusiness and Small Scale Farmers in Isan

The commercialization of agriculture also encouraged the expansion of agribusiness into Isan. According to Jarin, this expansion has 'had a lot of impact on northeastern peasants, especially in placing their subsistence production under monopolistic control of these companies' (Jarin 1995: 18). For example, Charoen Phokapan (C.P.), the largest agribusiness conglomerate in Thailand, has set up contracts with small farmers. Under the contract, C.P. provides credit to farmers for buying company breeding stock and feed. In return, farmers are bound to sell their produce to the company at a predetermined price. Such practices put farmers under the control of the company, which decides 'what will be produced, how and according to what standards it will be produced, and how much it will sell for' (Hewison 1989: 144). The presence of C.P. in Isan caused bankruptcies among small pig farmers and poultry breeders in the region, because they were unable to compete with the company, which has its own full-cycle contract farms and which easily dominates the market (Atiya 1992: 24).

Another kind of contract farming was carried out within the framework of the government's quadripartite agricultural projects. The quadripartite group comprised government agencies, agribusiness companies, farmers and the Bank of Agriculture and Agricultural Cooperatives (BAAC). The projects were promoted as parts of the government effort to reduce tapioca farming, which had excess production capacity (Santi Uthaipan, interview, 21 February 1998). This kind of contract farming was carried out on a large scale: for example, 20,000 farmers joined in the cashew nut project (The Action Plan, n.d.: 1). Under these projects, the BAAC provided loans for farmers to buy seedlings and certain types of chemicals from companies on the condition that the companies provided technical support, and bought qualified products from farmers at a guaranteed price. In practice, the companies ignored the conditions. They supplied farmers with unproductive seedlings and failed to provide technical support for them. As a result, the project turned out to be a disaster for farmers (Jarin 1995: 19).

Another quadripartite project involved silkworm breeding. Under the scheme, the government promoted the introduction of exotic silkworms, instead of encouraging the local species which villagers had traditionally raised for silk; 3,484 farmers borrowed 351.36 million baht from the BAAC to join the project. They allocated 47,404 rai of their rice fields to grow mulberry bushes to feed the silkworms. The farmers were told that they could sell their products at a guaranteed price to the companies, which supplied chemicals and silkworms to them. However, in 1991, two years after the project had begun, the government introduced a 'free trade' policy relating to trade in silk by abolishing the guaranteed price and lifted the quota on imported silk. These changes resulted in the bankruptcy of many farmers (National Committee on Farmers' Debt Management 1994: 1–2; Komon Ruenjit, interview, 23 May 1998).

Farmers who joined the cattle promotion programme also faced the same plight. The programme, which was allegedly aimed at improving the living standards of Isan farmers, was one of many programmes under the 'Green Isan' project initiated by the Army commander-in-chief, General Chavalit Yongchaiyudh in 1987 (Missingham 1996: 195–196). As with the other quadripartite projects, farmers were required to draw loans from the BAAC to buy Brahman cows from an import company. According to the programme, by raising Brahman cows farmers were supposed to receive attractive profits from selling the calves within a short period of time. After a year, the farmers found out that the cows were infertile. They demanded that the government take back the infertile or 'plastic' cows, and write off their debts to the BAAC (*Siam Rath Sudsapda*, 25–31 October 1993: 9). The government, however, blamed the farmers for failing to take proper care of the animals, and insisted that they must be responsible for the debts to the BAAC (*Bangkok Post*, 28 August 1993: 2). The failure of this and other programmes within the quadripartite projects became a rallying point of the SSFAI. A more controversial role of agribusiness that related to state projects was the commercial reforestation programme that finally led to the *Kho Jo Ko* scheme (see Chapter 3).

The Commercialization of Agriculture and Farmers' Debt

The penetration of capitalism undermined the subsistence economy in the countryside. To produce for the market, more and more farmers had to rely on credit from either private lenders, state institutions or both to buy fertilizers, pesticide, petrol and consumer goods. Traditionally, credit in rural areas was provided by informal lenders with very high interest rates. In 1969, the government set up the BAAC to provide credit for farmers (Ammar et al.

1993: 104). According to the BAAC, 4.8 million families around the country were indebted to the BAAC in 1998 and these debts amounted to 230 billion baht (*Matichon Sudsupda* 1998: 12).

The Internal Differentiation of Isan Farmers

Capitalist penetration into the Isan rural areas influenced both the subsistence economy and rural class structure. Commercialization of the Isan rural economy led to the internal differentiation of Isan farmers. However, the transformation of Isan rural society had taken place in a distinctive manner. Over the previous three decades, the rural community in Isan, as in other parts of Thailand, had experienced socio-economic changes that finally led to the disintegration of the subsistence economy. Nevertheless, such transformations were uneven and complex. As a consequence, there are now huge variations within rural society. As Baker has pointed out, because of such variations, it is almost impossible to 'generalize about Thai rural structure'. The solution, argues Baker, 'is to portray it as a spectrum' (Baker 2000: 12). At one end of the spectrum is the advanced commercial farmer. According to Baker, this kind of farmer is concentrated in the Central region and in smaller pockets elsewhere. 'His production', Baker notes, 'is relatively capital-intensive because of the use of machinery and expensive inputs. His main concern is pricing – of capital goods, inputs, outputs, and credit'. He is 'a long time client of the government's agricultural bank' (Baker 2000: 12). This type of farmer can be found in some areas of Isan. Since they can gain access to markets easily, such farmers engage in other kinds of agriculture apart from growing rice, such as raising livestock, fruit plantations, and vegetable farming. When compared with the production of farmers in degraded forest reserves, their production activities need more knowledge and technology and use a lot of pesticides and chemical fertilizers. Because of the relatively capital-intensive nature of their productions, their investments are higher. Of central importance to this type of farmer are the availability of credit for investments, prices of inputs (pesticides, fertilizers, machinery) and outputs (products). At the other end of the spectrum, Baker places the farmer who has no secure land title in the degraded forest reserves. This type of farmer 'has no secure land title and faces the threat of dislodgement by official or speculator'. Moreover, 'he has had neither the time nor opportunity to generate a capital fund, and he has no access to government loans because he has no land title' (Baker 2000: 12). It was estimated that in the 1980s some 970,000 families lived in degraded forest reserves in every region of Thailand; of these 250,000 families were in Isan, 520,000 families in the North, 108,000 in the South and 92,000 in the Central region (*Voice of Community*, October 1991: 9). Lack of land titles in degraded forest reserve areas is the major cause of land problems in Isan, while in other regions, such as the Central plain or the North, problems also arise from the tenancy system (Ammar et al. 1993: 100). As a result, the conflicts over land in Isan are not conflicts between landlords and tenants, but between the state and farmers. In recent years, these farmers have constantly faced the threat of eviction by the state, although during the campaign against the *Kho Jo Ko*, the government agreed to allow farmers to live in degraded forest reserves. But since then there have been efforts by officials to evict them from these areas. It is not surprising that this kind of Isan farmer has frequent conflicts with the state. However, it should be noted that state-versus-farmer conflicts over land rights happen not only in degraded forest reserves, but also in various parts of the region outside these areas. Most conflicts outside degraded forest reserves arise either because the government claims that farmers' lands belong to the Treasury department or was public land, or because the state forces farmers to leave their lands for dam projects.

Standing between these two types of farmers were 'various intermediate forms'. However, it was very difficult to plot the profile of groups (Baker 2000: 13). Prominent among them were farmers in the degraded forest reserves who 'had been legitimated' under the government's land reform schemes, and those who 'have negotiated stand-off arrangements with local authorities'. Another important group was farmers who had secure land rights and 'high involvement in the commercial economy, and yet with high vulnerability to climate and market' (Baker 2000: 13).

Baker's approach was useful in mapping out the big picture of rural social structures. However, it failed to understand the complex position of farmers in degraded forest reserves. It is undoubtedly true that the major concern of this group of farmers is land rights, though, this does not mean that they are not interested in 'income issues'. On the contrary, the price of agricultural produces is important for them because most upland crops produced in degraded forest reserves are for the market. Since they engage in commercial agriculture, farmers in the degraded forest reserves need capital for investment as do the advanced commercial farmers. They are also interested in accessing loans from the BAAC. As a result, they do not hesitate to join activities that will help them to obtain such loans (see Chapter 5). The complex position of farmers in the degraded forest reserves increases when intermediate forms are taken into account. Intermediate forms are the articulation of the two typical types with different degrees of interactions under various conditions. One prominent kind of intermediate form comprises those farmers who own a piece of paddy field with secure land rights in a lowland area, and a piece of land in a degraded forest reserve. The internal division of labour of the family involves growing rice for household consumption in the lowland area, while engaging in upland crops for cash in degraded forest reserves. Furthermore, many of them also engage in other sources of income generation, such as raising poultry or vegetable farming. Because their rice fields have land titles, they can access the loans of the BAAC. But since their paddy lands are quite small, they can get only a small amount of credit from the bank. More frequently, they have to turn to private lenders. Such farmers, while concerned with land rights in the degraded forest reserves, also regard credit and prices as vital to their livelihoods.

The failure of Baker to grasp the complexity of farmers in the degraded forest reserves led to another shortcoming. It prevented him from capturing the diversity of their politics. According to Baker, the politics of these farmers revolves around 'insecurity issues, particularly over access to land, water, and forests' (Baker 2000: 14). Their politics differs from that of intermediate farmers who have land rights and a high involvement in the capitalist economy, but are vulnerable to markets and the climate. According to Baker, their politics concentrated on prices and related issues (Baker 2000: 13–14). However, his analysis ran counter to what actually happened. Since the interests of farmers in the degraded forest reserves were not confined only to 'insecurity issues', but also involved 'income issues', so was their politics. The limitation of Baker's analysis will be made clear when discussing the internal politics within Isan farmers' movements in the next chapter.

The internal differentiation in rural Isan is further complicated because farmers are involved in economic activities outside villages. Generally, Isan farmers spend part of their time on their own farms and part of it in other economic activities. The form of involvement varies from place to place. In some areas, for example in Donglan, Khon Kaen province, income from working on sugar cane plantations in the Central provinces, or other provinces in Isan forms a major part of their household incomes (field notes, 1 August 1997). In other areas, such as villages near the provincial town of Mahasarakham, the major income comes from working in factories or working as street vendors in Bangkok and provincial towns (field notes, 8 September 1997). In many areas an important source of farmers' income comes from working in foreign countries (*Krungthep Thurakit*, 15 July 1998: 11).

This section has examined the impacts of capitalist penetration into the Isan rural economy. This penetration led to the end of the subsistence economy, the domination of agribusiness over small scale farmers, the increase of farmers' debt, and the internal differentiation of farmers. These changes on farmers' politics were to diversify farmers' demands. Farmers did not limit their demands only to land rights, but also addressed problems derived from commercialization of the rural economy, such as prices and related issues. The transformation of Isan peasant society examined in this section provides the economic background for understanding the struggle of the SSFAI from the radical period onwards.

THE SSFAI IN THE RADICAL PERIOD

The radical period of the SSFAI (1993–95) marked a new stage of the struggle of the organization in terms of organizational structure, strategy and tactics and demands, which led to a new form of political mobilization. The purpose of this section is to explore such developments and the results of the struggle in this period. It comprises two main parts. The first part examines objectives, organizational structure, strategy and demands of the SSFAI. The second part explores the major protests of the SSFAI during the period 1993–1995. The purpose of the first part is to give an overview of how the SSFAI organized itself, and of the leading ideas and demands of the organization in the struggle for the rights of Isan farmers. The second part explores the struggle of the SSFAI and offers a detailed study of its major protests in chronological order.

In Defence of Class Politics: The Objectives of the SSFAI

During the radical period, unlike in the earlier period, the SSFAI did not confine its objectives only to specific problems such as opposing the National Farm Bill. The new goals of the SSFAI were protecting the rights and interests of small scale farmers and strengthening their power and their organization, which would enable them to live equally with other classes in Thai society (SSFAI 1997: 1). The SSFAI, noted Bamrung, acted as the representative of the farmers, just as the Federation of Thai Industries, the Thai Chamber of Commerce, and the Thai Bankers Association acted for capitalists (Bamrung et al. 1994: 5).

The objectives of the SSFAI refute attempts to interpret the organization as a new social movement. Because the activities of new farmers' movements were involved not only in problems concerned directly with farmers, but also with new kinds of issues, such as ecology and ethnicity, some critics asserted that they were part of a worldwide trend of new social movements (NSMs) (Byres 1995: 2; Veltmeyer 1997: 140). Since the mid-1970s, the term 'new social movements' has gained popularity among theorists sympathetic to peace, ecology issues, women, and local autonomous movements (Cohen 1985: 663). 'New social movement theory', as Foweraker has noted, 'developed partly in response to what was considered to be an outmoded style of class analysis'. Its advocates criticized the social class theory of Marxism on the grounds that it had failed to catch up with the increasingly complex social relations of postmodern society (Foweraker 1995: 36). For Hellman, NSMs 'have nothing to do with the development of class consciousness or class conflict', and they are 'non political' because their members come from 'various social origins linked by issues cutting across class lines' (Hellman 1992: 55). As a result, NSMs based their organizations and activities on 'identity and consciousness rather than objective material position' (Brysk 1996: 39). The identity mobilization of NSMs clearly runs counter to the SSFAI's emphasis on farmers' social position. The way the SSFAI depicted farmers' position in society vis-a-vis that of capitalists was closer to the class analysis of Marxism than to the identity construction of the NSMs.

Organizational Structure and Strategy of the SSFAI during the Radical Period

To examine the organizational structure and strategy of the SSFAI during the radical period, the resource mobilization theory (RMT) will be employed as the starting point for discussion. The RMT, according to Canel, 'focuses on how groups organize to pursue their ends by mobilizing and managing resources' (Canel 1992: 40).

Resources can be of a material or non-material nature: material resources include money, organizational facilities, labour, means of communication; non-material resources include legitimacy, loyalty, authority, moral commitment, solidarity ... *Mobilization* is the process by which a group assembles resources ... and places them under collective control for the explicit purpose of pursuing the group's interests through collective action. (Canel 1992: 40)

Central to the RMT are political opportunity structures and mobilizing structures. However, as McAdam et al. point out, the combination of the two factors only affords social movements 'a certain structural potential for action', but they are not sufficient 'to account for collective action'. A third factor, framing processes, is needed to mediate between political opportunities and mobilizing structures. 'Mediating between opportunity, organization, and action are the shared meaning and definitions that people bring to their situation' (McAdam et al. 1996: 5).

Organizational Structure

In the previous chapter we tracked the dialectical relationship between political opportunities and social movements that resulted in a political environment favouring political mobilization. However, political opportunities could not guarantee the success of social movements. As McAdam et al. point out '"political opportunities" are but a necessary prerequisite to action'. For them, to seize such opportunities it was necessary for a movement to have a sufficient organisation (McAdam et al. 1996: 8). 'Social movement organizations', according to Kriesi, 'constitute crucial building blocks of the mobilizing structures of a social movement' (Kriesi 1996: 152). 'For the movement to survive', argue McAdam et al., movement activists 'must be able to create a more enduring organizational structure to sustain collective action. Efforts to do so usually entail the creation of the kinds of formal social movement organizations (SMOs)' (McAdam et al.,1996:13). SMOs played a crucial role in the struggle of the movement. 'Following the emergent phase of the movement … it is these SMOs and their efforts to shape the broad political environment which influence the overall pace and outcome of the struggle' (McAdam et al., 1996: 13). Organizational structure was very important to the struggle of the SSFAI. The empirical materials below deal with the implementation of a new organizational form during the radical period of the SSFAI.

Before the radical period, the SSFAI had no clear-cut organizational structure. It was simply a gathering of different groups that agreed to work together under the name SSFAI. After the protest in October 1993 (see below), the various groups held a meeting at Si Khiew district, Nakhon Ratchasima on 5 November 1993. The meeting marked a new phase of the SSFAI. It decided to turn the SSFAI into a new form of organization. Apart from electing Bamrung Kayotha as the secretary general, the meeting elected a committee and an executive committee of the SSFAI, which comprised 25 and 9 members respectively. In January 1994 however, the SSFAI decided to replace the two committees with a central committee to take charge of the activities of the organization. The central committee comprised a secretary general and one representative from every zone, a zone consisting of a group of provinces. The SSFAI in the radical period was divided into six zones:

Zone 1: Khon Kaen, Mahasarakham, Chaiyaphum

Zone 2: Roi Et, Mukdahan, Yasothorn, Amnat Chareon

Zone 3: Kalasin, Sakhon Nakhon, Nakhon Panom

Zone 4: Nong Khai, Nong Bua Lamphu, Udon Thani, Loei

Zone 5: Surin, Sri Saket, Ubon Ratchathani

Zone 6: Nakhon Ratchasima, Buri Ram

Each zone was run by a committee, which was elected from provincial representatives (the SSFAI held elections at all levels every year) (SSFAI 1994b: 1, 7; Jittima 1996: 145; *Thansettakit Khanmuang*, 23–25 December 1993: 13). However, according to an advisor of the SSFAI, the setting up of zone committees failed because in practice zone committee members mainly worked in their own provinces. Later, the SSFAI abolished the zones and zone committees, and zone representatives in the central committee were replaced by provincial secretaries (Ratsapa Namloaw, interview, 24 August 1997).

Apart from the central committee and the secretary general, other important posts within the SSFAI were those of general coordinator and advisor. The internal division of labour between secretary general and general coordinator was that the secretary general was responsible for external affairs (such as coordinating with allies, and holding press conferences) and protest activities, while the general coordinator acted as a link between the central committee and members in different areas. The result of this internal division was that although the secretary general became the symbol of the organization, he did not have real power to control the whole organization. It was the general coordinator who acted as the grassroots organizer and thus had more influence over local leaders and members.

Another group of leaders were advisors, appointed by the central committee and zone committee. Most of the advisors came from the ranks of allied organizations and school teacher activists. This kind of practice was common among Isan grassroots movements. Madsen wonders whether 'the status of "advisor" derives from the fact that Westerners on official duty in Thailand were classified as advisors', or derives from 'the front/cadre duality of the communist movement' (Madsen 1999: 5). In fact, the presence of advisors in Isan grassroots movements, including the SSFAI, reflected the history of grassroots movements in the region. Most of the advisors were intellectual activists (NGOs, school teachers, lawyers), who played an important role in the formation of grassroots movements. It was impossible to separate them from the movements, since they were an integral part of the movements themselves. Around the mid-1980s, there were efforts to build people's organizations in which farmers were able to assume leadership roles themselves. To achieve such goals, intellectual activists chose to act as advisors to facilitate the development of farmer cadres.

Even though the SSFAI adopted a more centralized form of organization, it still maintained some aspects of a network in the early phase of the radical period. The member groups were allowed to have a degree of relative autonomy. For example, within their areas they were able to organize protests independently under their own name, and only at the regional level were they required to act together under the name of the SSFAI (Bamrung 1993: 23). However, the need for a more efficient organization pushed the SSFAI in a more centralized direction. As Bamrung pointed out in 1995, 'now we have to speed up the attempt to establish a *strong and unified* organization for the people so that the government will really be interested in our problems' (cited in Yaowares 1995: A2; emphasis added).

Strategy and Tactics

Because the RMT pays great attention to resource management, strategy and tactics of social movements, it 'calls attention to the importance of strategic instrumental action' (Canel 1992: 45). Strategy is undoubtedly very important to social movements in pursuing their goals. However, movements face a 'unique dilemma'. According to McAdam and Snow, movements generally develop among less powerful groups within society, and organize outside formal political institutions, such as political parties and formal interest groups. They shun politics through 'proper channels' because they rarely access these institutions and the conventional forms of actions, for example, lobbying and electoral politics. In addition, they are also afraid that if they pursue their aims through formal politics, which is dominated by political and economic elites, they have to compromise. McAdam and Snow point out that this rejection poses a dilemma for movements. 'By opting politics by other means, movements must answer a difficult question: what should these other means be? How will the movement seek to overcome its relative powerlessness and press effectively for the realization of its interests?' (McAdam and Snow 1997: 326). This section will address these questions by looking at the strategy of the SSFAI during the radical period, which comprises four main components: building a strong people's organization, strengthening bargaining power by building alliances with other political forces, pressuring the state by marching on foot along the highway and self-reliance in funding.

a) The Right to Have Rights and the Necessity of People's Organizations

The SSFAI did not aim to achieve its objectives by seizing state power. The Assembly, according to Bamrung, adhered to peaceful, non-violent ideals from the start (Bamrung 1995a: 19). For them, the seizing of state power would lead to the abuse of power because 'the state is dictatorial in nature' (Nakon 1998: 11). Because of such beliefs, the SSFAI advocated working within the framework of the existing political system. However, this does not mean that the SSFAI sought incorporation into the existing order. Although it did not try to rewrite the existing political rules, the SSFAI demanded the 'right to have rights' in the decision-making process (Bamrung 1993: 24), which would lead to significant transformation of political practices. The 'right to have rights', according to Bamrung, was the key in the efforts to solve farmers' hardships. However, the establishment of the 'right to have rights' could not be conducted through representative democracy, but would materialize only through political mobilization within civil society.

For Bamrung, farmers' grievances were caused by the pro-industrial policy of the Thai state. 'So far', argues Bamrung, 'the state's development policy is destroying the livelihood of farmers, directly and indirectly'. For him, 'the state used farmers as a tool to develop industries without paying attention to the farmers' plight, leaving industrialists to take advantage of us farmers all the time' (Pravit 1993a: C1). In addition, 'small farmers' natural resources are violently and unfairly taken away to support the business and private sector' (*Thai Development Newsletter* 1995: 41). As a result, Bamrung noted, the countryside of Isan was in a state of bankruptcy:

Right now, we farmers can no longer survive… We are going bankrupt because of poor income and a lack of security in life. Young teens, both boys and girls flee to large cities. They get married, the husband becomes the security guard, the wife a vendor, and those who go abroad in search of work are cheated. The villages are left idle with no one. (cited in Pravit 1993a: c1)

Only children and the elderly are left in local communities now. What will our villages' future be with no one to sustain them? *We are being killed by government policy.* (cited in Supara 1995: 17; emphasis added)

Although the line of argument of Bamrung might seem to resemble the 'urban vs. rural' thesis of neo-populism (see Chapter 3), he stated clearly that the SSFAI did not oppose industrial development in general. It opposed government development policies only because these policies caused suffering among the rural population (Supawadee 1995b: 4).

According to Bamrung, when farmers tried to complain, the state ignored them because 'the century-old system looks upon farmers as stupid – a lower class and slaves who need to be ruled'. Electoral politics were also seen by him as hopeless. Farmers, argues Bamrung, could expect nothing from politicians because it was 'clear that political parties, in general, accept contributions from businessmen and industrialists. Because of that, all the parties' policies serve to benefit the latter' (Pravit 1993a: c1). To make the demands of farmers heard, Bamrung challenged traditional forms of representation. He proposed grassroots movements as an alternative to representative democracy. For him, to change the situation, farmers 'have to stand up and fight for our demands'. Only 'people's organizations', argues Bamrung, can force the state to 'listen' to farmers (Pravit 1993a: c1). Without pressure from below, the state would not pay attention to the plight of farmers (Yaowares 1995: A2).

Based on such assumptions, the SSFAI, under the leadership of Bamrung, singled out 'pressuring the government by political protest' as its main strategy in the struggle to solve farmers' problems (Bamrung 1995b: 19). The aims of political protest were two-fold. First, to pressure the government to solve the concrete problems of farmers, such as land rights and agricultural prices. Second, in the past farmers were unable to defend their interests because they were excluded from the policy making process. Therefore, the SSFAI demanded the 'right to have rights' in decision-making on agricultural and other policies that related to the rural sector. This was the most important demand of the SSFAI. According to Bamrung, the aims of the demands differed greatly from those of the farmers' groups sponsored by the state. State-sponsored groups confined their demands only to short-term material gains, such as capital, credit and fertilizers, but they did not question the policy-making process itself (Bamrung 1993: 24). To create a channel for participation in the policy-making process, the SSFAI demanded that the government set up a joint committee comprised of farmers, NGOs and academics and government officials for solving the problems of farmers (Jarin 1995: 5).

b) Building Alliances

The SSFAI's political mobilization strategy was strengthened by building alliances with other political forces. For Bamrung, without support from allies, farmers would be in a weak position, while wealthy businesses could hire the best lawyers and legal advice (Pravit 1993a: C1). Because of disagreements over strategy, most Isan NGOs, especially the AIFLRINL, did not cooperate with the SSFAI. They considered the political mobilization of the SSFAI to be a form of 'adventurism' that would lead farmers to disaster (*Phujatkan*, 2 March 1994: 14). However, the SSFAI still managed to secure support from various democratic groups, such as the Committee for Isan Environment, the Isan Human Rights Lawyers Club and from Bangkok NGOs, such as the Federation for Democracy. These groups helped the SSFAI mainly in political protests, while academics from various institutions were invited to provide farmers with counselling, information and analysis (Bamrung 1994).

The most important allies of the SSFAI were school-teacher activists in various provinces of Isan. As discussed in Chapter 3, most of them supported the idea of building peoples' organizations to campaign for farmers' rights and interests. After the collapse of the CPT, the efforts to organize a farmers' movement in Isan without help from the Isan NGO-CORD seemed impossible. However, the presence of teacher activists compensated for the absence of NGO support. They provided the SSFAI with valuable experiences both in terms of political campaigning and organizational skills. From the protest of the cashew nut growers in 1993 onwards, school teacher activists were prominent in the SSFAI. They came from different teacher groups, the most prominent among them being the Teachers' Organizations for Society Council (TOSC). According to Somkiat Pongpaiboon, general secretary of the TOSC and an advisor of the SSFAI, the TOSC was founded in 1991 with 66 member groups all over the country. Isan was its strongest base. The activities of the TOSC involved helping poor students who lacked opportunities in education, problems concerning agriculture and environment and promoting democracy (Somkiat 1995b: 3). This group of teachers acted as farmers' representatives in negotiations with the government and also helped the SSFAI to organize farmers in various villages of Isan. Actually, some of them were de facto leaders of the SSFAI. During the radical period, around 40 school teacher activists acted as the advisors of the SSFAI (*Bangkok Post*, 1 February 1995). However, the relationship between the SSFAI and the AIFLRINL and the Isan NGO-CORD improved in the later period of

Bamrung's leadership because they realised that cooperation would benefit all of them (Teepakon Kanwit, interview, 17 May 1998).

c) Pressure Produced by Marches: Framing Political Opportunities

The role of 'framing' in the struggle of social movements has drawn great attention among movement scholars (see, for example, McAdam et al. 1996: 261–356). 'Framing' means 'the conscious, strategic efforts of movement groups to fashion meaningful accounts of themselves and the issues at hand in order to motivate and legitimate their efforts' (McAdam 1996: 339).

McAdam has pointed out that the notion of framing is a remedy to the shortcomings of 'those broader structural theories, which often depict social movements as the inevitable by-products of expanding political opportunities (political process), emerging system-level contradictions or dislocations (some versions of new social movement theory) or newly available resources (resource mobilization)' (McAdam 1996: 339). The presence of the 'facilitating circumstances' can 'create a certain structural potential for collective action' but the realization of that potential 'depends on the actions of insurgents' (McAdam 1996: 339). As Gamson and Meyer point out, 'movements are active in structuring and creating political opportunity … Political opportunities are subject to framing processes' (Gamson and Meyer 1996: 276). To achieve their goals under the hostile and highly fluid environment, social movements have to rely on the strategic use of framing process. 'That is', argues McAdam, 'in trying to attract and shape media coverage, win the support of bystander publics, constraint movement opponents, and influence state authorities, insurgents depend first and foremost on various forms of signifying work' (McAdam 1996: 340). However, although the concept of framing is concerned with subjective sides of social movements, it would be wrong to treat it as something exclusively concerned with ideas of movement activists. It is not only ideas that constitute framing efforts of social movements; 'the actions taken by insurgents and the tactical choices they make' also 'represent a critically important contribution to the overall signifying work of the movement' (McAdam 1996: 341). In addition, if the efficiency of a social movement derives from its mobilization, the tactics and the actual activities in which it engages would become the most important component of a movement's overall framing work (McAdam 1996: 341).

The SSFAI makes great use of framing processes in its struggle. The framing work of the organization was designed to draw attention and win over the public at large, which would help to strengthen the bargaining power of the SSFAI. Marching along the highway was the main strategy for that purpose. Pressuring the government by political mobilization is common among social movements in Thailand. However, the SSFAI employed mobilization in a distinctive manner. Instead of organizing protests at one place, either in the capital city or provincial towns, like other organizations, the SSFAI chose to organize their major campaigns by marching from near the Isan–Central region border to Bangkok. The tactic was initiated during the anti-*Kho Jo Ko* campaign. However, as Baker points out, the march during this campaign 'had been a largely spontaneous response to the threat of mass forced evictions', while the protest of the SSFAI was 'planned as a deliberate attempt to force the government's attention to a long list of northeastern rural grievances' (Baker 1999: 12). It is worth noting that the 'march to the capital city' strategy was also adopted by farmers' movements in other countries. For example, in Brazil, the Landless Workers' Movement (MST) organized a march along the highways to Brasilia. However, while the march was the main means for the SSFAI to pursue its demands, it was one of the supporting measures the MST adopted to strengthen its main strategy, that of land occupation (Almeida and Sanchez 2000: 11–32).

Why did the SSFAI employ such a strategy? Because if they remained in only one place, their protests were unable to draw attention from the public. A march, by contrast, put their demonstrations into the headlines. According to a veteran reporter who followed the rallies closely, marches had become a focus of attention of the media because they believed that the government would use force to break up such protests in order to prevent the SSFAI from reaching Bangkok. Such actions would lead to political violence (Nares Yuwarat, interview, 22 February 1998). However, the SSFAI not only wanted their march to become the focus of attention, but also to produce a positive reaction from society. Such a reaction would increase pressure on the government (*Phujatkan*, 28 February 1994: 13).

The Thai state always accuses popular protestors of being 'troublemakers' and 'hired mobs'. To counter the state's accusation, the SSFAI determined that, first, its political mobilization must adhere to 'non-violent' principles and must not cause trouble to society (SSFAI 1994: 7). Second, during protests, the protesters had to have activities that were able to arouse interest and draw support from society. For example, on the march to Bangkok, farmers were assigned to carry posters to highlight their problems (Nares Yuwarat, interview, 22 February 1998). Third, the protests had to win over the media, which had an important influence on Thai public opinion. For movement theorists, media occupied a special role in framing processes. Since 'most movements lack the conventional political resources processed by their opponents', they therefore have to 'offset this power disparity by appeal to other parties. The media come to be seen … as the key vehicle for such influence attempts' (McAdam 1996: 346). 'Framing contests', as Zald points out, 'occur in face-to-face interaction and through a variety of media'. Movement activists 'have to change and mobilize bystander publics, many of whom may only know of the movement and its issues as portrayed in various media' (Zald 1996: 270). According to Gamson and Meyer, the media 'play a crucial role in defining for movement actors whether they are taken seriously as agents of possible change'. It 'spotlight validates the movement as an important player' (Gamson and Meyer 1996: 285). However, positive media coverage was not an end in itself. Movements 'courted the media for the role it might play in mobilizing public awareness of and support for the movement' (McAdam 1996: 349).

For the SSFAI, the most effective means to get positive coverage on the front pages of newspapers was simply to let reporters contact the farmers freely. Since farmers joined the march not because they were paid to do so, but because they were in trouble over a variety of problems, the more reporters had contact with farmers, the more they expressed sympathy with the farmers' cause. As a result, the government's accusations were countered by positive reports from the media (*Phujatkan*, 28 February 1994: 13).

However, as leaders of the SSFAI pointed out, marches not only increased pressure on the government, but also nurtured courage, integrity and solidarity among the farmers. Another advantage of the 'march to Bangkok' strategy was that it helped to solve problems for the leaders. If the rally was held at one place, the leaders had to think up new activities every day. Protests without activities caused inertia, lack of discipline and vacillation among the protesters, which undermined the strength of the protest itself. A march helped the leaders to overcome such problems. Every day, the farmers had to prepare themselves for unexpected incidents that might be caused by the authorities during the march. To cope with such situations, they had to remain alert, act with discipline and help each other, which boosted their solidarity. As a result, the sense of collective action was strengthened (Nakon Sriwipat and Somsiri Wongwinai, interview, 1 August 1997).

d) Self-Reliance in Funding

As mentioned above, the resources of social movements are of a material and non-material nature. This section looks at material resources of the SSFAI. Another important aspect of the strategy of the SSFAI was self-reliance in funding. There was a consensus within the SSFAI that one of the weak points of NGOs was their reliance on funds from outside sources. As a result, they were unable to act independently, because activities that their donors disliked would lead to fund suspension. Furthermore, reliance on funds from outside sources generated a bad attitude among members. It hampered their initiative and weakened their efforts in solving the difficulties they faced. According to one SSFAI leader, 'without funds from donors NGOs can do nothing' (Nakon Sriwipat, interview, 15 January 1998). In addition, NGOs – argued one advisor of the SSFAI – did not encourage farmers to rely on themselves. Despite promoting the idea of self-reliance, they acted as 'charity organizations' in practice. For example, they were typically responsible for all expenses during demonstrations, while farmers had no responsibility except joining the protests (Chaluen Chanasongkram, interview, 1 October 1997).

The SSFAI was determined to overcome such shortcomings. In its charter, the SSFAI emphasized that one of its objectives was building a strong farmers' organization based on the principles of independence and self-reliance (SSFAI 1997: 2). The self-reliance policy of the SSFAI was initiated by Bamrung during the protest in October 1993. Instead of seeking funds from outside, he relied on the resources of the farmers. During a rally, according to an advisor of the SSFAI, farmers were asked to bring food sufficient for their consumption, and they also had to donate 10 baht as funds for the protest. In addition, each member of the SSFAI was required to pay 100 baht as an annual membership fee. Such measures proved successful in solving the financial problems of the SSFAI (Somsiri Wongwinai, 8 January 1998). Even though the SSFAI emphasized self-reliance, it accepted material support from outsiders, including politicians. However, the support must have no conditions, because conditions would undermine its political autonomy (*Matichon*, 6 November 1993: 2).

The self-reliance policy of the SSFAI occupied a very important place in the history of the grassroots movements in Isan, because since the 1980s, Isan grassroots movements had been organized by NGOs. They relied on NGOs not only in political terms, but also concerning financial matters. As a result, NGOs were indispensable to their survival. The self-reliance policy of the SSFAI overcame such dependence. It encouraged the grassroots movements to develop to a new stage.

The Demands of the SSFAI

After the protest of cashew nut growers, the government showed no interest in solving farmers' problems as it had promised. In September 1993, the SSFAI planned a new demonstration to pressure the government actively to solve their problems. Before it organized a protest, the SSFAI prepared new demands by inviting academics to provide information concerning the problems, and then held a meeting among members to draft its demands. After that the demands were revised with help from leading economists, such as Ammar Siamwalla, Chermsak Pinthong and Rangsan Tanapornpan. According to Bamrung, the participation of academics assured that the demands of the SSFAI were not extreme, and were practicable (Bamrung 1993: 22, 24). These became later known as the demands of 'three main issues, nine problems'. However, by October 1995 the number of problems had increased to more than 80 (*Bangkok Post*, 25 October 1995: 4). Furthermore, new issues such as the environment and debt were raised. The demands of the SSFAI were those of postpeasants, who were faced with two types of problems. The first concerned land rights – the prototypical peasant problem. The second dealt with problems derived from the expansion of capitalism into the countryside, such as prices, debt and environment. As discussed above, problems like these reflected the transformation of peasant society into postpeasant society.

The First Issue: Problems Caused by State Policies

The first issue – problems caused by government policies – comprised four problems. The first was caused by dam projects. Based on the concept of community rights, the SSFAI proposed that before the construction of any dam, the state had to inform the public concerning the impact of the dam on village life. More important, the community must have a role in determining whether the proposed dam should be built or not. If it had to be built, villagers had to be consulted on how big it should be and how much the state had to pay as compensation to villagers. In addition, if there was conflict between the state and community, the conflict should be settled by a committee comprised of government agencies, farmers and academics. These principles were later applied to rock-blasting as well (SSFAI (n.d.).

The second and third problems, cashew nut growing and silkworm breeding, were caused by the quadripartite projects. The fourth problem was the failure of Brahman cow raising under the Green Isan Project. All of these state-sponsored projects failed to produce what the government had promised. The failure caused huge debt among farmers. The problem was, who should be responsible for the failure? For the SSFAI, the farmers should be exempt because they were persuaded to join the projects by state officials, who supplied them with inaccurate information. Moreover, the private companies involved also failed to keep their promises. Therefore, it was not fair to blame farmers for the failure of the projects. The SSFAI demanded that the government take responsibility for the farmers' debts, and provide funds to help restore the farmers' careers (Tunya 1994: 24).

The Second Issue: Land and Forestry Conflicts

The second issue concerned problems related to land and forestry conflicts between villagers and the state. This group of problems mainly involved disputes over land rights in the degraded forest reserves, and disputes over public land and Treasury Department land. As mentioned above, Isan farmers in different areas still faced the threat of eviction from their lands by the state, even though the *Kho Jo Ko* project was terminated in 1992. As a result, the right of farmers to live in the so-called 'forest reserves' was still central to their struggle. The SSFAI shared with NGOs the idea of prioritizing community rights over local natural resources. According to a leading member of the Assembly, the SSFAI believed that 'man can co-exist with the forest', and the community had rights to participate in community forest management (Ken Fanglit, interview, 13 March 1998). It is interesting to discover that this kind of idea is not alien to Isan. When the government passed the forest reserves law in 1938, Isan MPs protested against the law on the ground that it destroyed the traditional subsistence method of Isan's rural populations, who made their livings from the forest (*Phujatkan*, 9 September 1996: 2).

Concerning this issue, the SSFAI demanded that (a) the government stop promoting eucalyptus planting in the national reserves under the land reform programme to avoid environmental destruction, and support community forests that benefit local communities; (b) the government review national forest policy and allow conservationists and academics to participate in the reviewing process; (c) the government allow the community or community organizations to take part in forest conservation via the Community Forest Law; (d) the government issue land title deeds to farmers, whom the state wrongly blamed for encroaching on forest reserves or public land; and (e) the government allow local communities to participate in solving conflicts over land and forest, issue land title deeds and implement land reform (SSFAI (n.d.); Tunya 1994: 24; *Bangkok Post*, 23 October 1994: 3).

The Third Issue: Agricultural Prices

The third issue concerned the problems of low prices for three kinds of agricultural produce: tapioca, paddy and pigs. The Assembly opposed the current laissez-faire policy on this issue. According to Bamrung, to declare a free trade policy that prevented the government from subsidizing farmers would lead to the destruction of poor farmers, who were unable to compete with giant conglomerates (Atiya 1992: 24). As a result, the SSFAI demanded some kind of protection or subsidies from the government. Concerning tapioca prices, the SSFAI called for a fixed price of 1 baht per kilogram without a 10 per cent deduction. It also demanded that the government set up places for gathering raw tapioca as recommended by farmers. In addition, the police should stop extorting money from farmers when they delivered their crops to merchants. Concerning the paddy problem, the SSFAI asked the government to stop charging interest on mortgaged paddy from 1 October 1993; and concerning the problems related to pig raising, the SSFAI raised the same issues as the protest of the Pig Raisers' Cooperatives in March 1993 (SSFAI 1993; Jarin 1995: 45).

According to Bamrung, in addition to the eight problems over three issues there was the protest against the government's agricultural policy in controlling small farmers through the establishment of the National Farm Council. While the first eight problems reflected the specific problems of each group, the last problem was the common problem of all groups (Bamrung 1993: 22). In the

January 1995 protest, the SSFAI raised two new issues: debt and the environment.

The Debt Issue

In 1995, the Assembly singled out debt as one of the important issues for Isan farmers. According to Bamrung, farmers' debts had increased sharply in recent years, partly due to the falling price of agricultural products and the high interest rate of the BAAC loans. Apart from demanding that the government write off debts caused by the quadripartite projects, as mentioned above, the SSFAI called for a 15-year suspension on loan repayments. They also asked the government to provide low-interest loans for farmers. However, they argued that government loans should be provided through farmers' organizations (such as cooperatives), and that the state should allow farmers to participate in the decision-making process in order to reduce the chances of failure, which was important to prevent farmers from building up new debt in the future (*Phujatkan*, 30 January 1995: 2).

Environmental Issues

As discussed above, the struggles of postpeasants did not operate in the political space of specific localities; they operated in a global space. As a result, they could appropriate some global issues, for example the environment, as part of their own campaign. The SSFAI, as an organization of postpeasants also engaged in ecology politics. The environmental problems raised by the Assembly consisted of problems caused by the rock-blasting industry and salt mining. However, in the later period, problems caused by dam projects were also included under environmental issues. Actually, most of the dam problems raised by the Assembly, such as the Lam Sae, Sirindhorn and Pong Kun Petch dams, were struggles for land, and central to the demands was land compensation (*Phujatkan*, 25 January 1993: 8). To portray the struggle for land as a struggle for the environment was an effort to turn weakness into strength (Brysk 1996). By doing so, rural activism could build alliances with environmental movements in the city.

Underlying the demands of the SSFAI discussed above were the rights and participation of the community in the decision-making process. According to Bamrung, the participation approach of the SSFAI 'shocked' the Cabinet when it was raised in meeting in November 1993. In their opinion, the demands of the SSFAI aimed at 'sharing power' with the state (Bamrung 1993: 24). Such demands were unacceptable to the bureaucrats. They declared in a meeting with SSFAI representatives that they would prefer the nation to disintegrate than allow farmers' representatives to take part in decision-making processes (Nakon Sriwipat, interview, 26 January 1998). The authorities reacted in such a way because it challenged the philosophy of the state in dealing with villagers. For

Chaiyan Ratchakul, deputy director of the Thai Studies Research Institute of Thammasat University, the Thai state has 'for decades had one philosophy in common – "You do what we say"' (cited in Pravit 1993b: c1).

The demands of the SSFAI discussed above had significant implications for democratic deepening in Thailand. As we saw in Chapter 1, Thai electoral politics was dominated by business interests. The subordinate classes were excluded from meaningful participation in the political process, except casting their votes. Moreover, their basic rights were not fully acknowledged and often violated by the state. The SSFAI demand for the right to participate in decision-making processes was an important step for democratic progress because, as Pateman points out, popular participation was the core of democracy (Pateman 1970), and it would help to increase popular control over state power and undermine the exclusionary nature of Thai democracy. The demand for rights to participation in the decision-making process was an action that Charles Taylor called the politics of recognition. According to Taylor, the guiding idea 'has been the equalization of rights and entitlements. What is to be avoided at all costs is the existence of "first-class" and "second-class" citizens' (Taylor 1994: 37). For Fraser, this kind of politics 'aimed at overcoming subordination by establishing the misrecognized party as a full member of society, capable of participating on a par with the rest' (Fraser 2000: 3). Apart from demands for recognition, the SSFAI also demanded material benefits (redistribution) such as land rights and compensation. However, it would be wrong to view such demands as purely redistributive issues. For example, while the struggle for land rights was the fight for a piece of land, the heart of the struggle was the campaign against arbitrary state policies. It was the action to protect the basic rights of ordinary citizens and social justice. Moreover, the SSFAI also demanded democratic rules and procedures in dealing with problems raised by the organization.

MAJOR PROTESTS OF THE SSFAI DURING THE RADICAL PERIOD

The aim of this section is to explore the implementation of strategy and tactics in the major protests of the SSFAI during 1993–95. While the previous section covered the guiding ideas of the organization, this section examines how such ideas were implemented in practice. As a result, what is presented below is a series of events relating to contests between the SSFAI and the state. The events will be presented in chronological order around the following questions: What were the measures the SSFAI implemented during their protests? How did the government respond to the protests? What were the outcomes of the contests between the two sides? The struggles of the SSFAI described in this section will provide a point of reference for a discussion of the search for new strategies in the following chapter. However, before exploring the major protests of the SSFAI during the radical period, it will be useful to look at the political context of the protests.

The Political Context of the SSFAI Protests during the Radical Period

The protests faced hostile reactions from the Thai state. The hostility of government officials arose from their negative attitude towards the political rights of the citizen. Although Thailand was ruled by elected governments after September 1992, officials still regarded extra-parliamentary political activities as a form of 'mob rule', which caused trouble for the nation. According to Prime Minister Chuan Leekpai, people who resorted to 'mob rule' had no respect for the laws and regulations of society and did not care whether their protests caused trouble to other people. Chuan took such a stance towards extra-parliamentary politics because he had a very narrow view of democracy: democracy was equal to parliamentary activities. For him, problems ought to be solved only in parliament by MPs. If MPs ignored the demands of the public, it was the fault of voters because they had voted for bad MPs (Prapas 1998: 123). Chuan's negative attitude towards extra-parliamentary politics also derived from his educational background. Chuan was a former lawyer 'who follows the law to "the letter" and with "rigidity"' (*Thai Development Newsletter*, July–December 1999: 38). His principles in running the country were that the law must be upheld and officials must be in charge (Baker 2000: 24). As a result, Chuan and his party, the Democrats, preferred the status quo rather than pushing for change (McCargo 1997b: 124).

Chuan's attitude was shared by military leaders and bureaucrats. Army Commander-in-Chief Wimol Wongwanich criticized those who organized political protest as people 'who want to cause rifts and do not want peace restored in society' (*Bangkok Post*, 1 April 1993: 3), while Pong Leng-ee, the Forestry chief, asserted that 'organised mobs' were Thailand's 'new enemy'. They posed similar problems to those created by communist armed struggle in the past. For Pong, mobs were more dangerous than organized crime activities because 'they undertake illegal action openly, while "dark influence" is afraid to break the law' (*Bangkok Post*, 23 May 1993: 21).

Moreover, the hostility of the authorities towards the SSFAI also arose from the political situation at that time. In the early 1990s, some elements of the Thai state were still concerned about a possible revival of the CPT. The emergence of the SSFAI engendered suspicions among officials for a number of reasons. First, prominent SSFAI figures were left-wing political activists from the 1970s, and some of them had joined the CPT's armed struggle in the jungle during the late 1970s and early 1980s. Second, the SSFAI operated in many former CPT areas. Third, the SSFAI adopted a political strategy similar to the leftist movements of the 1970s; that is, it emphasized political protest and building a strong mass organization (Nakon Sriwipat and Somsiri Wongwinai, interview, 1 August 1997).

However, there were constraints on state hostility towards the SSFAI. The authorities were afraid that if they used force, they would face another 'Bloody May'. As Pong points out, the officials did not 'take action against these "mobs" in the past because they feared that they would join the communists. Today, we dare not take legal action against them because we're afraid it will lead to a riot' (*Bangkok Post*, 23 May 1993: 21). Another factor that influenced government policy towards the SSFAI was the 'politics of compromise'. Before the 1980s, the Thai countryside was under 'a "climate of fear" in which violent attacks or death by assassination, rather than mere official rebuke or arrest, is a possible, ultimate sanction' (Turton 1987: 99). Actions considered legitimate for citizens in a democratic society, such as 'demanding rights from the government', or 'urging others to demand rights and to resist oppressive or corrupt on the part of officials' were viewed by the government as 'communist activities' which were illegal and would result in severe repression. To deter 'communist activities', the government set up the Village Scouts and several paramilitary Volunteer Defence Forces at the village level for 'intelligence gathering, informing, surveillance, with the attendant elements of harassment, provocation, and intimidation' (Turton 1987: 92–96). Such practices, prevalent in the countryside before the 1980s, were gradually reduced after the introduction of the Prime Minister Decree 66/23 in 1980. As was pointed out in Chapter 3, the Decree was implemented to prevent leftists and other activists from joining the armed struggle of the CPT by allowing them to engage in peaceful political activities outside the jungle. As a result, the government had to tolerate the existence of the grassroots movements. The combination of factors mentioned above, though generating a hostile attitude towards the SSFAI, also prevented the government from suppressing it forcibly.

Civil Society as the Space for Democratic Struggle: the Radical Strategy in Practice

Civil society was an important political arena for the struggle for democratization in Thailand. To contain state suppression and fight for democratic rights, ordinary citizens had to organize themselves within civil society. Civil society, as Cohen and Arato have pointed out, 'has become the indispensable terrain on which social actors assemble, organize, and mobilize' (Cohen and Arato 1994: 502). Civil society was the main arena for the struggle for 'the right to have rights' for the SSFAI. The empirical materials in this section will address the major protests of the SSFAI from 1993 to 1995, which brought the organization to national prominence. The section will focus on the strategies the SSFAI employed to enhance its bargaining power and the government reactions to these strategies. In doing so, it is necessary to illustrate the implementation of these strategies through a detailed narrative.

Members: The Pillar of SSFAI's Major Protests

It is important to acknowledge the contribution of SSFAI members to the success of the protest. As mentioned above, marches along the highways were the main form of SSFAI's major protests during the radical period. The marches were organized to draw public attention in order to build up pressure on the government. The strength of such protests was based on active participation of ordinary members. Without their unity, determination, courage, sacrifice and discipline, the major protests of the SSFAI were unthinkable. It was the members who marched under the burning sun of Isan for weeks. It was they who confronted and broke down the blockade of the armed commandos. Their actions were the key to winning media attention, crucial for the success of SSFAI's major protests.

The October 1993 Protest

The first major protest of the SSFAI during the radical period occurred four months after the cashew nut farmers' protest. It was a reaction to government failure to solve the farmers' problems, which they had promised to address during previous protests. The protest was held in Kalasin province on 19 October 1993 (SSFAI 1994: 5) and moved to Lam Takong reservoir in Si Khiu district, Nakhon Ratchasima province (*Bangkok Post*, 2 November 1993: 2; *The Nation*, 25 January 1995: A4). Lam Takong, according to Charoon, 'became to the farmers a haven and strategic stronghold' for numbers of reasons. The reservoir, located some 197 kilometers from Bangkok, making it possible for protesting farmers to march on Bangkok at any time. The site was also close to markets and had a good water supply (Charoon 1995: B 4). More important, Lam Takong was situated alongside the Friendship Highway, one of the busiest highways in Thailand, linking Bangkok with Isan. It was an ideal place for the SSFAI to demonstrate for its causes in order to draw public attention. Another reason for the SSFAI choosing Lam Takong as the site for mobilization was that significant numbers of its members were in Si Khiu. So the organization was able to call on a 'reserve army' any time during the protest (Nakon Sriwipat, interview, 11 July 1997).

This time the government applied more pressure on the demonstrators. In villages, village headmen, sub-district chiefs and local authorities threatened to arrest those villagers who joined the SSFAI protest. They also spread a rumour that there would be violence at the rally, and farmers who joined the demonstration would be killed. In some areas, officials made direct threats to the families of the SSFAI leaders (SSFAI Yasothorn Provincial Committee, interview, 30 September 1997). At the rally site, hundreds of military-trained rangers, border patrol police and local police were sent to keep a close watch on the rally (*Bangkok Post*, 2 November 1993: 2). In addition, according to the SSFAI provincial general secretary of Yasothorn, the government also sent local officials, such as district officers, to threaten the protesters and force them to go home (Uthai Potduang, interview, 25 February 1998). The threat of force was combined with the accusation that the protest was a 'hired mob' paid for by the opposition parties (*Daily News*, 5 November 1993: 29). At the time of the protest, the opposition parties were preparing to launch a no-confidence debate. According to one opposition leader, the protest and the censure debate happened at the same time by chance (*Daily News*, 5 November 1993: 19). However, if this time the SSFAI did not deliberately plan to organize their protest during the no-confidence debate, in the future they did adopt this strategy because they believed it would increase their bargaining power (Somsiri Wongwinai, interview, 7 January 1998).

The SSFAI, however, was not scared by these government moves. On the contrary, the Assembly was determined to deploy more offensive tactics towards the government in order to gain more concessions. The SSFAI reacted to the government threats by setting up its own security unit. The majority of unit members were young farmers, and they were coordinated by student activists. Their duties were to guard the rally against the threat from government authorities and keep a close eye on plainclothes police officers who sneaked into the rally. In addition to the setting up of the security unit, the protesters were organized into groups of ten, and each group had one representative to coordinate with other groups. These measures were designed to facilitate security and prevent confusion among protesters. To maintain discipline, the farmers were forbidden to drink alcohol during the protest (Somsiri Wongwinai, interview, 2 November 1997).

Road blockades were one of the tactics the SSFAI employed to pursue their demands on a number of occasions. On 1 November, for example, when the governor of Nakhon Ratchasima province, Damrong Ratanapanich, refused to provide drinking water, medicine and mobile toilets at the rally site, the SSFAI blocked the Friendship Highway for 20 minutes and threatened to block the road longer if the governor still did not respond to its demands (*Daily News*, November 2, 1993: 15). Road blockades were very effective in drawing attention from the government, but at the same time very unpopular among the public. According to a poll conducted by Suan Dusit Teachers' College, road blockades ranked second among 'the most unpopular mobs' (*Daily News*, 4 February 1998: 13). Aware of the negative aspects of the blockade, in the later period the SSFAI had a policy of avoiding road blockades during protests.

The most important measure that the SSFAI adopted during the October 1993 protest was the 'march to Bangkok' strategy. This measure became the main tactic of the organization in pressuring the government during the organization's radical period. The decision to pressure the government by marching to the capital city turned the Friendship Highway near the Isan–Central region border into a new site of contest between the SSFAI and the state. The SSFAI decided to march along the Friendship Highway to Bangkok after learning that the Cabinet had rejected the idea of a joint committee they had proposed, and planned to set up government committees that excluded farmers from the decision-making process.

The government was particularly afraid of protests in Bangkok. After negotiations with SSFAI leaders in Bangkok, the government agreed to set up the joint committees as proposed by the SSFAI, to look into the problems of farmers, and promised to raise the issue with the Cabinet within 30 days (*Bangkok Post*, 5 November 1993: 1). However, as in the past, the government did not take the agreement seriously. It was just a tactic to defuse the demonstration. As a result, no progress was made by the government. On the contrary, it tried to undermine the SSFAI by threatening their leaders and spreading rumours to cause confusion within their rank and file (SSFAI 1994: 6). This insincerity on the part of the government inevitably led to new protests by the SSFAI.

The Long March (I)

The SSFAI decided to organize a new round of rallies at Lam Takong on 4 February 1994. In this protest, the SSFAI not only demanded from the government serious action in solving their problems as promised, but also raised seven new cases. All of these, except the Lam Sae Dam case, were concerned with conflicts over land rights in the degraded reserves and public land (SSFAI 1994: 15–16).

The inactivity of the government after the previous protest indicated that more pressure was needed. To increase the pressure on the government, the SSFAI modified its strategy in the February 1994 protest. After gathering at Lam Takong for three days, SSFAI leaders decided to split their forces into two groups. The first group consisted of 200 farmers and their representatives, who were sent to Bangkok in advance to rally in front of Government House. The second group, the main force, adopted the 'march to Bangkok' strategy (Jarin 1995: 46). Although the SSFAI had employed this strategy before, it did not occupy such an important position as in this protest. Previously, the strategy was employed as a supporting part of their protest, but this time it became the main strategy in efforts to bargain with the government. On 7 February, a convoy of 80 *etan* – small, slow and noisy two-stroke engined farmers' trucks – stretching more than one kilometre, left Lam Takong. This marked the beginning of the historic march of the SSFAI. Avoiding criticism from the public, this time they did not obstruct traffic on the Friendship Highway, using only one lane of the highway (*Bangkok Post*, 8 February 1994: 1).

It was not only the SSFAI that applied more pressure on the government; the government also adopted tougher measures against the SSFAI. In the downtown area of Pakchong, about 10 kilometres from Lam Takong, some 20 policemen tried to stop the SSFAI's convoy. The SSFAI, however, was able to break the blockade by instructing a group of security guards to encircle the police and let the main force go through. The police tried to stop the march of the SSFAI again the same afternoon at the crossroads to Khao Yai. They blocked the highway with half a dozen large trucks loaded with some 30 tonnes of rice. The farmers, however, were not afraid of any obstacle created by the authorities. They showed their determination and unity by pushing the trucks aside. After their successful clearing of the highway, they were confronted by more than 200 Border Patrol police and 100 anti-riot police from the Crime Suppression Division at Klang Dong, Pak Chong district, about 60 kilometres from Lam Takong. The SSFAI decided to end their first day of marching by camping at a temple near the highway (*Bangkok Post*, 8 February 1994: 1).

The police action signalled the beginning of tougher measures designed to stop the rally. On 8 February, while the farmers prepared to move from the temple grounds, some 250 Border Patrol police, anti-riot police and commandos armed with tear-gas and clubs blocked their way. Tension rose when 60 commandos formed barricades near the protesters (*Matichon*, 10 February 1994: 13). Afraid that tear-gas would be used to break them up, the SSFAI instructed the farmers to prepare to defend themselves by using wet *pha khao ma* (bathing cloth) to wrap around their head or waist. By parking tow trucks on the road, police successfully prevented the convoy of farmers' vehicles from continuing. Such blockades, however, failed to stop farmers from continuing their protest. The SSFAI declared that the march to Bangkok would continue by foot and would not be called off until the government responded to its demands (*The Nation*, 9 February 1994: A2). This decision meant that the protesters had to march on foot, but also without food, which was seized by police along with their trucks (Keunpetch 1994: 6).

The march on foot set up a new and dramatic contest. The SSFAI planned their march not only to overcome the police blockade, but also to gain political support from society. The protesters were protected by young farmers who acted as security guards. Children and women, carrying pictures of the king and queen and national flags, were assigned to lead the march (Nakon Sriwipat, 14 December 1997). As Baker points out, such an act was a move to affirm loyalty and deny any attempt at rebellion (Baker 2000: 19). However, there were two more important functions for women and children at the front of the march. First, for security reasons, their presence made it difficult for police to use force against the protesters. The women members of the SSFAI had special duties during the march. They formed a special unit called 'the ankle-length skirt squad'. Their task was to deal with police who blocked the road. If men were employed to confront the police, the SSFAI was afraid that it would turn into violence. However, police were reluctant to push and shove women in front of reporters who followed the march closely. Second, for political reasons, the presence of women and children helped to win sympathy from people along the highway and the public at large. Some children took to the protest stage to explain why Isan farmers had to march to Bangkok. Most of the children who joined the protest had parents among the protesters. However, some of them were outsiders who came from the Khru Tim Boon-ing Foundation School in Buri Ram province. The school was named after a school teacher activist, who was assassinated in the 1980s because of his social and political activities. School officials encouraged the students to participate in the rally because they saw it as one way of raising the political consciousness of the youngsters (Sirimas 1994: C1). According to Somsiri, the role of children was specially emphasized when the SSFAI wanted to arouse its members and appeal to the public. In addition to women and children, old villagers played their part in the SSFAI's scheme for winning political support. The picture of an old farmer carried by young villagers on a stretcher specially made for him from a gunny bag and wooden poles had a strong impact on society (Somsiri Wongwinai, interview, 7 January 1998).

Before the march began, the SSFAI faced the problem of how to handle the protest. A march of 2,000 to 3,000 protesters, which extended about 2–3 kilometres, needed communication lines between leaders and marchers. The SSFAI communicated with the protesters during the march through an amplifier sound system on a pickup truck. According to Kuenpetch, it was impossible to handle the march without an amplifier, so the SSFAI decided to take the pickup truck with them. Since police blocked the highway, the SSFAI instructed farmers to carry the pickup truck across a roadside ditch to the other lane (Kuenpetch 1994: 6). The SSFAI then began their march towards Bangkok. After about three hours of marching, they faced another blockade by some 400 Border Patrol Police commandos at a bridge across the Muak Lek canal on the Central Plain–Isan border. The SSFAI decided to camp about 200 metres from the blockade (*Matichon*, February 10, 1994: 13). That night, they held an urgent meeting to discuss the situation, because there was a report that the officials planned to use force to break up the protest before the marchers crossed the border. There were two options for the SSFAI: either to give up the march to Bangkok and negotiate on the government's terms, which meant that they would not go beyond the previous protest, or to continue the march until the government accepted their demands. The SSFAI chose the latter (Nakon Sriwipat, interview, 14 December 1997).

The march was resumed on the morning of 9 February. The commandos, however, still blocked the highway. In efforts to persuade them to change their mind, some protesters kneeled to beg the commandos to open the highway (*Daily News*, 11 February 1994: 17). When the commandos refused, they had to avoid the blockade by walking across the Muak Lek canal. The route was not so difficult for the marchers, but for the pickup truck, farmers once again had to lift it up and carry it across the canal. After crossing, they managed to walk in the heat for 20 kilometres before camping at Thub Kwang in Muak Lek district of Saraburi province. On the way to Thub Kwang, the SSFAI received food and water, donated by villagers who lived near the highway (Kuenpetch 1994: 6) – an evidence of the success of their efforts to win over the public.

Although the police did not try to stop the march again after they crossed the canal, the SSFAI was still worried that the government would use force against the protesters, especially after learning that students who helped their colleagues by protesting in front of Government House had been arrested (*Bangkok Post*, 10 February 1994: 10). As mentioned above, on 7 February, the SSFAI had sent a group of farmers to hold a demonstration in Bangkok. In the capital, they were supported by a group of students from the Student Federation of Thailand (SFT). On 9 February, North Bangkok Metropolitan Police arrested 64 students and seven other people at the protest scene. They were accused of instigating disorder. According to the police, the students had to be separated from farmers because the situation was about to turn chaotic when the farmers did not cooperate with the government. Yet at the time of the arrests, farmers' representatives led by Werapon Sopa were negotiating with officials at the Agriculture Ministry. Werapon called off the negotiations only after learning about the arrests. He declared that farmers would not negotiate with the government again 'unless all arrested students are released' (*Bangkok Post*, 10 February 1994: 3). All students were later released and they returned to join the protesting farmers in front of Government House (*Matichon*, 12 February 1994: 12). Anti-protest activities not only occurred in Bangkok, but also in Saraburi. Late at night on 10 February, leaflets were secretly distributed at the camp site accusing the protesters of being a 'hired mob', of which the leaders got paid 10,000 baht per day, and the protesters 500 baht (*Daily News*, 12 February 1994: 11).

Contrary to the government's intention, these moves designed to isolate the SSFAI drew more sympathy for the organization. In Bangkok, the arrests were criticized by democratic organizations such as the Campaign for Popular Democracy and the Federation for Democracy. They demanded that the government treat the students and farmers properly, in accordance with democratic principles (*Bangkok Post*, 11 February 1994: 1). The labour movement also vowed to support the protest. The Labour Congress of Thailand declared that five major labour organizations would help the farmers step up pressure on the government by staging a demonstration on 19 February (*The Nation*, 14 February 1994: A5).

It was difficult for the government to ignore the demands of the SSFAI, since the SSFAI was not only capable of organizing 'protracted' protests against the state, but also successful in winning support from the public at large. Their activities received positive coverage in most major newspapers. For example, while the government accused the protest of being a 'hired mob', *Thai Rath*, the most popular newspaper in Thailand, contended that it was impossible for a 'hired mob' to walk for 100 kilometres (*Thai Rath*, 11 February 1994: 17). When the rally went on, more and more newspapers criticized the government for its insincerity in solving the farmers' problems. The SSFAI finally won concessions from the government. The Agriculture Minister agreed to solve all the problems identified by the SSFAI and agreed to set up a joint committee to follow up on the implementation of the agreement. The SSFAI, however, insisted that they would call off their protest only when the Cabinet approved the agreement (*Bangkok Post*, 15 February 1994: 3). On 15 February, after the Cabinet acknowledged the agreement, the SSFAI ended their 17-day rally (*Bangkok Post*, 16 February 1994: 3). The government action was just another tactical move to defuse the rally. Cabinet acknowledgement was completely different from a Cabinet resolution and had no legal status at all.

After the protest, the government was not active in tackling farmers' problems as promised; only the problems derived from the Brahman cow raising project were seriously addressed (Jarin 1995: 51). However, the protest had a very important impact on the development of the SSFAI. It attracted thousands of farmers to join the SSFAI. According to one young farmer, who later became a leader, he joined the organization because he was impressed with its bargaining power and the ability of the organization to mobilize thousands of farmers. It convinced him that the SSFAI could solve all farmers' problems (Ronachit Tummong, interview, 3 April 1998). Two main groups of farmers joined the SSFAI after the protest. The first group comprised farmers in conflict with the state over land rights. During the eight months after the protest, the SSFAI received petitions from some 20,000 families of Isan farmers who had problems with land rights (*Phujatkan*, 25 January 1995: 2). This group, according to Nakon, was the most resolute and committed to the SSFAI's goals. They formed the backbone of the SSFAI (Nakon Sriwipat, interview, 11 July 1997). The second group joined the SSFAI because they wanted cheap credit and free ponds from the Readjustment of Farming Structure and Production System Programme (RFSPSP). During the protest in February 1994, the government agreed to allow some 3,000 members of the SSFAI to join the project. The SSFAI used this opportunity to recruit new members (*Phujatkan*, 6 May 1995: 14). It must be noted that the RFSPSP occupied a special position in the history of the SSFAI; it helped to increase the membership of the SSFAI dramatically but also led to a major conflict that split the organization (see Chapter 5).

The Long March (II)

On 26 September 1994, the Central Committee of the SSFAI held a meeting in Kalasin to assess the progress of the work of the joint committee nine months after the February protest. They agreed that government officials had clearly shown that they did not want to solve problems; therefore, it was necessary for the Assembly to prepare for a new protest. The meeting proposed that in addition to the demands relating to the original nine problems, new demands would focus on 'land rights and debt' (SSFAI 1994c: 5, 6). The Assembly also raised new problems concerning the environment. According to Somkiat Pongpaiboon, an Assembly advisor, the plan for a new protest, dubbed the '*Dao Krajai* (scattered stars) Operation', comprised three main activities: organizing a series of protests in different provinces of Isan, marching along the Friendship Highway and organizing an extended protest at a suitable rally site. Originally, the SSFAI planned to hold a new rally in February 1995, but the organization revised its plan when Chuan and the Democrats faced a crisis from the land reform scandal. The objective of this reform was to grant land ownership documents to poor and landless farmers. But Suthep Thueksuban, a deputy agriculture and cooperatives minister, issued land documents to four wealthy business people in Phuket. Suthep's action faced strong opposition from the public. The Assembly, according to Somkiat, saw the vulnerability of the government as a good opportunity for a political offensive, so it decided to organize its protest earlier than previously planned (Somkiat 1995c: 3).

The SSFAI organized a new protest in January 1995. According to an organizer, the new protest was the best prepared of the major campaigns of the SSFAI. From October to December 1994, the Assembly held several meetings with their members in every zone to discuss and explain the objectives, demands and strategy and tactics of the protest. Every zone was also told to prepare for a 'protracted' campaign, and had to prepare enough rice and food for such a campaign. Furthermore, campaign duties were assigned among members, and because the main form of protest was 'marching on foot to Bangkok', a rotation system was planned to rotate forces during the march. Apart from internal preparations, the Assembly gave priority to social understanding of its activities. Articles explaining objectives and the necessity for a new rally were distributed. The main target of the SSFAI's public relations campaign was the media (Nakon Sriwipat, interview, 2 August 1997).

From 13–23 January 1995, the SSFAI gathered in Roi Et, Mukdahan and Loei, and then moved to the hotbed of the last two campaigns, the Lam Takong reservoir. The Assembly adopted the same strategy as the previous protest, but with more strength and determination. Moreover, this time it singled out Chuan and his party, the Democrats, as the main target of criticism. According to an advisor of the SSFAI, such a move was a reaction to the intransigence of Chuan towards the Assembly's demands in the previous protests (Ratsapa Namlaow, interview, 18 July 1997). The SSFAI demanded that Chuan meet them to hear their problems, otherwise they would move their campaign to Government House (*The Nation*, 25 January 1995: A4). They also wanted the Prime Minister to sign an agreement guaranteeing that the government would take prompt action to solve their problems (*The Nation*, 29 January 1995: A5). In addition, the agreement would have to be written in the form of a contract to ensure that the government complied with their demands (*Bangkok Post*, 27 January 1995: 1).

The move drew a strong reaction from Chuan and ministers from the Democrat Party. Chuan questioned the intentions behind the campaign and asserted that the government had already solved most of the farmers' problems. Hence, he suspected that the farmers were not really suffering, and there could be a hidden agenda behind their rally (*The Nation*, 26 January 1995: A1; *Bangkok Post*, 26 January 1995: 1). The Democrat secretary-general and Interior Minister, Sanan Kachornprasart, suggested that there might be people 'behind' the farmers trying to cause trouble (Naowarat and Suphavadee 1995: 5). He also accused Bamrung of organizing protests only for money. 'He mobilises such protests once a year or his purse will empty' (*Bangkok Post*, 28 January 1995: 3). Sanan went further by suggesting that the CPT had infiltrated the SSFAI and was behind the whole campaign, and that it would lead to violence (Naowarat and Supavadee 1995: 5). He warned that 'if any problem occurs … they must bear responsibility… They can't blame the government if villagers are left to die' (*The Nation*, 7 February 1995: A4). Sanan also claimed that the SSFAI's English name 'Voice of the Voiceless' (which was not true) was being used to seek money from foreign countries (Naowarat and Suphavadee 1995: 5). Leaflets were distributed to protesters claiming that Bamrung must be held responsible for causing national unrest and that his actions would eventually lead the mass demonstrations to fizzle out (*Bangkok Post*, 27 January 1995: 1). The government, in addition, spread rumours that the protest was backed by the opposition parties (Kiatisak 1995, B6).

Apart from verbal attacks, Sanan ordered provincial governors in Isan to stop the SSFAI from arriving in Bangkok. He insisted that such action was important before the situation got out of control (*Bangkok Post*, 24 January 1995: 1). Another Democrat leader, Sampan Thongsamak, the Education Minister, ordered a disciplinary investigation into the activities of any school-teacher activists who got involved in the demonstration (*Bangkok Post*, 1 February 1995: 6).

The government, however, was unable to gain the upper hand over the Assembly in its efforts to influence public opinion. Newspaper and TV news reports mainly conveyed the farmers' side of the story. For example, after the meeting of the committee overseeing government aid for farmers, the media reported only Bamrung's opinion, and carried no report on the government perspective (*Bangkok Post*, 28 January 1995: 1). While the government accused the SSFAI of being 'trouble-makers', the *Bangkok Post* editor asserted that the Assembly 'are not troublemakers ... but desperate souls who are badly in need of help'. Instead of agreeing that the government had already solved most of the farmers' problems, he warned that 'farmers may have a high degree of tolerance but their patience does have its limits, especially if pledges continue to be broken' (*Bangkok Post*, 25 January 1995: 4). Such a situation led the Interior Ministry to order the authorities to launch a public relations campaign through various channels, such as special TV programmes, advertisements in newspapers and leaflet distribution (*Bangkok Post*, 28 January 1995: 1).

Despite this strong reaction, the government was not ready to handle 'protracted' protests. Apart from the fact that Chuan and his party were in crisis because of the land reform scandal, the Assembly was this time stronger than during the previous protests. As discussed above, after the February 1994 protest, the SSFAI expanded rapidly, was able to mobilize bigger rallies and able to reinforce its forces with thousands of farmers if necessary. More than ten thousand farmers joined the January 1995 protest. The strength of the Assembly was also enhanced by the experience from political struggle during the previous two years (Somsiri Wongwinai, interview, 6 March 1998). In such a situation, the government had no choice but to compromise. After the commandos sent to block the Friendship Highway were unable to stop the march of the SSFAI, Chuan decided to invite Bamrung and other leaders to negotiate with him in Bangkok (*Bangkok Post*, 29 January 1995: 4). Following the negotiations, Chuan set up a joint committee of farmers' representatives and officials to discuss the Assembly's demands (*Bangkok Post*, 30 January 1995: 1). After a 12-hour negotiating session both sides reached an agreement on 3 February. However, the SSFAI was still not convinced that the government would not break the agreement again, because the government seemed too ready to accept its demands. An advisor of the Assembly asked: 'Will we have to organize protests again?' (Somkiat 1995d: 3). The government did indeed fail to keep their promises as the Assembly had suspected. The Assembly threatened to hold a new round of protests in Bangkok in May 1995 (*The Nation*, 17 May 1995: A1). However, the SSFAI called off a planned new rally when the Chuan government collapsed (Nakon Sriwipat, interview, 14 December 1997).

ENVIRONMENTAL PROTESTS AND POLITICAL VIOLENCE AGAINST THE SSFAI

During the January 1995 protest, the SSFAI raised a group of problems concerning the environment, including the pollution from rock-blasting and salt mining. The most prominent case of environmental protest by the Assembly was the struggle against rock-blasting in Loei province. On 13 January, some 5,000 villagers from 18 villages of Phanoi sub-district, Wang Sapung district, Loei province, staged a protest demanding permanent closure of three quarries that caused health and environmental hazards. According to a protest leader, the farmers had been affected by nearby rock blasting at night and round-the-clock stone milling. Dust from the blasting had made many farmers suffer from lung ailments and damaged crops (*Bangkok Post*, 23 January 1995: 3; *The Nation*, 25 April 1995: A2).

The protest faced strong reaction from the quarries' owners. One of the quarries, Surat Quarry Co, belonged to Surat Timsuwan, known as 'the godfather of Wang Sapung', a five-time chairman of Loei provincial council, and Tossapol Sangkhasap, a five-time former Chat Thai MP for Loei. Surat and his family held a majority share in the quarry. High-ranking military officers, policemen, politicians and businessmen were among other shareholders (*The Nation*, 30 July 1995: B7). Surat was an influential figure who enjoys the backing of certain politicians and government officials. One prominent figure acquainted with Surat was Sanoh Thienthong, secretary-general of Chat Thai, the core government party. It was said that several national politicians were under Surat's patronage. Before engaging in the rock-grinding business, Surat was in the logging business with an influential figure known as 'Sia Yae', the godfather of Ang Thong province, and another godfather, Wisit Thaethiang. Initially, Surat tried to win over villagers by promising to pay 80,000 baht a year to the sub-district council, 3,000–5,000 baht a month to each of 18 village schools and another 2,000 baht a month to every village in Pha Noi sub-district (Suvit 1995: 19; *Bangkok Post*, 15 July 1995: 1). The offer was opposed by the protesters. When the government revoked the licences of the quarries, Surat declared that he would fight back against the protesters in 'every way' (*Bangkok Post*, 27 April 1995: 3).

On 11 July, Prawien Boonnag, a coordinator of zone 4 of the SSFAI who led the protest, was killed by a deputy village headman who had been Surat's employee for 20 years. Three days after the killing, the provincial governor, Pathai Wicharnpreecha, handed a summary of the details of the murder case to the Interior Deputy Permanent Secretary, stating that the assassination was not politically motivated, nor was it masterminded by local influential people as many suspected. The SSFAI, however, disagreed with such a conclusion. They believed that Prawien was killed because of his campaign against the operation of stone quarries. They contended that the assassination was systematically organized and that some local officials and influential figures were involved (*The Nation*, 30 July 1995: B7; Suvit 1995: 19; *The Nation*, 16 July 1995: A1; *Bangkok Post*, 15 July 1995: 1). Another possible cause of the murder was related to the 2 July 1995 general election, in which Prawien had been a candidate for Loei's Constituency 2. During the campaign, he had a serious conflict with Tossapol. It was believed that Tossapol failed to win election partly because of Prawien's strong criticism during the campaign (McCargo 2000: 101).

To assure transparency of the case, the SSFAI demanded that the government transfer Pathai out of the province because he failed to remain neutral in the Prawien case (*Bangkok Post*, 18 July 1995: 1). They also asked for the replacement of Loei police investigators with Crime Suppression Division (CSD) police from Bangkok, because local police were subject to the manipulation by local influential figures, which would lead to a distortion of the facts behind the case (*Bangkok Post*, 19 July 1995: 18). Another point of concern was that Surat and Pathai had close connections with new Prime Minister Banharn Silapa-archa's party, Chart Thai Party. Surat was a major supporter of the Chart Thai Party who organized a political base for Banharn in Loei, and Pathai's elder brother was a former Chart Thai MP (*Krungthep Thurakit* [Isan Section], 21 July 1995: 12). To prevent Banharn from taking sides, the Assembly had to apply strong pressure on the government. The Assembly strongly warned Banharn, who succeeded Chuan as prime minister in July 1995, that if the case was not handled fairly, the government would collapse (*Phujutkan*, 21 July 1995: 15).

The SSFAI supported its threats by planning to organize a protest with 36 democratic organizations and human rights groups from Isan, Bangkok and the North, which would turn out to be the biggest protest in the history of the Assembly. The warnings of a mass protest were not just empty words. More than 10,000 people from all over Isan and other regions attended the funeral for Prawien (*Bangkok Post*, 20 July 1995: 3). The campaign clearly gained momentum and went beyond local problems, becoming a national issue impossible for the government to ignore. The CSD, which was assigned to handle the Prawien case, finally issued a warrant for the arrest of Surat. On 28 August 1995, Surat surrendered himself to Loei police and was released on bail after hearing the charges (*Bangkok Post*, 29 August 1995: 3). But the efforts to seek justice for Prawien were defeated by the Loei prosecutors, who decided to drop the murder charge against Surat (*Bangkok Post*, 31 October 1995: 6).

SOME ACHIEVEMENTS AND LIMITATIONS OF THE SSFAI PROTESTS DURING THE RADICAL PERIOD

The struggle of the SSFAI during the radical period was undoubtedly the most impressive struggle in the history of the organization, and also one of the most creative in the struggles of grassroots movements in Thailand. However, there were limits to the struggle of the SSFAI. The most important achievements and limitations from 1993–95 are the focus of this section.

Achievements

The first achievement of the SSFAI's struggle during the radical period was transforming the Assembly from an ad hoc network into the strongest farmers' organization in Thailand. When set up in 1992, the Assembly had only one problem to deal with; by 1995 it was dealing with 80, and the membership of the organization had increased to about 50,000 (*Bangkok Post*, 25 October 1995: 4).

The struggle of the SSFAI from 1993 to 1995 did not only help to expand the organization, but also created a new group of leaders. According to one, two groups of the 'new generation' of leaders emerged during the radical period. The first group comprised farmers who later rose to provincial committee or central committee posts. The second group consisted of student activists who worked in the secretariat. After the split within the Assembly (see Chapter 5), this second group joined the Assembly of the Poor (AOP), and some of them became leaders of that organization (Ronachit Tummong, interview, 13 October 1997).

Although the struggles of the organization failed to solve farmers' problems, they helped increase the bargaining power of farmers to the degree that the state was unable to arbitrarily drive farmers from their lands in degraded forest reserves areas. In other words, they created a stalemate between the state and farmers. While farmers were unable to pressure the state to grant them land rights, the state was also unable to move them off their lands.

The next achievement of the SSFAI during the radical period was gaining recognition from the state as a political actor. As we have seen, in the course of struggle the Assembly was able to overcome the threat of force from the state and press the government to recognize it as a farmer representative, who has to be dealt with respectfully. However, recognition as a political actor did not only mean the acknowledgement of the SSFAI's existence, but also certain rights of the organization. The government accepted the right of participation and representation of the Assembly by setting up joint committees between the SSFAI and the government to tackle farmers' problems raised by the Assembly. The recognition of the SSFAI's rights can be viewed as a process of broadening of citizenship and the claim of new political spaces.

Another important achievement of the SSFAI during the radical period related to the changing attitude of farmers towards their rights. According to an organizer of the SSFAI, a difficult task in the early period of the Assembly was to persuade farmers to join protests, because many feared that if they took part in demonstrations, they would be arrested or killed by officials. However, after they participated in rallies and other activities of the SSFAI, their fear gradually disappeared (Nakon Sriwipat, interview, 14 December 1997). Farmers clearly recognized their rights and power in bargaining with the state. According to the SSFAI committee of Yasothorn, before joining the SSFAI they thought that only officials had the right to speak, while farmers simply had a duty to follow orders. As members of the Assembly, they learned that farmers had '*sitthi*' (rights), and if their rights were violated by the state, it was legitimate for them to protest. However, when they and other villagers first joined protests, they were quite afraid. But their confidence grew when protesters were able to overcome threats from the authorities, and especially when the authorities had to comply with their demands. Victories over people whom they had long regarded as their 'masters' nurtured courage (SSFAI Yasothon provincial committee, interview, 1 July 1998). This kind of transformation in farmers' consciousness, which was very difficult to create through other channels, is one of the crucial elements for democratic progress in Thailand.

Further transformation also took place within the meetings of the joint committee. As mentioned above, the government was insincere in solving farmers' problems through joint committees, and only a few problems were solved by such committees. However, the setting up of joint committees brought new dimensions to the relationship between farmers and officials. Meeting with government officials was a new experience for farmers. The atmosphere within meetings of joint committees was quite different from that of meetings held during protests. During protests, farmers' representatives entered meetings with the support of protesters outside the meeting room, and they concentrated mainly on pressuring government officials to comply with their demands; but the meetings of the joint committee were mostly held after protests, which meant that farmers' representatives had to deal with officials by themselves. This situation made inexperienced SSFAI representatives, especially at district and village levels, nervous. However, during protests, the SSFAI successfully pressured the government to accept that farmers' representatives had equal status with the authorities within a joint committee. As a result, meetings of the joint committees were conducted under different rules from the past. Formerly, what was right or wrong was determined solely by government officials, but within the meetings of joint committees, SSFAI representatives had the right to challenge government claims and were able to alter officials' decisions. Although not helping farmers solve their immediate problems, such new rights helped to strengthen farmers' confidence and helped them overcome the attitude that the authorities were their superiors. The experience of farmers in Khon Kaen illustrated this point clearly. According to Bunyoung Bucha, having equal status with the officials within the joint committee was unbelievable for him. At the first meeting, the presence of a district chief scared him. However, experience in the meetings helped him to gain more confidence. He began to view government officials as 'ordinary persons' who were not superior to him, and he started to argue with them (Bunyoung Bucha, interview, 10 January 1998).

However, in challenging government officials' claims within a joint committee, SSFAI representatives had to support their arguments with evidence. As a result, before a meeting, farmers had to prepare their own evidence and arguments and propose new alternatives to the government's solutions. This was a learning process for farmers. It helped to increase farmers' knowledge and enabled them to think more independently (a Nong Ya Plong farmer, interview, 10 January 1998).

Limitations

The most obvious limitation of the struggle of the SSFAI during the radical period was that although the protests were strong enough to force the government to sign agreements to solve farmers' problems, they were unable to prevent the government from breaking such agreements. The government always broke its promises after the SSFAI called off the protests. However, this problem did not happen only to the SSFAI; it was a common problem of Thai grassroots movements (Sanitsuda 1992a: 29). How could the movements overcome this dilemma? One organization that tried to solve this problem was the AOP. Since its strategy to prevent the government from breaking agreements will be discussed in Chapter 5, this part will focus on another issue, the limitations of the 'march to Bangkok' strategy.

As shown above, this 'march to Bangkok' strategy was crucial to the success of the SSFAI during the radical period. However, there was a shortcoming; its success depended not only on the strength of the SSFAI, but also on resultant government hostility. The threat of force that led to the contest between the police and the SSFAI played a major part in strengthening solidarity among protesters, enhancing their enthusiasm and courage and turned the marches into the focus of public attention, which in turn helped to increase the bargaining power of the SSFAI. Without government hostility, the long marches along the highway, which used to be the SSFAI's most powerful weapon, became isolated and quiet events. As a result, these protests were unable to draw public attention and also failed to arouse farmers' enthusiasm. The limitations of the 'march to Bangkok' strategy clearly showed in the February 1998 protest of the SSFAI, when the government did not try to interfere with the protest. The ineffectiveness of the strategy on this occasion forced the SSFAI to search for a new strategy.

Another important shortcoming of the SSFAI during the radical period was the organization's failure to raise political consciousness of ordinary members to an extent that enabled them to exert their influence on the organization's leaders. The radical period was the best time for the SSFAI to educate its members in political awareness, and farmers could engage in the organization's activities at all levels because during that time they joined the SSFAI with high enthusiasm and dedication to the course of the organization. However, the SSFAI did not grasp that chance. As a result, the activities of the organization were largely decided by leaders, and this tendency grew in the later period (see Chapters 5 and 6).

SUMMARY

This chapter has examined the SSFAI in the radical period (1993–95) in terms of organizational structure, objectives and strategy, demands and major protests. The SSFAI was a new farmers' movement that operated in a socio-economic background different from that of a classic farmers' movement. In terms of demands, the organization raised not only land rights, but also a set of problems caused by the state and capitalism. During 1993–95, the SSFAI addressed three sets of problems caused by state policies: problems concerning land, forestry conflicts and problems of low prices for agricultural produce. Later, the Assembly also tackled debt and environmental problems. The problems raised by the SSFAI reflected the internal differentiation of Thai farmers, which derived from the transformation of a subsistence peasant community into a postpeasant society.

The main objective of the SSFAI was to defend the long term interests of farmers. Although the organization demanded short term material benefits, such as compensation and debt moratorium, the most fundamental issue was the right to participate in the decision-making process. The Assembly singled out the political mobilization of a people's organization from below as a vehicle to pursue its objectives, and rejected the idea that such goals could be achieved through representative democracy, because the policies of existing political parties served only to benefit the business sector. To strengthen the struggle of its people's organization, the SSFAI emphasized the importance of building alliances with other democratic organizations, of enhancing the organization's bargaining power through marches, and of self-reliance in funding. To achieve the demands and objectives of the organization, the SSFAI also adopted a new organizational structure, involving a more centralized form of organization. However, in the early phase of the radical period, group members still retained their autonomy at the local level. Only at the regional level did they have to act together under the banner of the SSFAI. Later, the need for more efficient organization pushed the SSFAI in a more centralized direction.

To pressure the government to tackle the problems of farmers, the Assembly staged more than 50 minor and major protests. In its major protests, the SSFAI adopted a 'march to Bangkok' strategy. These marches were designed to attract public attention, and increase pressure on the government. In order to achieve this purpose, the marches had to win over the media, which would be crucial in gaining support from society. During the radical period, the SSFAI held three major campaigns. Their rallies faced a hostile reaction from the elected government, which regarded extra-parliamentary politics as mob rule. The SSFAI was accused of being a 'troublemaker', 'hired mob' and a 'communist instigator'. The government tried to end protests by sending forces to block the highway and threaten the marchers in order to prevent the Assembly from making progress towards Bangkok. The SSFAI, however, managed to overcome government threats. The major campaigns of the Assembly ended up with promises from the government to solve all problems raised by the Assembly. But the government's promises were just tactical moves to end the campaigns without serious commitment. As a result, after the protests no major progress was made.

The struggle of the SSFAI during the radical period produced some important achievements. First, its mobilizations transformed the SSFAI from an ad hoc network into the strongest farmers' organization in Thailand. Second, the 1993–95 campaigns created a group of new leaders. Third, they prevented the state from using force to drive farmers off their land. Fourth, they helped farmers to realise their rights and power in bargaining with the state. Fifth, they helped the Assembly to win recognition from the state. Nevertheless, the campaigns of the Assembly during the radical period failed to make significant progress in solving farmers' problems. Another deficiency was inherent in the 'march to Bangkok strategy'. The weak point was that its success depended on government hostility. Without threats from the government, the strategy lost its strength. The organization's failure to raise political consciousness of ordinary members to the extent that enabled them to exert their influence on the organization's leaders was another weak point of the Assembly in this period.

The success of the SSFAI during the radical period was accompanied by conflict within the organization. This conflict finally led to a split, whose causes and results are the main focus of the next chapter.

CHAPTER 5

Conflicts, Splits and Experimentation with a New Strategy

The successes of the SSFAI in the radical period were followed by conflicts within the organization. Signs of conflict emerged when Bamrung Kayotha planned to organize another major protest in Bangkok during the no-confidence debate against the Chuan government in May 1995. The plan was opposed by Assembly leaders from various zones. According to Prawien Boonag, it was unnecessary to organize a protest in Bangkok if the Assembly was able to demand that the relevant officials attend to solving problems in provincial areas. Because most farmers were poor, they did not have enough money to pay for transportation costs and other expenses in Bangkok. Another Assembly leader, Niramit Sucharee from Roi Et, proposed that rallies should be organized in provinces where problems occurred (*Phujatkan*, 11 May 1995: 1). As a result, Bamrung's plan to stage a massive demonstration outside Parliament, involving thousands of farmers, did not materialize. Only about five hundred farmers joined him in the capital city (*The Nation*, 18 May 1995: A3). The differences between Bamrung and other Assembly leaders emerged again in the protest organized by Bamrung in October 1995. Again, Bamrung's aim was a massive protest in which more than ten thousand farmers would participate, but in the event only about four thousand farmers joined in. Bamrung considered the protest to be a failure on the part of the SSFAI.

At the end of the protest on 13 October, Bamrung decided to resign as secretary-general of the SSFAI, five months before his term was due to end, citing concerns over his personal safety (Supawadee 1995: 4; *Bangkok Post*, 23 October 1995: 3, *Phujatkan*, 19 October 1995: 14). However, he later revealed that he resigned because of a 'difference in work philosophy' (*The Nation*, 13 March 1997: A 3). The resignation was followed by conflicts that finally split the SSFAI, a split that led to experiments with a 'compromise strategy' by the SSFAI, and a 'confrontation strategy' by another grassroots organization, the

Assembly of the Poor. The tasks of this chapter are to examine the causes and consequences of the conflict and the implementation of these two competing strategies. The chapter is organized into four sections. The first section analyses the conflict within the SSFAI. The second explores the founding of the AOP and the split in the SSFAI. The third discusses the implementation of a 'compromise strategy' by the SSFAI and a 'confrontation strategy' by the AOP. The final section compares similarities and differences between the two, and assesses the strengths and weaknesses of the two competing organizational structures and strategies.

CONFLICTS WITHIN THE SSFAI

This section comprises four parts. The first part discusses the underlying causes of the conflict within the SSFAI. The second part explores another source of conflict within the SSFAI, conflict over strategy. The third part addresses conflicts over forms of leadership. The final part of the section looks at the result of these various conflicts.

1. The Causes of Conflict: Income vs Land Rights?

The only work to focus on the conflict so far is Chris Baker's article, 'Thailand's Assembly of the Poor: Background, Drama, Reaction' (2000). Baker viewed these conflicts within the context of the changing political economy of the Thai peasantry. Basing his analysis on Prapas's account (Prapas 1998), Baker concluded that the conflict within the SSFAI 'was not simply a product of leadership squabbles and outside interference (although both were present), but reflected a deeper differentiation within the peasantry' (Baker 2000: 27). According to Prapas, the SSFAI concentrated its demands on debt and credit, and was not interested in land rights problems in the post-radical period. As a result, most of the farmers concerned about land rights left the organization to join the AOP (Prapas 1998: 58). Based on the above account, Baker went beyond Prapas, who argued that the SSFAI had turned from an organization concerned with land rights and other issues that related to their members, into an interest group which was concerned only with income issues, such as debt and credit, because Nakon Sriwipat, the new leader who succeeded Bamrung, had changed the policy of the organization (Prapas 1998: 58). For Baker, such a change had deeper causes than just leadership changes. It was rooted in the political economy of the Thai peasantry. The conflict in the SSFAI reflected the different material interests of two groups of farmers, which finally led to the split within the organization. Farmers who were more involved in the market economy (income issues) stayed in the SSFAI, while the 'frontiersmen', whose main concern was land rights (an asset security agenda), resigned to join the AOP.

At one level this appeared as a typical leadership dispute, but at a deeper level, this was a much more fundamental split between two different causes and two different groups of people. From this point on, the more settled farmers and the income disputes were represented by organizations descended from So Ko Yo Oo [the shortened name of the SSFAI in Thai], while the more insecure farmers and asset disputes grouped under the Assembly of the Poor (Baker 2000: 15).

For Baker, differences within the peasantry had a significant influence on the strategy of the organizations. Because of such differences, argues Baker, 'the two groups moved decisively apart and adopted significantly different strategies'. The farmers from marginal areas, who lacked land rights, adopted an agitational strategy; the more secure farmers, who already secured their land rights, 'moved away from protest and agitation towards a strategy of negotiation with local officialdom and with government' (Baker 2000: 15), and they 'were being gradually drawn into the expanding world of formal democracy politics (local government, MPs, political parties)' (Baker 2000: 27).

Baker's conclusion runs into difficulty because his account contradicts what actually happened. The conflict within the SSFAI was not a conflict between two different groups of farmers, which finally turned the Assembly into an organization of 'income-concerned' farmers as Baker claimed. First of all, there were 'income-concerned' groups that resigned from the SSFAI after the conflict. Two prominent figures, Bamrung and Werapon Sopa, who left the SSFAI to join the AOP, were the leaders of 'income-concerned' groups. Bamrung was a leader of the Isan Pig Raisers' Cooperatives, while Werapon led the Cassava Farmers' Group; both had organized the network of rice farmers' groups. These groups joined the SSFAI because they wanted better prices for their products. More importantly, it was Bamrung who challenged the NGOs by asserting that the price issue was just as important to small-scale farmers as the land rights problem (see Chapter 3). After joining the AOP, both Bamrung and Werapon were still concerned with the 'income' agenda. When Bamrung led the protest of the AOP in February 1997, he simultaneously helped the Cassava Farmers' Group, comprising farmers who had left the SSFAI with him, to protest against the low price of cassava (*Krungthep Thurakit* [Isan Section], 21 February 1997: 2). Later, both Bamrung and Werapon, as representatives of the AOP, cooperated with the SSFAI and other organizations campaigning for a moratorium on farmers' debt (see Chapter 6).

Second, after the split, the SSFAI continued to rally on both 'income' (debt) and 'asset' (land rights) agendas. Most of the 'insecure' farmers did not leave the SSFAI, as Baker and Prapas claimed. Actually, Prapas's own account demonstrates that this claim was inaccurate. According to Prapas, the members of the SSFAI in 12–13 areas who faced land rights problems followed Bamrung to join the AOP (Prapas 1998: 77, 98). But in 1996, the SSFAI dealt with land rights in more than 50 areas (*Phujatkan*, 6–7 January 1996: 7). On 30 March 1996, when Nakon was elected as the secretary-general of the SSFAI, land rights was one of the important problems that he raised with the government (*Phujatkan*, 29 May 1996: 9). Actually, as shown in Table 1 below, the number of land rights problem raised by the SSFAI increased after the Bamrung period. The importance of farmers who lacked land rights was acknowledged by Nakon. According to him, farmers who lacked land rights formed the backbone of the SSFAI. They were the most resolute group among the organization's members (Nakon Sriwipat, interview, 11 July 1997). When the SSFAI later split into three groups, the new groups led by Auychai Wata (the Assembly of Isan Farmers (AIF)) and Kamta Kanbunchan (the SSFAI (1)) focused their campaigns on cheap credit from the Readjustment of Farming Structure and Production System Projects (RFSPSP) during the Chavalit government, although later they rallied more over land rights. When the SSFPI rallied on the issue of credit from the RFSPSP, this did not mean that the organization represented the interests of farmers who were concerned solely with the income issue. For example, the majority of 16,000 members of the SSFAI who joined the projects in 1995 were farmers who lacked land rights (SSFAI 1995: 1). More interestingly, the SSFAI in the post-Bamrung period did not again raise the price issues that they had addressed during the radical period. According to Nakon, campaigning on agricultural prices was a waste of time, because in practice only traders got benefit from such campaigns (Nakon Sriwipat, interview, 11 July 1997). The information from the government-appointed committee below shows the issues and numbers of problems raised by the three organizations and the AOP in February 1999. It clearly demonstrates the importance of land rights problem to all of them. So the view that the SSFAI solely represented the interests of farmers concerned just with 'income' issues is not sustainable.

On strategy issues, Baker's analysis did not fare any better, since again it did not correspond to reality. His account had two shortcomings. First, it was only partially true when he asserted that under Nakon, the SSFAI gave up its agitational strategy to pursue a more compromising approach by negotiating with the state. The negotiation strategy with which Nakon wanted to experiment lasted only about 14 months (March 1996 to May 1997). In late May 1997, he organized two protests in Sri Saket and Khon Kaen (*Krungthep Thurakit* [Isan Section], 2 July 1997: 1, 14); after that, the SSFAI organized dozens of protests, including the major protest in February 1998 (see Chapter 6). On the contrary, it was the AOP that Baker singled out as the champion of the protest strategy that failed to stage a single major protest from 1998 to 2000, after its famous 99 days protest in 1997.

Second, Baker contended that the SSFAI under Nakon adopted a strategy of negotiation because it was an organization of 'income-concerned' farmers.

Table 1: The demands of the AOP, the SSFAI, and other organizations (Submitted to the Chuan government in February 1999)

Organization	Issues	Number of problems
AOP	Forestry and land	87
	Dam projects	14
	Others	21
SSFAI	Forestry, land and environment	151
	Debt	1
	Cooperatives	1
	Farmers Rehabilitation Bill	1
SSFAI (I)	Forestry, land and dams	99
	Debt	1
AIF	Forestry, land and environment	23
	Cooperatives	1
	Means of production and ponds	1

Source: The Joint Committee for Solving the Problem of Isan Farmers (1999), 'The Problems Raised by People's Organizations' (Typescript) (in Thai).

But, as shown above, the SSFAI did not represent only 'income-concerned' farmers; more importantly, it was dominated by insecure farmers whose main concern was land rights. The decision to adopt the negotiation strategy was influenced by other factors rather than the composition of its membership (see below). This invalidates Baker's analysis of the causal linkage between the internal differentiation of the peasantry and the strategies adopted by different groups. Actually, it is very difficult to generalize about the relationship between economic interests and political choices. It seems logical when Baker assumes that farmers whose lives were not threatened by the state would avoid confronting the authorities, and prefer to access the decision-making process by formal channels via elections. It also seems logical that farmers who constantly struggled with threats to their survival would prefer extra-parliamentary politics because of their lack of resources. In the real world, however, farmers do not always follow such logic. Protests can be used by both 'income-concerned' and 'insecure' farmers. For example, new farmers' movements in India, which are dominated by 'income-concerned' farmers, chose to advance their interests by political mobilization rather than negotiation (see Chapter 1). In the Isan case, the main organization of 'income-concerned' farmers, the Thai Farmers Foundation (TFF), deals solely with the debt problem. Initially, the TFF worked through negotiation mechanisms. Frustrated with the indifference of officials to their demands, Asok Prasansorn, the chairman of the TFF, considered staging a protest. But because of lack of experience, the TFF did not have enough confidence to pursue this new tactic. However, after it became an ally of the SSFAI in October 1996, the TFF adopted a more aggressive approach. In 1997, it staged a road blockade during its protest in Khon Kaen province (Asok Prasansorn, interview, 7 December 1997). In 1999, the TFF joined the People's Organization of Isan (POI), which consists of six organizations, including the AOP and the SSFAI (The Manifesto of the POI, 1999). The strategy of the POI was to pressure the government by protest and other extra-parliamentary means (see below).

If protest is not confined to 'insecure' farmers groups, nor is electoral politics limited only to 'income-concerned' farmers. Political protest was the best way to build the popularity of Isan farmers' leaders, who were involved in local or national elections. Because of the lack of resources (both money and political connections), it was very difficult for farmers' leaders who wanted to succeed in formal politics to compete with politicians from business circles or other backgrounds. To gain support from rural populations, they turned to the only political capital they had, political mobilization. As a result, it was common that farmers' leaders who succeeded in 'formal democratic politics' in Isan had started out as *'punam* mob' (leaders of protests). More importantly, most of the protests organized by farmers' leaders-cum-politicians arose from insecurity rather than income agendas. One politician of this type was Suchat Srisung, who led the protests against salt mining in Mahasarakham province (see Chapter 3). His role in the protests boosted his popularity among farmers in affected areas. It helped him to win a seat on the Mahasarakham provincial council in October 1990. Suchat joined the SSFAI as a representative of anti-salt mining networks in 1992. He later entered national politics and won a seat in parliament to become an MP for Mahasarakham in July 1995 (*Krungthep Thurakit* [Isan Section], 18 October 1996: 5).

If the conflict within the SSFAI was not derived from the internal differentiation of farmers, as Baker claimed, then what were the real causes of the conflict? Central to the conflict were differences over strategy and the system of leadership. The conflict was personified by the clash between Bamrung and Nakon.

2. The Conflict over Strategy

The differences over strategy within the SSFAI centred around the question of what was the best way to realize the objectives of the Assembly. Should the Assembly continue its confrontation approach, or should it be more compromising and flexible? Another important point of conflict concerning strategy was the question of the relationship between the SSFAI and electoral politics. What was the proper relationship between the Assembly and parliamentary politics? Should Assembly members participate in formal politics or not? The debate within the Assembly also raised the question of cooperation between the SSFAI and its allies. How close should such cooperation be? The final issue concerning the conflict over strategy was the question addressing the proper balance between political mobilization and economic activities. To pursue its objectives, should the Assembly rely only on political mobilization, or should it require strong economic foundations as well? This section will examine the above issues.

Protest or Negotiation?

The first question discussed here is what was the best approach to realise the objectives of the SSFAI: protest or negotiation? Such a question was not new to social movements in Thailand in general and Isan grassroots movements in particular. During the 1970s, the question was posed in terms of 'reform or revolution?' and the student movements, which dominated the social movements at that time by advocating a revolutionary approach. In the 1980s and early 1990s, as discussed in Chapter 3, the question used the metaphor of 'hot' and 'cool' issues among Isan grassroots movements. 'Hot' issues involved mass mobilization for street protests, while 'cool' issues focused on local needs, which would help to improve the community in the countryside. Mass mobilization tactics were criticized on the grounds that they gained only empty promises from officials, while exhausting farmers and activists themselves. In return, the 'hot' faction contended that in the previous 20 years the 'cool' tactics had brought farmers nowhere. The answer to the problems of the poor could not be found in the villages, as the 'cool' faction believed; it was necessary to work with other democratic forces to change government policy (Sanitsuda 1994: 33).

The debate over strategy within the SSFAI differed slightly from the two debates mentioned above. From 1993 onwards, the SSFAI advocated a 'political offensive' strategy. However, around 1995 a conflict over strategy developed after a series of protests, major and minor, during 1993–95, had failed to produce concrete results in solving farmers' problems (see Chapter 4). Such a situation led to the debate over strategy within the SSFAI. One side, led by Bamrung, insisted that the Assembly had to continue to apply pressure on the government by political mobilization. For him, only through street protest could farmers pressure the state to comply with their demands. He rejected negotiation with the government as another possible way for solving the problems of farmers. What politicians do, contended Bamrung, is only to deceive farmers (*The Nation*, 13 March 1997: A3). Negotiation in Bamrung's scheme of things was a minor element in the protest package; it could take place only as a concluding part of political mobilization (Prapas 1998: 151).

The logic of such a conclusion led to a more aggressive strategy. Since the chances of success lay only in holding protests, it meant that in the future pressure had to be increased in order to get results. In the past, protests had failed because pressure was not strong enough. To make sure that the government would give concessions to farmers, it was necessary to organize bigger protests with more determination. This logic was reflected in the protests of the AOP (see below).

The other side of the debate, led by Nakon, advocated a new approach in dealing with farmers' problems. Nakon believed that Bamrung's strategy would lead to disaster (Nakon Sriwipat, interview, 11 July 1997). He saw danger in the political offensive approach of Bamrung from two sources: the lessons from the student movement in the 1970s and his own experience as general coordinator of the SSFAI.

During the 1970s, as mentioned in Chapter 3, the student movement adopted a confrontation strategy for social transformation. Such a strategy boosted the 'ultra-left' tendency within the movement. Street protest was the only means they employed. They rejected any kind of negotiation, even for political gain; as a result, the tactics of the movement became inflexible (Pornpirom 1987: 16). Parliamentary politics were also rejected on the grounds that such politics 'naturally protect the interests of the capitalists' (Morell and Chai-anan 1981: 169). The 'ultra-left' tendency of the student movement also showed in its advocacy of a tripartite alliance of workers, farmers and students, which they considered 'progressive' forces, combined with a refusal to cooperate with other political groups (Morell and Chai-anan 1981: 169; Zimmerman 1978: 60). Furthermore, the movement engaged in too many issues ranging from the problems of slum dwellers, labour disputes, farmers' hardship, high prices of commodities, arbitrary behaviour of officials, corruption and opposition to US military bases. This wide-ranging involvement was criticized by the government and the public at large as intending to cause political conflict within society. The movement, moreover, not only involved too many issues, but also organized too many protests. For example, during the period from November 1973 to September 1974, there were 323 demonstrations in various provinces outside the capital city (Morell and Chai-anan 1981: 157–167). The ultra-left tendency of the social movements of the 1970s was best described by Dr Puey Ungphakorn, a former rector of Thammasat University:

They have pushed too hard, demonstrated indiscriminately on too many issues … they have not developed a flexible strategy of differential response to various issues, dealing quietly with some while raising hell about others … they went immediately to the streets or to the newspapers every time they unearthed a problem. This strategy has turned off many in the center. As for the public support they had after October 14 … It's gone. (Cited in Morell and Chai-anan 1981: 174)

Such a strategy created enemies and alienated the students from society (Morell and Chai-anan 1981: 172–176). It drew strong hostility from the state both in terms of propaganda and physical violence. In response, the social movements insisted on a confrontation strategy 'in the belief that each stage of political struggle meant a struggle in the advancement of the political consciousness of its members' (Pornpirom 1987: 19–21). The reaction created conditions for the military to stage a bloody coup on 6 October 1976 to destroy the movements (see Chapter 3).

The lessons from the failure of the social movements in the 1970s played an important part in the debate over strategy within the SSFAI. Avoiding the mistake of the 'ultra-left' strategy was a main concern of Nakon. He believed that if the Assembly wanted to be successful, the organization had to prevent itself from repeating the same mistakes (Nakon 1996a: 1). For him, the confrontation approach of Bamrung, if continued, would lead to the destruction of the SSFAI. Such an approach not only led to frequent protest; it also helped to increase hostility from the authorities. For example, no matter how important the problems at stake, leaders tended to resort to protest every time they faced problems without considering other alternative means. They also preferred to force authorities to comply with their demands without trying to persuade them. Such tactics engendered unnecessary tension between farmers and officials. In addition, they treated all government officials as 'adversaries'; as a result, they did not make efforts to win over 'sympathetic' or 'rational' people among the authorities (Nakon Sriwipat, interview, 11 July 1997). More importantly, argued Nakon, the frequent protests of the SSFAI would undermine social support and alienate the Assembly from society. If such a situation occurred, it would be dangerous for the organization. Because it would provide conditions for the state to campaign against the SSFAI, it would result in state terror against the Assembly, as happened against the student movement in the 1970s (Nakon 1996a: 1; Nakon 1996b: 2).

Another source of Nakon's rejection of the confrontation approach of Bamrung came from the reaction of farmers to frequent protests. As the general coordinator responsible for coordinating and organizing farmers in different zones to join the rally, Nakon had first-hand experience of the problems. Frequent protests without progress created a burden on farmers, who had limited money and food, and it demoralized and exhausted them. The success in pressuring the government to accept the Assembly's demands during major protests gave hope to farmers that their problems would be solved, yet every time the promises turned out to be just tactical moves to end the protests. After the January 1995 protest, complaints about the slow progress in solving their problems increased among farmers. It was more difficult for local leaders to persuade farmers to join new protests (Nakon Sriwipat, interview, 11 July 1997).

To overcome problems and dangers from the confrontation approach, Nakon proposed that the Assembly should learn to cooperate with the state in the efforts to solve the problems of farmers. A less confrontational approach overcame the 'ultra-left' tendency of the student movement, allowed the Assembly more room to manoeuvre and helped to solve the problems derived from frequent protests. For Nakon, cooperation between the farmers' movement and politicians had both positive and negative consequences. Such cooperation 'builds more potential, while making the people's movement rely on the bureaucratic system' (*The Nation*, 13 March 1997: A3). His idea was widely misunderstood as a move to give up demonstrations (for example, Baker 2000: 15). In fact, he pointed out that the struggle of the SSFAI required not only protest but also negotiation. Both forms of struggle were equally important. For him, protest without negotiation would fail to solve farmers' problems, and negotiation without support from the bargaining power of protest would also definitely fail. The importance of protest and negotiation depended on the situation; therefore, it was not appropriate to emphasize protest as the main form of struggle all the time. The Assembly should be more flexible and employ a varied form of pressure on the state. If possible, argued Nakon, the Assembly should choose to negotiate with the authorities first, because it was appropriate to the current situation of the organization, in which members were tired of demonstrations, and it also helped to save the organization's limited funds. However, when negotiations failed, the SSFAI must not hesitate to pressure the government with protests (*Phujatkan*, 3 April 1996: 7). Nakon summarized his strategy as 'pressure, negotiation, and participation in problem solving' (Nakon 1996b: 3).

Nakon's ideas about protest and negotiation were not unique among Isan activists. For example Decha Premrudelert, a leader of the Isan NGO-CORD, also pointed out that protest was 'costly and the government's resultant promises are often empty', so he tried to 'avoid street protests as much as possible'. A more effective means, for Decha, was to 'lobby policy makers or officials behind the scenes rather than challenge them on streets' (Sanitsuda 1994: 33). Another Isan activist, Pakpum Witanteerawat, the secretary-general of the AIFLRINR and an AOP advisor, argued that the struggle of the poor needed both protest and cooperation with the government and politicians. Protest only created bargaining power for the poor; it did not solve problems by itself. After the government complied with the demands of the movements, it was necessary for the poor to cooperate with the state to solve their problems (Pakpum Witanteerawat, interview, 6 October 1997).

The SSFAI's Strategy Concerning Electoral Politics

Closely related to the 'protest-negotiation' issue discussed above was the question concerning the relationship between the SSFAI and electoral politics. The debate over the relationship between people's organizations and electoral politics began before the founding of the SSFAI. As discussed in Chapter 3, there was a group of political economists who believed that it was necessary for the poor to set up a political party, or get involved in parliamentary politics to defend their interests, while another faction insisted on building up people's organizations to create pressure from outside. This debate recurred within the SSFAI.

The idea of building a people's organization had become the guiding idea of the SSFAI, but some members still saw participation in electoral politics as a channel to pursue farmers' interests. Occasionally, however, the Assembly seemed to endorse the idea of participation in electoral politics. For example, it supported the idea that when the Assembly became strong enough, it would set up its own political party, a party of farmers, to defend the interests of the poor in parliament (*Phujatkan*, 11 May 1995: 1). Furthermore, the SSFAI allowed activists-turned-politicians to work as their advisors in the early period. According to Bamrung, the Assembly had no objection to politicians who wanted to help farmers (*Phujatkan*, 20 February 1995: 8). A number of activists-cum-politicians joined the SSFAI, among them prominent persons like Auychai Wata, Niramit Sucharee, Somyong Kaewsupan, Chuang Kamlae and Prawien Boonnug. Auychai was a public relations officer of Mahasarakham's Primary Educational Office. Niramit, Somyong and Chuang were members of the provincial council and contractors in Roi Et, Khon Kaen and Nong Bua Lamphu respectively. Prawien was a primary school teacher in Loei. In the 1995 general election, Auychai and Prawien were the Muan Chon Party candidates in their own provinces, while Niramit was the Chat Pattana Party candidate in Roi Et. All of them failed to be elected. It should be noted that not all members of this group were involved in electoral politics. Some influential figures had other occupations: Kamta Kanbunchan was a farmer and contractor in Buri Ram, and Supot Agkrarapram was a primary school teacher in Mahasarakham (field notes, 10 September 1997).

Nevertheless, in 1995, the SSFAI passed a resolution demanding that members and advisors who wanted to contest elections at any level must resign from the Assembly (*Phujatkan*, 6 June 1995: 1). The move reflected concern over the rising number of Assembly advisors participating in electoral politics. According to Bamrung, becoming politicians could not solve farmers' problems. He cited the case of Somboon Buranont, a Yasothorn-based former advisor of the SSFAI, who became a Palang Dharma MP and an assistant secretary to the Agriculture Minister in 1992. According to Bamrung, when the SSFAI staged a protest, all Somboon was able to do 'was prepare mobile toilets for the demonstration' (*The Nation*, 13 March 1997: A3). 'Good people' in parliament, contended Bamrung, were unable to solve the problems of society because parliamentary rule was a corrupt political system (*Phujatkan*, 6 June 1995: 1). Furthermore, Bamrung considered the participation in electoral politics of some SSFAI leaders as an action that 'undermined people's power', because those leaders who wanted to become MPs tried to build their personal political base instead of strengthening people's organisations (*Krungthep Thurakit* [Isan section], 15 March 1995: 7).

Nakon, who wanted to avoid the mistake of the social movements in the 1970s, disagreed with Bamrung. As mentioned above, the rejection of parliamentary politics during the 1970s was viewed as an 'ultra-left' policy that failed to take advantage of all potential channels of support available to the movements. Nakon had no doubt that electoral politics was corrupt, but he believed that it also provided opportunities for the people's movement. As a result, he opposed the idea of banning Assembly members from participating in electoral politics. He believed that if some members of the SSFAI succeeded in electoral politics, it would help to increase the bargaining power of the Assembly (*The Nation*, 13 March 1997: A3). Such a belief was illustrated in the promises of Assembly advisors, who competed in the July 1995 general election. They promised that if elected, they would donate part of their salary to the SSFAI, help to strengthen farmers' organizations, join the struggle of farmers and raise farmers' problems in parliament (*Phujatkan*, 26 May 1995: 3).

The Relationship between the SSFAI and Its Allies

Another issue concerning strategy that led to conflict within the SSFAI was the question of the relationship between the SSFAI and other democratic organizations. Although the leaders of the SSFAI recognized the importance of cooperation with other democratic organizations, they disagreed on how close such cooperation should be. Bamrung emphasized close cooperation. For him, farmers had to build alliances with other democratic organizations fighting beyond farmers' short term benefits. 'The Assembly', contended Bamrung, 'should not defend only its own interests, but has to fight for democracy as well'. This was because it was impossible for farmers to solve their problems under the existing politico-economic structure, in which power was concentrated heavily in the hands of the state (Bamrung 1994: 3).

Based on such ideas, Bamrung, who acted as the representative of the SSFAI in coordinating with its allies, decided to join political activities organized by Bangkok NGOs on various issues such as the anniversary of the 1992 May events and political reform (*Thankanmuang*, 14–16 April 1994: 18; Bamrung 1994: 3; The Nation, 27 April 1995: A8).

Bamrung's move, logically, should have helped to strengthen the SSFAI in terms of the political consciousness of its members and the relationship with its allies. However, in practice it weakened the organization because it led to conflict within the SSFAI. The conflict arose because when Bamrung decided to join political activities organized by the allies of the Assembly in Bangkok, the SSFAI had to send a large number of Assembly members. Bamrung's decision was opposed by Nakon. As with the problem of frequent protests, one source of Nakon's objection was the lesson of the student movement. According to Nakon, the involvement of the SSFAI in issues that did not directly relate to farmers' problems would face the same reaction from society as the student movement of the 1970s, which campaigned on 'too many issues' that did not directly relate to students. As a result, the protests of the SSFAI would be perceived as irrational political activities intended only to cause trouble to society (Nakon Sriwipat, interview, 11 July 1997). Nakon's fear was not without foundation. For example, Sujit Boonbongkarn, dean of the Faculty of Political Science at Chulalongkorn University, criticized the SSFAI when Bamrung pledged solid backing for Chalad Vorachat, who staged a hunger strike to pressure the Chuan government to take action over the land reform scandal. According to Sujit, 'it's inappropriate to protest whenever they're dissatisfied' (*The Nation*, 27 April 1995: A8). Such views were typical of many in the Thai elite.

Moreover, Nakon disagreed with Bamrung on this issue because it increased the burden on farmers. According to Nakon, the members of the Assembly were already after the January 1995 protest tired from frequent protests and unhappy with the idea of participating in any kind of activities in Bangkok. Attempts to take them to Bangkok only engendered a strain in the relationship between leaders and members. Equally importantly, Nakon was not enthusiastic about the idea of participating in political activities in Bangkok, because he felt that Bangkok NGOs treated the Assembly as an unequal partner. According to Nakon, Bangkok NGOs expected the SSFAI to respond to their demands on every issue, and were furious when the Assembly refused. For him, cooperation between the SSFAI and its allies should be conducted on an equal basis. Whether the Assembly should participate in activities organized by its allies or not had to be based on the decision of the SSFAI itself, not on a decision by outsiders. Furthermore, the Assembly also had the right to decide on how to join the activities; allies must not impose instructions on the SSFAI. To his mind, the Assembly should concentrate its campaigns on the problems of farmers. In other activities organized by allies, the SSFAI ought to play only a supporting role. The Assembly should send only a group of representatives to Bangkok, not a large number of its members (Nakon Sriwipat, interview, 11 July 1997; Nakon, 1996b: 3).

The Relationship between Political Mobilization and Economic Activities

The relationship between political mobilization and economic activities was another issue of debate. According to Nakon, the SSFAI had to build its economic base alongside political struggle. During the radical period, he argued, the SSFAI emphasized only political mobilization. Members were urged to sacrifice their household economic activities for the political struggle of the organization. The economic difficulties that arose from this practice were ignored. Over-emphasis on political activities caused hardship to members, who spent most of their time on political mobilization but not enough time earning their living. Many had to borrow money for political activities, which caused conflict with their families, and some had to give up their political activities. For Nakon, if such a tendency continued, in the long run it would be impossible for the organization to survive and maintain its political strength. He believed that a strong organization needed both a resilient political base and sound economic foundations (Nakon 1996 b: 1–2). According to Nakon, to solve the economic problems of members, the SSFAI had to concentrate its efforts on organizing cooperatives. However, Bamrung disagreed because he did not believe that cooperatives would succeed under the existing law in Thailand (Bamrung 1996: 20).

3 The Forms of Leadership

Another point of conflict between Bamrung and Nakon concerned forms of leadership. The argument over this issue centred around the role of Bamrung as secretary-general of the SSFAI. Under Bamrung, decisions within the SSFAI were made by the secretary-general (*Phujatkan*, 20 March 1996: 6; *Matichon*, 1 April 1996: 4). This practice became an object of dispute; according to Nakon, one of the weak points of the leadership system of the SSFAI under Bamrung was the lack of collective leadership. As a result, important issues that should have been decided by the committee of the SSFAI were decided by one person, the secretary-general. For example, the decision to join political activities organized by NGOs in Bangkok was made solely by Bamrung without consulting with the SSFAI committee. Such actions caused conflict and undermined unity. If the power of the secretary-general was left unchecked, argued Nakon, it would lead to an over-concentration of power in the hands of one person, which would destroy democracy within the organization. To prevent this, it was necessary for the SSFAI to introduce a new leadership system. Nakon proposed to reduce the power of the secretary-general and set up an executive committee to take charge activities. Under the new leadership system, only the executive committee could authorize the action of the SSFAI, while the secretary-general was merely responsible for day-to-day work under the guidance of the executive committee (Nakon Sriwipat, interview, 11 July 1997).

The Defeat of Bamrung

The debate ended up with a victory for Nakon. After the resignation of Bamrung in October 1995, 13 out of 16 committee members elected Nakon to take charge of the organization as acting secretary-general (*Bangkok Post*, 23 October 1995: 3). Why was a flamboyant leader like Bamrung defeated by an almost unknown leader like Nakon? First of all, because of his advocacy of a confrontation strategy, Bamrung had alienated himself from farmers and local leaders, who were tired from the numerous protests of the previous three years. The second factor for his defeat derived from his style of leadership. According to other leaders of the SSFAI, they supported Nakon because Bamrung tended to lead the SSFAI by himself without adequate consultation with them and local leaders. Moreover, Bamrung, as secretary-general, tried to order them to follow decisions with which they disagreed. These disagreements finally led to a conflict. Because of the negative impact of the 'one man' leadership of Bamrung, they decided to support the 'collective leadership' system proposed by Nakon (Ken Fanglit, Ratsapa Namlao, interview, 27 February 1998). The third factor related to the division of labour within the SSFAI. As mentioned in Chapter 4, the SSFAI assigned the secretary-general to be responsible for leading protests, while the general coordinator coordinated with members. Because of these arrangements, Nakon, who had spent most of his time in villages, was able to develop close relationships with local leaders and members. Bamrung, by contrast, even though nationally famous because of his role in the protests, lacked his own power base among members because he rarely worked with them. As a result, when the conflict between both sides broke out, Nakon, who not only proposed the strategy that reflected the mood of the members of the organization at that time, but also worked closely with them, was able to gain support from the majority of members. The fourth factor that influenced the outcome of the Bamrung–Nakon conflict was the policy towards electoral politics. The anti-politicians-cum-activists policy of Bamrung generated a conflict between him and a group of leaders who were already involved or wanted to become involved in electoral politics, while Nakon's positive attitude towards electoral politics gained support from this group. This support had important implications for the balance of power within the SSFAI because from 1995 onwards the influence of the group increased significantly (see below). When the SSFAI set up a new leading body, the executive committee, several important politicians-cum-activists such as Auychai Wata, Niramit Sujaree, Kamta Kanboonchan, Chuang Kamlea, Thawon Lokam and Supot Agkrarapram were elected to the nine-member executive committee in January 1996, while Auychai became the chairman of the committee (The Executive Committee of the SSFAI, 5 March 1996). In the election for secretary-general in March 1996, Auychai played an active role in organizing members of the SSFAI to support Nakon (*Krungthep Thurakit* [Isan Section], 29 March 1996: 1).

FOUNDING OF THE ASSEMBLY OF THE POOR (AOP) AND THE SPLIT IN THE SSFAI

Bamrung's defeat did not end conflicts within the SSFAI. Rather, the organization faced new conflicts after the founding of the AOP. This section considers the first split in the organization – the impact of the founding of the AOP on the conflict within the SSFAI that led to the split. The first part of the section provides a factual account of the founding of the AOP. The second addresses the role of the SSFAI in the founding of the AOP. The third looks at the SSFAI–AOP conflict. The final part discusses the end of SSFAI–AOP cooperation and the resultant split in the SSFAI.

Founding of the AOP

The AOP was founded on 10 December 1995 in Bangkok at a regional meeting of NGOs from 10 countries (Australia, Cambodia, India, Indonesia, Japan, Malaysia, Nepal, Philippines, South Korea and Thailand) (AOP 1998: 23). The objectives of the meeting were to exchange experiences among NGOs/POs in the region, and to discuss problems of the poor and solutions to those problems (*Krungthep Thurakit* [Isan section], 12 December 1995: 4). The meeting proposed that there should be campaigns to remind society about the problems of the poor at regional, national and international levels; and that in the efforts to solve the problems of the poor, there should be no obstacles to the poor from different organizations working together to achieve such aims. Only through the collective effort of various organizations would the poor be able to strengthen their bargaining power and to pressure the state to implement favourable policies (Somkiat 1995e: 8). Under the influence of such ideas, the AOP aimed to represent the poor more broadly. Although the majority of its demands addressed problems in Isan (74 out of 125 cases in 1997) (Prudhisan 1998: 266) the AOP, unlike the SSFAI, did not limit its operation to one particular area, but operated in every region of Thailand, and did not only address issues relating to agriculture, but also non-agricultural issues.

The AOP is a network of farmers and the urban poor (slum-dwellers and workers) coordinated by NGOs. The members of the AOP basically come from the poor, who face problems ranging from dam construction and large scale development projects to land and forest conflicts, industrial hazards and occupational diseases (Bantorn and Boonthan 1999: 48; Madsen 1999: 4). Another important aspect of the AOP is its range of international connections. According to Ichinohe, the AOP is part of an international NGO network with registered branches in Australia, Bangladesh, India, Japan, Laos, Malaysia, Nepal and the Philippines (Ichinohe 1999: 46). In addition, the AOP is a member of the International Coordinating Committee for Southeast and East Asia of the Via Campesina, the network of world farmers' movements (Bantorn and Boonthan 1999: 50).

The Role of the SSFAI in the Founding of the AOP

It is a misunderstanding to assume that the AOP was a product of the split within the SSFAI (for example Baker, 2000: 15; Missingham 1999: 55). Actually, the SSFAI played an important role in the preparations for the founding of the AOP. According to Werapon, the SSFAI was contacted by groups of the urban and rural poor from other regions during the major protests in 1994 and 1995. These groups wanted to join the organization, but the SSFAI was unable to accommodate them because the organization dealt only with problems in Isan. To overcome this limitation, it was necessary to form a new organization that operated at a national level. This idea led to the establishment of the AOP. Initially, the SSFAI was expected to be a core organization with the AOP (field notes, 25 January 1998). The SSFAI was involved in the events that led to the founding of the AOP. The SSFAI, as one of the organizers of the meeting, sent its provincial secretary-general and representatives from every province to participate in the meeting that led to the establishment of the AOP. The aim of this participation was to submit problems and demands to the government after the meeting (Nakon 1995: 6). During the meeting, Nakon was invited to chair the panel on the problems raised by the SSFAI (*Krungthep Thurakit* [Isan section], 12 December 1995: 4), and the activities and organizational structure of the SSFAI become the focal point of discussion (Somkiat 1995e: 8). In addition, the SSFAI also joined other activities organized by the AOP after the meeting; for example, Werapon and a group of SSFAI members joined a demonstration organized by the AOP in Bangkok during the ASEM (Asia–Europe Meeting) Summit in February 1996 (*Phujatkan*, 4 March 1996: 15).

The Conflict between the SSFAI and the AOP

SSFAI–AOP cooperation, however, rested on a fragile basis because of the conflict between the two sides. Most of the AOP leaders were NGO activists who had been involved in the activities of the SSFAI as advisors or allies. They disagreed with Nakon and some leaders of the SSFAI on a number of issues, especially on the compromise strategy. They criticized the idea of negotiating with politicians and officials, and questioned the intentions behind such an idea. They viewed the implementation of the new strategy as a sign of co-optation by the state (*Krungthep Thurakit* [Isan section], 29 March 1996: 4, 7). They also saw the election of activists-cum-politicians, such as Niramit, Chaung and Auychai to executive committee posts as a betrayal of farmers' interests, which would turn the SSFAI into the 'political tool' of *nakleuktang* ('electioneers') (Pakpum Witranteerawat, interview, 6 October 1997). Nakon, as mentioned above, criticized NGOs on several grounds, including the fact that they did not treat the SSFAI as an equal partner. As the general coordinator of the SSFAI, he opposed the plan to join the activities organized by NGOs in Bangkok. Such a move ran counter to the main tactics of the AOP, which viewed protests in Bangkok as the most effective means to pressure the state (see below). According to Nakon, the differences between the SSFAI and the AOP over the site of protest became a vital factor that contributed to the split (field notes, 20 April 1998).

Nakon's ideas were echoed by Auychai when he explained the relationship between the SSFAI and the AOP. For Auychai, the SSFAI was an independent organization that did not want to join the AOP. The SSFAI preferred to work with the AOP as an ally, able to make decisions by itself, rather than following the AOP's instructions. However, while Nakon and Auychai refused to join the AOP, Bamrung and his group clearly declared that they would join it (*Krungthep Thurakit* [Isan section], 29 March 1996: 29).

The End of the SSFAI–AOP Relationship and the Split in the SSFAI

The relationship between the SSFAI and the AOP did not come to an end until the SSFAI secretary-general election in March 1996. The AOP still hoped to maintain a good relationship with the SSFAI, if Nakon failed to win the election. Although Bamrung (who had planned to run for secretary-general again) withdrew from the election because he realized that it was impossible for him to beat Nakon (*Krungthep Thurakit* [Isan section], 29 March 1996: 4), Werapon, a close friend of Bamrung's who was ready to cooperate with the AOP, contested the post (*Krungthep Thurakit* [Isan section], 29 March 1996:7). The relationship between the SSFAI and the AOP reached an uncompromising point when Werapon lost to Nakon. The defeat of Werapon led to the first split in the SSFAI. After the election, the NGOs withdrew their support and collaboration, while Bamrung, Werapon and a group of SSFAI members left to join the AOP (*Krungthep Thurakit* [Isan Section], 16 April 1996: 1, 4). The SSFAI reacted by refusing to get involved in the protests organized by the AOP in Bangkok (*Krungthep Thurakit* [Isan Section], 16 August 1996: 1).

IMPLEMENTATION OF TWO COMPETING
ORGANIZATIONAL STRUCTURES AND STRATEGIES

This section studies the struggle of the SSFAI by comparing it with that of the AOP. The conflict between the SSFAI and the AOP led to the implementation of two different strategies. While the SSFAI decided to experiment with a compromise strategy, the AOP chose to implement a confrontation strategy. Moreover, the AOP also adopted a new organizational structure that it believed could overcome the types of problems caused by the centralized structure of the SSFAI. The implementation of two different organizational structures and strategies by the SSFAI and the AOP offered interesting and valuable lessons for the struggle of social movements in Thailand. The main purpose here is to evaluate the strengths and weaknesses of the two competing organizational structures and strategies. The section is organized into four main parts. The first provides the political context of this implementation. The second explores the SSFAI's experimentation with a 'compromise strategy'. The third looks at the AOP's organizational structure, strategy, nature of the organization, and its implementation of a 'confrontation strategy'. The fourth part tries to assess the strengths and weaknesses of the two organizations.

The Rise to Power of Chavalit

The implementation of a 'compromise strategy' by the SSFAI and a 'confrontation strategy' by the AOP was conducted with a political context different from that of the major protests of the SSFAI in the radical period. As shown in Chapter 4, the SSFAI's protests faced hostile reactions from Chuan Leekpai and the Democrats during the 1993–95 period. However, the resignation of Chuan in May 1995 led to changes in the government's policies towards the SSFAI and other grassroots movements. During the Banharn premiership (July 1995–November 1996), the government did not threaten popular protests with force. Moreover, it adopted a more cooperative stance in solving farmers' problems (*Phujatkan*, 19 October 1995: 14). The government's policies towards grassroots activism changed further when Chavalit Yongchaiyudh succeeded Banharn as prime minister in December 1996. The reasons for this change lay in Chavalit's strategy to become Thailand's prime minister. On 11 October 1990, Chavalit, who had recently retired from the post of Army Commander-in-Chief, founded the New Aspiration Party (NAP). The NAP was a political instrument for Chavalit to become prime minister. According to McCargo, the NAP first tried to build its political base among local officials and village headmen in Isan (McCargo 1997b: 128). Later the rural poor in the region became the main target of the party. The NAP tried to build its popularity among the Isan populace by representing itself as the 'champion of Isan'. In the July 1995 election, Chavalit stood in Nakhon Phanom, a province in northern Isan. He adopted the slogan 'Chavalit for premier representing Isan' (*Bangkok Post*, 3 July 1995: 2), and promised that if successful, he would 'make the region become prosperous' (*Bangkok Post*, 11 June 1995: 1). Later however, the NAP tried to represent itself as the voice of the poor as a whole rather than confining itself to one particular region. 'The poor', stated Chavalit, 'must be taken care of; this belief is the heart of the party' (*Bangkok Post*, 19 July 98: 6).

As McCargo pointed out, in the 1995 election the NAP mainly relied on the old-fashioned exercise of 'amnat and ittiphon' ('power and influence') as well as vote-buying (McCargo 1997b: 129). However, in the later period the party also relied on winning over grassroots groups and former CPT members in Isan (field notes, 29 May 1998). It seems that the NAP adopted such a policy because of Chavalit's positive impressions of the efficiency of organized political groups in building political support and carrying out political tasks, which he had experienced during the anti-insurgency operations. The SSFAI and the AOP, which were able to organize tens of thousands of poor farmers all over Isan, were among the priority groups that Chavalit wanted to win over in the efforts to expand his political base in the region. The importance of the two organizations to Chavalit's political scheme was shown on Chavalit's first day in office as prime minister, when leaders of the SSFAI and the AOP were invited to discuss farmers' problems with him (Fairclough 1996: 20). To win over the two organizations, Chavalit had to adopt a policy different from that of Chuan. While Chuan refused to solve farmers' problems, arguing that their actions were illegal because they ran counter to existing law, Chavalit declared that 'if it is a problem of the people, even just one person, it still needs to be cared for' (*Thai Development Newsletter*, July–December 1999: 41). Chavalit also assessed that his government would give priority to the grievances of farmers rather than points of law (Prapas 1998: 171). Chavalit's policies offered opportunities for the SSFAI and the AOP to win major concessions from the government. However, it also contained potential dangers of co-optation.

The SSFAI and the Experiment with a New Strategy

In this context, the SSFAI experimented with a 'compromise strategy', which emphasized problem solving through negotiation rather than protest. To understand the results of this experiment, it is necessary to look at the rise to power of activists-cum-politicians within the SSFAI, because this had important implications for the success or failure of the compromise strategy.

The Rise of Activists-cum-Politicians within the SSFAI

The influence of activists-cum-politicians within the SSFAI increased in the period just before the resignation of Bamrung, when it successfully recruited thousands of new members under the RFSPSP. However, they did not play a dominant role in the organization. When conflicts with Bamrung arose, they had not challenged him directly. They chose to support Nakon rather than nominate someone from their own group to contest the secretary-general's post. However, after the resignation and departure of Bamrung, their power rose significantly because he was the main opponent of activists-cum-politicians in the SSFAI. His departure meant that the major obstacle to their rise to power was cleared.

Another factor that contributed to the rise of activists-cum-politicians was the withdrawal of support from allies. Previously, allies had played an important role in negotiating with the government. When its allies withdrew their support, the SSFAI had to become more self-reliant. This situation enhanced the importance of activists-cum-politicians, because they were capable of negotiating and dealing with the government. Moreover, their role within the organization also increased because it was assumed that such a strategy would work, if the organization was able to build good relationships with political parties and officials. As a result, the importance of the activists-cum-politicians, who had close relationships with political parties, increased accordingly (Ratsapa Namloaw, interview, 8 July 1998). Another important factor that contributed to the rise of activists-cum-politicians was that they became the main source of funds for the SSFAI. They regularly donated money to the organization, and sometimes gave funds to advisors and leaders. By doing so, their influence within the organization increased considerably, because from 1995 onwards the SSFAI faced difficulty in collecting fees from its members. Their influence increased to the extent that even leaders who had conflicts with the activists-cum-politicians were reluctant to criticize them (Ronachit Tummong, interview, 11 July 1998).

The factors mentioned above led to the rise of activists-cum-politicians within the SSFAI. As noted earlier, when the SSFAI set up its executive committee, a new leading body, Auychai was elected chairman of the committee. Apart from Auychai, five other politician activists were elected members of the committee. This meant that they formed the majority of the nine-member executive committee. This was the first time that they had dominated a leading body of the SSFAI. The executive committee was elected by the central committee on 20 January 1996. As discussed above, it was set up in an effort to promote collective leadership within the organization. Decisions formerly made by the secretary-general now had to be authorized by the executive committee before they could be implemented (The Executive Committee of the SSFAI 1996: 1).

The rise of activists-cum-politicians meant that the experiment with a 'compromise strategy' was doomed from the beginning, because to pursue a strategy of compromise, the organization risked co-optation. Only a high-integrity organization can maintain its independence while making trade-offs with the state. If its leaders are concerned with their self-interest, it is easy for them to sacrifice the movement's interests for their own politico-economic gain.

The SSFAI and the Implementation of a Compromise Strategy

On 5 March 1996, the executive committee issued an official statement about the SSFAI's policy towards protests. It claimed that after the protest in October 1995, the Banharn government had shown its willingness to solve the problems of the SSFAI, and there was satisfactory progress in some areas. The SSFAI therefore decided that it would solve its problems through a joint committee made up of government representatives and the SSFAI. Only in the areas where local officials were unresponsive or insincere concerning the demands of the SSFAI would the SSFAI apply pressure on them. Nevertheless, such actions would be confined to the areas where problems occurred. The SSFAI would organize a major protest only when there was evidence suggesting that the government and local officials had refused to solve its problems (The Executive Committee of the SSFAI 1996: 1–2).

The statement above signalled the implementation of the compromise strategy, which developed further after the resignation of Banharn in September 1996. Since the compromise strategy was based on the view that it was possible to solve farmers' problems by negotiation with the government, it presupposed interaction between the organization and the government for its success. Within the confrontation strategy framework, the success of the movement mostly depended on the pressure that it was able to apply to the government. The main concern of the organizers was to mobilize strong forces to pursue their objectives; the relationship between the government and the movement was of secondary importance. But in using a compromise strategy, the relationship became more important: it actually became the main focus of attention. The success of the movement depended on how to influence the government's decisions through persuasion, or other kinds of incentive actions.

During the run-up to the general election of 17 November 1996, the SSFAI considered its policy towards political parties. There were two rival parties that might be expected to win the election, the Democrats and New Aspiration Party. According to Nakon, the SSFAI did not support the Democrat Party because its leader, Chuan Leekpai, had failed to solve farmers' problems when he ran the country previously (*Bangkok Post*, 10 November 1996). The SSFAI's stand towards the Democrats reflected the organization's experience with the Chuan government during the radical period (1993–95) (see Chapter 4). Among the grassroots movements in Thailand, the SSFAI was not the only group dissatisfied with the Chuan government. For example, a year earlier, Sulak Sivaraksa, a prominent social critic and NGO advisor, criticized Chuan for his indifference to the plight of the poor. In the 1995 election he urged people not to vote for the Democrats (*Phujatkan*, 1 July 1995: 23). The Democrats were also branded an undemocratic government by the Confederation for Democracy, a civic group that had led the popular uprising against the military-backed government in May 1992 (*The Nation*, 26 April 1995: A1).

The SSFAI's policy towards the New Aspiration Party (NAP) was more complicated. It had general guidelines for its members that they should vote for candidates whom they believed would help to solve their problems. But if they were unable to decide whom to support, they should vote for NAP candidates (Nakon Sriwipat, interview, 14 December 1997). According to an advisor of the SSFAI, the NAP was favoured because its major political base was in Isan. It was believed that in order to gain popularity, the NAP would have to help Isan farmers to tackle their problems (Chaleun Chanasongkram, interview, 5 October 1997). However, there were differences among SSFAI leaders over implementation of the guidelines. While one group, led by Nakon, followed the guidelines by emphasizing the independence of the SSFAI from any political party, another group, led by Auychai, adopted only the second part of the guidelines and actively campaigned for the NAP.

During the 1996 election, Auychai cooperated with primary school teacher groups in Isan to organize campaigns to support the NAP under the slogan 'An Isan MP for Prime Minister – Oppose Chuan' (*Krungthep Thurakit* [Isan section], 15 October 1996: 1). He even proposed producing SSFAI posters bearing this slogan, but this was rejected by Nakon and other leaders (*Phujatkan*, 23 April 1997: 5). The main reason for teachers to support the NAP was because they were satisfied with the education policy of the party. The NAP did not only change the regulations to allow C-6 teachers to get promotion to C-7 level without having to gain extra academic qualifications: it also promised to allocate a budget amounting to 300 billion baht for improving the education system and teacher welfare (*Phujatkan*, 21 October 1996: 14).

Auychai supported the NAP because he had a close relationship with Chingchai Mongkoltham, a leading figure in the party from Kalasin province. Chingchai had been a teacher activist in the late 1970s. In 1979, he resigned from his job and ran for parliament in his home town. Chingchai joined the NAP in 1994, served the party as a political strategist and played a key role in building up the NAP's political base in Isan (Ampa 1997). In 1995, he became deputy education minister. Chingchai appointed some Isan teacher activists, including Auychai, to his personal staff. As a result, Auychai was a farmers' leader but he also worked for a politician (*Phujatkan*, 23 April 1997: 5). The relationship between Auychai and Chingchai served the objectives of both sides. For Auychai, Chingchai was a political patron who would help increase his chances of winning a seat in parliament, an objective he had failed to realise in the past. For Chingchai, Auychai, who worked with farmers' and teachers' groups, would be very helpful in his efforts to incorporate those groups into the NAP's political base.

The role of Auychai during the election led the public to conclude that the SSFAI was supporting the NAP (*Bangkok Post*, 8 November 1996). This situation caused concern to Nakon. A week before the election, Nakon gave an interview to clarify the SSFAI's position. He told the interviewer that the SSFAI 'has never agreed to support any party. Whoever is in power must help solve our problems'. He also added that Auychai's statements that the SSFAI would support the NAP were only a personal opinion (Wut 1996). However, although Nakon did not approve of Auychai's stand, he still hoped that the SSFAI would be able to gain concessions from the NAP, which relied on Isan farmers to win the election (78 out of 125 of the NAP's MPs were in Isan) (Chaluen Chanasongkram, interview, 5 October 1997).

Such hopes did not seem unrealistic. After winning the election, Chavalit held a meeting with the SSFAI in Khon Kaen on 29 December 1997, and on 22 January 1998 he authorized establishing a joint committee for solving the problems of the SSFAI (*Phujatkan*, 23 April 1997: 5). Moreover, one month later, Chavalit declared before some 50,000 SSFAI members who had gathered in Khon Kaen that he would solve their problems 'once and for all' (*Bangkok Post*, 25 February 1997), and would even 'prefer to die', if he failed to solve their problems. In a meeting with the leaders of the SSFAI, Chavalit agreed in principle on every issue raised by the organization, especially on the debt issue. He agreed to help farmers to clear debts amounting to 100 billion baht. Chavalit's overture, according to Nakon, surprised the leaders of the SSFAI because they did not expect that Chavalit would agree to all of their demands (*Krngthep Thurakit* (Isan section), 25 February 1997: 6: *Siam Rath*, 26 February 1997: 14). Because of this surprise offer, Nakon described the meeting with Chavalit a 'remarkable success', although he did not forget to remind Chavalit that farmers would rally again if they felt they were being neglected by the government (*Bangkok Post*, 25 February 1997).

THE POLITICAL ECONOMY OF THE READJUSTMENT OF FARMING STRUCTURE AND PRODUCTION SYSTEM PROGRAMME

One of the SSFAI's demands that Chavalit approved was to allow SSFAI members to join the Readjustment of Farming Structure and Production

System Programme (RFSPSP) in 1997. Participating in the RFSPSP became a point of conflict that led to another split within the SSFAI.

The government launched the RFSPSP in 1994 to reduce the land areas used for the production of rice, cassava, coffee and pepper, which faced problems of overproduction, insufficient water supply and competition in the international market. Under the programme, farmers received loans and the means of production (ponds, fish stocks and chickens) for starting new kinds of agricultural production, including orchards and flowering trees (The Office of the RFSPSP 1994: 1).

The SSFAI participated in the RFSPSP in 1994. As discussed in Chapter 4, during the protest in 1994 one group of problems raised by the SSFAI concerned the low price of agricultural products. The authorities tried to solve the problem by inviting SSFAI members to join the RFSPSP; 3,300 members participated in the programme in 1994, and the number increased to 16,100 in 1995 (SSFAI 1995: 1).

It should be noted that there were differences among SSFAI leaders' attitudes towards the programme. According to Bamrung, the RFSPSP was not useful for farmers in the long run (*Krungthep Thurakit* [Isan section], 15 August 1994: 3). However, he conceded that the programme had good objectives (*Krungthep Thurakit* [Isan section], 27 December 1994: 12). Bamrung's position ran contrary to the attitude of the majority of SSFAI leaders, who believed that the RFSPSP was very useful for farmers in the long term (*Phujatkan*, 6 February 1995: 14). In 1994, when the difference between both sides was not so big, Bamrung also tried to help SSFAI members gain access to the programme (*Krungthep Thurakit* [Isan section], 27 December 1994: 12). Nevertheless, in 1995 Bamrung came out to criticize the SSFAI's participation in the RFSPSP as bad strategy because it created debt for farmers. 'The real strategy of the SSFAI', argued Bamrung, 'is to solve debt problems for farmers, not create new debt for them' (*Phujatkhan*, 19 October 1995: 14).

Participating in the programme, the SSFAI faced a number of problems. First, in some areas local authorities refused to allow members of the SSFAI to join the RFSPSP (SSFAI 1994d: 2). Second, the majority of SSFAI members were unable to access loans from the Bank of Agriculture and Agricultural Cooperatives (BAAC), because their lands did not have title deeds as required by the bank (SSFAI 1995: 1). Third, the means of production such as chicken and fish stocks that SSFAI members received from the programme were more expensive but the quality was inferior to that generally available on the market, and they were delivered late, nearly at the end of the farming season (September) (SSFAI 1994e: 1; *Phujatkan*, 30 December 1994: 7). According to Nakon, the means of production supplied under the programme was more expensive and of low-quality because of the corruption of Agriculture and

Cooperatives Ministry officials. Some of them set up companies to get contracts from the programme, and then supplied low quality but expensive goods to farmers, while others received money from contractors and ignored the quality of goods delivered (Nakon Sriwipat, interview, 14 December 1997).

The SSFAI reacted to difficulties in getting loans from the RFSPSP by organizing protests in different provinces of Isan (*Bangkok Post*, 15 May 1995: 6). On the price of the means of production, the central committee decided that the organization should expose the corrupt practices of officials to society (SSFAI 1994f: 3). More importantly, in order to gain greater influence over the implementation of the programme and prevent corrupt practices among the Agriculture and Cooperatives Ministry officials, the SSFAI demanded participation in the subcommittee on agricultural development that supervised the implementation of the RFSPSP. The government complied with this demand and appointed SSFAI members to the subcommittee at provincial and district levels (Nakon Sriwipat, interview, 14 December 1997). The SSFAI instructed its representatives, who worked within the subcommittee, to check the quality and price of the 'means of production', and to make sure that the bids for contracts were conducted fairly (SSFAI 1996: 2).

This move, designed to prevent corruption among Agriculture and Cooperatives Ministry officials, turned out to provide opportunities for corrupt practices among some SSFAI leaders, most of them politicians-cum-activists within the organization. As members of the subcommittee, they had the power to obstruct any bid from contractors, so the Agriculture and Cooperatives Ministry officials and contractors needed to win them over (Nakon Sriwipat, interview, 14 December 1997). Sums of money, or gifts such as pickup trucks, were offered in exchange for cooperation. As a result of such corrupt practices, a group of politicians-cum-activists who represented the SSFAI within the subcommittee became quickly rich (SSFAI provincial committee of Nong Bua Lamphu, interview, 7 December 1997). Corrupt practices related to the RSFPSP also took place in another form. For instance in Roi Et, in addition to 110-baht annual fees, SSFAI members were asked by district leaders to pay another 500 baht to guarantee access to loans from the RSFPSP. This case, which was raised in the media, led to an investigation from the organization, and the district committee was ordered to return the extra fees to members (*Bangkok Post*, 20 April 1995: 6).

CONFLICT AND SPLIT

Corrupt practices relating to the RSFPSP became a point of conflict between the Nakon group and a group of politicians-cum-activists led by Auychai.

When Chavalit won the election, the Auychai group came up with another even more corrupt idea. Before meeting with Chavalit in Khon Kaen, they drew up a new plan aimed at monopolizing all benefits from the RSFPSP that the government would have assigned to the SSFAI. At a meeting in Udon Thani province, Kamta, Niramit, Chuang and Somyong, proposed themselves for membership of the economic committee of the SSFAI. Had their proposal been accepted, they would have become responsible for all of the organization's expenses, in exchange for the right to handle all of the RSFPSP resources that the government allocated to SSFAI members. This move drew criticism from other leaders, who had already learned about some of their corrupt practices (Ronachit Tummong, interview, 15 July 1998). When Chavalit approved the RSFPSP for SSFAI members in the 1996 fiscal year, the Auychai group allocated a quota of the RSFPSP among themselves. This action increased conflict within the SSFAI (Somsiri Wongwinai, interview, 14 December 1997).

This move of the Auychai group was countered by the Nakon group, which urged the government to allocate the budget of the RSFPSP through cooperatives set up by the SSFAI. The proposal was aimed at preventing corruption by individuals and, at the same time, increasing income for communities. According to this plan, private contractors were replaced by cooperatives. Cooperatives would supply means of production for the programme by buying them from cooperative members, and cooperatives would dig ponds by themselves. In this way, the programme would help to increase incomes of farmers and local cooperatives (Nakon Sriwipat, 14 December 1997).

The corrupt practices of politicians-cum-activists within the SSFAI forced Nakon and other leaders to rethink the relationship between the farmers' organization and politicians. They now realized that politicians-cum-activists who participated in the mass movement had their own objectives, which were impossible to compromise with the interests of the masses. They joined the grassroots movement only to build up their political bases to pursue their self interests. The best way to protect farmers' organizations from this group of people was to prevent them from running the organization. So Nakon and other leaders planned to make a change in SSFAI rules preventing politicians and civil servants from competing for the leading posts of the organization (Nakon Sriwipat, interview, 14 December 1997).

When the Auychai group learned about the proposal of Nakon and other leaders, they made a counter-move with the help of their political patron, Chingchai. In March 1997, Chingchai, as the chairman of the Centre for Solving the Problem of Isan Farmers – set up by Chavalit in February 1997 to solve the problems raised by the SSFAI – appointed Auychai vice chairman of the Centre, giving him power second only to that of Chingchai himself. Nakon was only appointed the secretary of the committee, which meant that he had no power at all in the Centre (*Phujatkan*, 23 April 1997: 5). This move allowed Auychai to represent himself as the highest leader of the SSFAI, and permitted him to influence the policies of the SSFAI towards the government in the problem-solving process.

On 31 March 1997, the Auychai group made another move that led to a split between the two sides. They held a meeting at the house of the SSFAI secretary-general of Mahasarakham province, Boontom Uthaipan. According to a press release issued by Auychai, the meeting passed a resolution to sack Nakon from the post of secretary-general, because of his 'lack of transparency in management and finance' (*Phujatkan*, 22 April 1997: 11). However, the real problem behind the move was their dissatisfaction over Nakon's proposals concerning the RSFPSP. According to Boontom, the idea of letting cooperatives take charge of the RSFPSP was unacceptable to people who attended the meeting, because they played an important role in the protests that forced the government to allow the SSFAI to join the programme. They felt as though they were being robbed by this proposal and they decided to sack Nakon (Boontom Uthaipan, interview, 1 October 1997). On 16–17 April 1997, the Nakon group reacted by holding a meeting of the central committee to elect new executive committee members to replace those, whose terms had ended in February 1997. The meeting barred politicians and civil servants from any post in the SSFAI, and the Auychai group was expelled from the organization (*Krungthep Thurakit* [Isan section], 18 April 1997: 1, 4).

As a result, the organization was split into two groups, both using the name SSFAI. Both sides claimed legitimacy, but when dealing with the government Auychai got the upper hand because Chingchai and Chavalit recognized his group as the representatives of the SSFAI in the joint committee between the SSFAI and the government, while rejecting the Nakon group (*Krungthep Thurakit* [Isan section], 29 May 1997: 2). When Nakon demanded that the government set up a new joint committee between his group and the government, separated from that of Auychai, Chingchai replied that the government had already set one up, so it was impossible to create a new committee, and the government would only solve problems through the existing committee (*Krungthep Thurakit* [Isan section], 25 April 1997: 6). As a result, when Nakon contacted local officials to negotiate on the problems of the SSFAI, he was told that they could not negotiate with him, either because they did not know who the real representatives of the SSFAI were, or because they would negotiate only with SSFAI representatives who were recognized by Chingchai (Somsiri Wongwinai, interview, 14 December 1997).

The SSFAI implemented the compromise strategy with high hopes, but it turned out to be a tragic error for the organization. The split ended the experiment and led to the pursuit of different objectives and strategies by conflicting groups. These differences will be explored in the next chapter. For now, attention will turn to the implementation of a 'confrontation strategy' by the AOP.

THE ASSEMBLY OF THE POOR AS A NEW FORM OF POPULAR POLITICS

From the beginning, the AOP was the antithesis of the SSFAI in terms of organizational structure and strategy. The AOP adopted a new form of organization and a new strategy, which it believed could overcome the deficiencies resulting from the organizational structure and strategy of the SSFAI. What were the main points of difference the AOP and the SSFAI?

Organizational Structure

According to Prapas, to understand the organizational structure of the AOP, it is necessary to look at the problems that arose from the organizational structure of the SSFAI. The SSFAI, argued Prapas, set up its organization along centralized lines. Such a form led to the concentration of power in the hands of a few leaders, especially the secretary-general. The centralization of power enabled leaders to decide the activities of the organization without consulting members. Sometimes such actions caused severe damage to the reputation of the organization as whole. For example, when leaders chose to cooperate with politicians, it cost the SFFAI its support from wider society because it was viewed as evidence that the SSFAI had been co-opted. Furthermore, the fact that the activities of the organization were decided by leaders generated dependency and a tendency towards inertia among members. Instead of actively participating in the organization, they tended to wait for leaders to make decisions and solve their problems for them (Prapas 1998: 93–95, 221). The centralized structure also led to other undesired outcomes. According to Pakpum, an AOP advisor in Isan, a centralized structure inevitably led to conflicts and splits within an organization. Moreover, since power within a centralized organization was concentrated in the hands of leaders, it enabled them to use their power for their self interest, which would lead to corruption within the organization (Pakpum Witranteerawat, interview, 6 October 1997).

The AOP, argued Prapas, learned from the mistakes of the SSFAI and tried to avoid similar problems. Instead of setting up a centralized organization, the AOP adopted a decentralized network (Prapas 1998: 221). According to Banthorn Ondam, a senior advisor of the AOP, the best organizational structure for a grassroots movement was a loose network, not a centralized organization, because the strength of local movements lay in their localities

(Baker 1999: 20). A decentralized network was designed to prevent not only conflict between local groups who participated in the AOP, but also the monopoly of power in the hands of the leaders. The AOP had no central office-holders such as secretary-general; the highest decision making body of the AOP was the meeting of representatives from each member group, called the 'assembly of *pho khrua yai*' (big chiefs) (Prapas 1998: 99). Moreover, the AOP's decentralized network made it more difficult for the state 'to play a trick by "buying", or "co-opting", or "shooting down" leaders, because leadership was so collective that it could protect each individual leader from any risky situation' (Bantorn and Boonthan 1999: 49).

The assembly of *pho khrua yai* was supported by 40–50 advisors. These advisors consisted of NGO activists, academics and experienced village leaders. The advisors helped the *pho khrua yai* to prepare documents, topics and issues, demands and also to negotiate with the government. In the case of important negotiations, for example those with the prime minister, the AOP was represented by advisors who did the actual face-to-face talking.

Another important organ of the AOP was a secretariat run by a group of NGO workers. The secretariat acted as coordinator between local groups. In addition to coordinating work, the secretariat was responsible for public relations activities aimed at promoting a good understanding between the AOP and society through the media during protests. It gathered information and monitored the attitudes of society towards protests and government responses to the demands of the AOP, on behalf of advisors and *pho khrua yai*. The secretariat also produced leaflets for campaigns and issued press releases to explain or respond to criticism from government and other sources (Prapas 1998: 101, 182).

Strategy

The AOP rejected the compromise strategy of the SSFAI under Nakon. It did not believe that the problems of the poor could be solved by 'lobbying' officials or politicians. The AOP declared itself to be an 'autonomous social force' independent from any political party. It believed that only when the poor mobilized themselves as an independent force were they able to pressure the state to respond to their demands (Prapas 1998: 148–152; Suthee 1997: 12–13). However, protests in the past had failed to produce results. For example, the SSFAI protests under Bamrung ended with empty promises. Even though the government agreed to form a committee to tackle the SSFAI's problems, the government took no action after protesters returned home. If the leaders of the AOP insisted that protest was still the best means for the poor to pursue their demands, how could they overcome such a problem? To remedy the deficiencies of the SSFAI's protests in the past, the AOP refused to solve its problems through negotiation within a committee set up by the government. The AOP determined that it would not call off its protests until negotiations with the government had reached final decisions on every issue, and were ratified as a cabinet resolution, which instructed local officials to take action immediately (Prapas 1998: 151, 157–158). To achieve such objectives, the AOP had to apply more pressure on the government by organizing massive protests, in which tens of thousands of AOP members participated. According to Wanida Tantiwittayapitak, a prominent leader of the AOP, the government would not respond to the demands of the AOP if the numbers of protesters were less than ten thousand (Prapas 1998: 152). Massive protest was also able to draw the attention of the media. When the problems and demands of the AOP were regularly reported in the media, they would become a public issue, which was difficult for the authorities to ignore (Prapas 1998: 154). Second, they decided to keep pressure on the government by using protracted protests. According to the meeting of *pho khrua yai*, a protracted protest was required to pressure the government during negotiation, which would take time before agreement on every issue could be reached (Prapas 1998: 158). Third, instead of organizing its protests in the provinces as the SSFAI had done in the past, the AOP held its protests in front of Government House in the capital city.

The AOP's protracted protests were strengthened by two important means. The first was to build broad-based alliances. According to an important advisor of the AOP, Suthy Prasartset, the AOP was able to achieve such an objective because it was not dependent on a political party or government officials, but operated as an independent political force (Suthy 1998: 13). The AOP formed an alliance with 206 democratic organizations. Those organizations helped to raise protest funds and to pressure the government to negotiate with the AOP. Second, protracted protests could be strengthened by gaining public support through the media. The AOP used the media as a channel for conveying its grievances and problems with society in order to win over public opinion. Support from the public would prevent the state from using force against the protests and also increase pressure on officials to respond to AOP demands (Prapas 1998: 175–176, 181–182). Even though the efforts of the AOP to overcome the shortcomings of the SSFAI's strategy during the radical period by organizing a protracted protest on a massive scale in Bangkok were new, the idea of strengthening protests by winning public support through the media and building alliances with other democratic organizations was not different from that of the SSFAI.

The Protest of the AOP: A Confrontation Strategy in Practice

This section will focus on the 99-day protest in 1997, because here the AOP managed to achieve all the elements it considered vital to its strategy: the number of protesters, the time period of the protest, and the support from allies, media and the public. In addition, the AOP also succeeded in pressuring the government to comply with its demands in full. It was the strongest protest of the AOP to date, which can be used as a test case for its strategy.

In 1996 and 1997, the AOP organized two major protests in Bangkok. The first was held from 26 March to 22 April 1996. It was joined by more than 11,000 members of the AOP from 21 provinces. After nearly a month of protest in front of Government House, the government agreed to resolve 47 grievances cited by the AOP. The agreement between both sides was ratified as a cabinet resolution. Nevertheless, no progress was made afterwards (AOP 1998: 28).

When the first major protest proved ineffective, the AOP prepared for a larger protest. On 9 December 1996, it was planned that the next protest should have not less than 20,000 protesters, and the protest must last 1–3 months (Prapas 1998: 158). Because the protest involved a large number of people and a long period of time, the timing was vital. Learning from the past, the AOP concluded that the protest had to be organized after the rice and upland crop-harvesting season (after December). After harvesting farmers were free from their farm work, which enabled the AOP to mobilize them in large numbers. Organizing protests after harvest also partly helped to solve the food supply problem, since farmers could store food from their harvest for consumption during the protest. However, the protest had to finish before the rainy season, which begins in May, because this was the time for farmers to return to their farms to grow new crops (Prapas 1998: 161). Apart from the timing, protracted protest needed a rotation of forces. Since villagers had to earn their living, it was quite difficult for them to participate in protracted protests without a break. So the AOP divided its members into groups and rotated them every 2–3 weeks (Prapas 1998: 158).

After about two months of preparation, the AOP staged another protest in Bangkok on 25 January 1997. It turned out to be the strongest protest of the AOP so far. Some 20,000 protesters from 35 provinces took part, and it continued for 99 days (AOP 1998: 30). The AOP organized the protest like a final showdown. It declared from the beginning that the protesters were determined to stay in the capital city until all the problems raised by the AOP were solved, however long it might take (Chakrit 1997).

To achieve this objective, the AOP organized itself for a long peaceful protest. Members were instructed to raise protest funds. Following the SSFAI's example, the AOP asked members to be responsible for food and other expenses during the protest. The AOP also raised protest funds by collecting a 100 baht fee from every member (Banthorn and Boonthan 1999: 48). However, unlike the SSFAI, the AOP did not collect annual membership fees from farmers, because that increased the burden on them (field notes, 6

October 1998). Another important task was setting up a security unit to look after the safety of the protesters, and to impose discipline to prevent disturbances (Prapas 1998: 169). There were also units responsible for activities on the stage, finances, art and a team of spokespeople who were to report 'updates from the negotiation with the government, to hold press conferences every day, and to respond to the accusations that might affect the movement'. Another important unit was the campaign team responsible for explaining the problems of the AOP to the urban public and gathering donations from sympathetic city dwellers (The Friend of the People 1999: 54). However, the organizers of protracted protest not only had to deal with day-to-day problems, but also with the state of mind of protesters, since, as Banthorn and Bunthan had pointed out, protracted protest 'always leads to tension, boredom, and exhaustion'. To cope with such phenomena, the AOP set up a political school to boost the morale and political understanding of its members. The school involved lectures by academics, lawyers, human rights activists, journalists and social workers (Bantorn and Boonthan 1999: 48). The measures mentioned above played a significant role in strengthening the protest and turned it into a well-disciplined rally. A government official admitted that the protest was well-organized, 'which was very hard for any outsider, or even a member of government, to interfere with' (Suvit 1997). Such strong self-organization provided a reliable base for the protracted protest of the AOP.

The protracted protest was also strengthened by support from the media and the public. The AOP, as noted above, saw public support as an important factor that helped to legitimize its activities and increase pressure on the government. To gain public support, the AOP carefully organized its public relations efforts to draw public attention, clarify its position and promote better understanding towards the organization. These worked rather well. During the 99 days of protest, there were 128 articles, interviews and reports on the activities of the AOP in newspapers, the majority of which gave positive coverage of different aspects of the protest, such as living conditions of the protesters at the rally site, protest fund raising and the ideas of protest leaders. This coverage helped outsiders to understand the actual situation. As a result, negative questions frequently asked in the past, such as, 'who was behind the protest?' or 'what would protest leaders gain from organizing the protest?' were rarely raised (Prapas 1998: 133–135).

Positive coverage in the media helped the AOP to gain support from the public. However, public support also came from the discipline of the protest and the work of the campaign team, who went out to explain the problems of the protesters to the urban public (The Friend of the People 1999: 54). The support of the public for the AOP showed in terms of donations. During the 99-day protest, the AOP gathered 1,876,196 baht from donations of which

104,804 baht came from its members and 408,792 baht from its allies. The donations mainly came from the Bangkok middle classes. However, donations also came from politicians (145,000 baht) (Prapas 1998: 168). According to Baramee, an advisor of the AOP, the AOP had a policy of accepting donations from any source, including politicians. Nevertheless, the donations had to have no conditions (Baramee Chairat, interview, 6 October 1997).

The AOP started to negotiate with government representatives on 27 January. The meeting appeared promising when Prime Minister Chavalit Yongchaiyudh assured the AOP that the government would solve the problems raised. However, no progress was made after the meeting. On the contrary, there was criticism from high ranking officials. The AOP reacted by encircling Government House on 4 February, which prompted the government to resume negotiations (Prapas 1998: 171–173). Nevertheless, pressure on the government was not created by the AOP alone. It was also created by the support of its allies in Bangkok. In March, when negotiations with government representatives faltered, AOP allies from 108 groups sent their representatives to urge the prime minister to negotiate with the AOP. The move led to a meeting between the AOP and the prime minister a day later, which resulted in agreement on a number of issues, especially on land-forest disputes (Prapas 1998: 175–176).

The progress of negotiations, however, took a new turn when Chavalit asserted that the government was unable to solve the problems of the AOP in cases that ran counter to existing law. The AOP reacted by intensifying its campaign. This culminated in the blockade of Government House for more than two hours on 8 April, which forced the government to restore the momentum of negotiations that finally led to agreements between both sides on every issue. The agreements were then ratified as cabinet resolutions. The AOP called off its protest on 2 May 1997 (Prapas 1998: 178–181).

During the 99 days of protest, the AOP had official meetings with the authorities 38 times (Prapas 1998: 186). The meetings were organized once or twice a week, equal to about six hours a week, with a maximum of four topics for discussion (Suvit 1997). The 38 meetings resulted in nine cabinet resolutions (4, 11, 18, 25 February, 11, 18 March, 1, 17, 29 April), and 12 follow-up committees were created to monitor the progress of the agreements (AOP 1998: 30–31). The resolutions accepted the right of long-settled villagers to live in areas that the government called 'national reserves' (Baker 2000: 23). Moreover, the government agreed to allocate a 4.6 billion baht fund for assistance and compensation to AOP members for damages caused by various government projects. The AOP, according to Prudhisan, was also successful in pushing to initial stages three important bills, 'which could go some way towards tipping the power balance more to the benefit of the poor'.

These were the Community Forest Bill, the Plant Species Protection Bill and the Protection of Occupational Health Bill (Prudhisan 1998: 269).

The concessions achieved by the AOP were hailed as 'the beginning of a new chapter of Thai history' (The Friends of the People 1999: 54). According to Baker, 'such concessions were totally unprecedented', not only in terms of the budget promised to the AOP, but also because 'the concessions had broken the constraints of law and procedure which were biased against the poor' (Baker 1999: 15). However, most of these concessions did not materialize. When the Chavalit government resigned in November 1997, only 18 out of 125 issues had been resolved, while 90 issues were still being processed, and there had been no progress at all on another 17 issues (Prapas 1998: 188). Moreover, when Chuan Leekpai succeeded Chavalit as prime minister, all the concessions made by the Chavalit government were reversed (Baker 1999: 16).

THE SSFAI AND THE AOP: A COMPARISON

This section examines the similarities, differences, strengths and weaknesses of the two contesting organizations, the SSFAI and the AOP, by focusing on three issues: organizational structure, strategy and the nature of the organization.

Organizational Structure

The first issue addressed here is the form of organization. As discussed above, even though they had severe conflicts with each other, the SSFAI under Nakon and the AOP shared the view that the negative impact of the concentration of power in the hands of the secretary-general during the radical period had to be overcome by collective leadership. While the AOP proposed horizontal networks as a form of collective leadership, the SSFAI set up an executive committee to counter-balance the power of the secretary-general. The setting up of the executive committee, however, failed to prevent the concentration of power in the hands of one individual. It created a new centre of power in which the chairman of the executive committee became another influential figure. As a result, it created dual power within the SSFAI centred around the secretary-general and the chairman of the executive committee. When conflict within the organization emerged, both sides claimed the authority to lead the organization. As a result, instead of helping to strengthen collective leadership, the new leadership system created the conditions for more severe conflict within the SSFAI.

The horizontal network adopted by the AOP appeared able to overcome the problems created by the organizational structure of the SSFAI. Because the AOP was a 'cooperation network' (Wanida 1999, 51), no one was able to act as its sole leader. The decentralized structure also helped to prevent differences among member groups from developing into severe conflicts, because each group had the power to make decisions concerning its internal affairs. Because of the fact that activists in Thailand were prone to conflicts, this kind of organization was more suitable for a grassroots movement than a centralized structure, such as the SSFAI. However, a decentralized structure created a different set of problems. As Bamrung pointed out:

> There are still a lot of internal problems in the Assembly of the Poor because various groups that composed it are still focusing on their own problems rather than looking at the whole picture. (Cited in *Bangkok Post*, 9 January 1997)

The lack of unity that arose from the decentralized structure was considered by some factions within the AOP as a weak point that needed to be changed. They proposed to change the AOP structure into some kind of centralized organization, which would be able to provide better coordination of local groups, and to gain stronger bargaining power (Baker 2000: 26).

Another aspect frequently mentioned as an important difference between the SSFAI and the AOP was that decision-making within the SSFAI was concentrated in the hands of leaders at different levels who functioned along vertical lines, while the activities of the AOP were decided by each group of farmers themselves (Prapas 1998: 95, 99). There is no doubt that decisions within the SSFAI were made by the committees at different levels of the organization. But decision-making within the AOP was more ambiguous. Even though decisions within the AOP had to be decided by *pho khrua yai* in principle, in practice there was no clear-cut divide between *pho khrua yai* and advisors who actually made decisions. According to Werapon, advisors drew up policies and then presented them at the meeting of *pho khrua yai*. If disagreement emerged, matters were decided by a majority vote. However, more often than not, *pho khrua yai* accepted the policies proposed by advisors (Werapon Sopa, interview, February 5, 1998). One of the *pho khrua yai* in Khon Kaen explained the relationship between advisors and *pho khrua yai* as follows. When problems occurred, *pho khrua yai* would take them up with advisors. After solutions for problems were suggested, *pho khrua yai* would explain the solutions to their group members. If group members disagreed with the proposed solutions, *pho khrua yai* had to consult the advisors, and then come back to explain the new solutions to their group members (Term Kotsuno, interview, 9 January 1998). So, although *pho khrua yai* had the power to make final decisions, if their decisions were shaped or influenced by advisors, it was very difficult to say that *pho khrua yai* had sole decision-making powers concerning the activities of the AOP. In addition, the relationship between advisors and *pho khrua yai* also took place in another context. Within member groups, most advisors were NGO workers who organized and led the groups, while *pho khrua yai* were group members. As a result, in such a context, decisions concerning the group's policies were determined by advisors rather than *pho khrua yai*. Actually, the advisors of the AOP, who were at the same time NGO leaders, were in effect another group of AOP leaders. Their roles and powers were different from those of *pho khrua yai*. Although they were policy makers in the organization, their powers were restricted by *pho khrua yai*. This balance of power was wisely designed to perform two functions; it helped to compensate for the lack of expertise in negotiation and policy matters among farmers, and it prevented the concentration of power in the hands of NGO intellectuals.

Strategy

This section compares the strategies pursued by the SSFAI and the AOP by focusing on points of contestation between both sides. Most of the literature on this issue tends to argue that the strategies of the two organizations were greatly different from each other (Prapas 1998, Baker 2000). Close scrutiny, however, suggests that after the implementation of two opposite strategies in 1996, the two organizations made some revisions, which resulted in a convergence of strategies. As discussed above, while the SSFAI under Nakon proposed a compromise strategy as a means to solve farmers' problems, the AOP advocated a confrontation strategy. The compromise strategy emphasized negotiation, and meant that protests would be held only when necessary. Protests, moreover, had to be limited to the areas where problems occurred. The experiment with the compromise strategy of the SSFAI had been disastrous. It not only led to co-optation by politicians, but also to conflicts and splits within the organization.

What were the results of the implementation of the confrontation strategy of the AOP? There is no doubt that mainly through protracted protest on a massive scale, the AOP gained recognition from the government. The protests helped to enhance its bargaining power, which finally led to major concessions from the Chavalit government. However, a protracted protest on a massive scale also had problems of its own. The target of the AOP during the 99-day protest was to solve all of its problems. As mentioned above, the Chavalit government complied with the AOP's demands, but when Chuan succeeded Chavalit as prime minister, he reversed most of Chavalit's concessions. Such a reversal had a strong effect on the AOP. To organize a protracted protest on a massive scale meant that an organizer had to restrict the choice of acceptable outcomes to complete victory. Since such a protest requires a high level of sacrifice and is bound to exhaust protesters both mentally and physically, there is no reason to organize such a protest if it does not achieve what is expected. Moreover, since the target of the organizers is victory, protesters will be mobilized to join the protest with high hopes that their problems would be solved by it. And if the protest then fails to deliver its objectives, it will generate despair among rank and file participants, making it difficult to organize that kind of protest again. Chuan's policy reversals had this kind of impact on the activities of the AOP from 1997 to 2000.

The reversal of Chavalit's concessions by Chuan turned victory into defeat. The negative impact of Chuan's actions on the morale of AOP members can be properly understood if one looks at what happened before. After a hard-fought 99-day struggle, the AOP was finally able to declare a victory. All the grievances that villagers had held for a long time would be solved soon. In some areas, AOP members organized parties to celebrate their victory (Yang Wongkraso, interview, 10 March 1998). Nevertheless, such hopes disappeared six months later when Chuan refused to acknowledge the agreements made by Chavalit with the AOP. The reversal stunned AOP members because they believed that their hard-fought efforts had already paid off. When the opposite proved true, it meant that if they wanted to solve their problems, they had to start again from the beginning. This was a source of real despair for them. As a result, it was very difficult for the AOP to persuade them to participate in a protracted protest on a massive scale again. Moreover, the setback not only had a demoralizing effect, but it also produced differences and conflicts. After the 99-day protest, the AOP threatened to mobilize major protests many times, but not one large-scale protest materialized. Protracted demonstrations now seemed less attractive not only because the government could easily reverse agreements, but because of the way the new government reacted. The Chuan government tried to discourage grassroots movements from pressuring the government by applying the same policy to every group, no matter how big or small a protest it organized. This policy made big protests pointless (field notes, February 1998).

The Chuan reversal forced the AOP to adjust its strategy on a number of points. First, before and during the 99-day protest, the AOP criticized the idea of solving farmers' problems through negotiations within a joint committee of government and farmers' representatives, as proposed by the compromise strategy of the SSFAI. The AOP insisted that its problems must be solved by protests. However, Chuan's actions forced the AOP to accept a joint committee as a mechanism for tackling its problems. Sometimes, the AOP clung to such an approach more than the SSFAI. In February 1998, for instance, while the SSFAI staged a month-long protest in Nakon Ratchasima province, the AOP still tried to solve its problems at the negotiation table (see Chapter 6). Also, when the AOP organized further protests after the 99-day protest, it adopted the 'scattered stars' strategy of the SSFAI with some modifications, rather than its own massive protest approach (Baker, 2000: 26). As discussed in Chapter 4, the strategy was first proposed for the protest of the

SSFAI in January 1995. The heart of the strategy was to organize small protests simultaneously in different areas of the provinces. As a result, when the AOP adopted the 'scattered stars' strategy, the organization not only had to abandon its massive protest, but also change the site of protest from Bangkok to the provinces. The changes in the scale and site of protests brought the strategy of the AOP closer to that of the SSFAI. As mentioned above, the SSFAI rejected the idea of organizing protests in Bangkok by arguing that since problems occurred in Isan, they should be solved locally. Moreover, the SSFAI also refrained from staging major protests, but organized small-scale protests with limited objectives instead. However, in the Pak-Moon-dam and 16-problem protest, organized by a section of AOP members led by Wanida, the AOP combined elements of the 'scattered stars' strategy with a protracted protest approach. Two protracted protests were organized at Pak Moon dam in Ubon Ratchathani and Rasi Salai dam in Sri Saket. At the same time, protests lasting only one day or a few days were held in various parts of Isan. In the final stage, the protests moved from the two dams to Bangkok. In term of participants, this round of protests was minor for the AOP, in which only some 1,000-3,000 farmers participated. However, in length, they surpassed the 99-day protest. From beginning to end, this round of protests lasted more than one year (March 1999–July 2000) (*Thai Development Newsletter*, July–December 1999: 43–45; *Bangkok Post*, 2000).

In sum, failed in practice both strategies. The experimentation with a compromise strategy of the SSFAI led to co-optation by politicians and to splits within the organization. The implementation of the confrontation strategy of the AOP also proved unsuccessful. Although such a strategy did not have the same danger of co-optation as the compromise strategy, it led to demoralization among AOP members. These failures forced the two organizations to revise their strategies, which resulted in strategy convergence.

SUMMARY

This chapter has analysed the causes and consequence of conflict within the SSFAI, and the differences between the SSFAI and the AOP on strategies and organizational structure. The causes of conflict in the SSFAI lay in differences over strategy and form of leadership. The first issue in the debate over strategy was the question of the best way to realize the aims of the SSFAI. For Bamrung, farmers could pressure the state to comply with their demands only through political mobilization. Nakon, however, argued that a more flexible and compromising approach was needed for addressing farmers' problems. Another important strategy issue was the question of the relationship between the SSFAI and electoral politics. Should the SSFAI allow its members to participate in electoral politics? For Bamrung, participation of some SSFAI leaders would not solve farmers' problems; on the contrary, it undermined people's power. Nakon disagreed with Bamrung. He contended that although parliamentary politics was corrupt, it provided opportunities for the people's organization. If some members of the SSFAI were elected as MPs, it would help to increase the bargaining power of the organization. The relationship between the SSFAI and their allies was the other point of conflict between both sides. According to Bamrung, farmers had to build a close relationship with their allies because it was impossible for them to solve their problems without struggling for democracy. Bamrung's idea was opposed by Nakon, who proposed that the SSFAI ought to concentrate on farmers' problems. The final issue concerning conflict over strategy between Bamrung and Nakon was the relationship between political mobilization and economic activities. On this issue Nakon criticized Bamrung for his over-emphasis on political mobilization, which caused hardship to farmers. Nakon singled out the building of agriculture operatives as a means to overcome this problem. Concerning the leadership issue, Nakon pointed out that there was a danger that the decisions of the organization would be made by one person, the secretary-general. In his mind this tendency ought to be overcome by replacing the existing leadership system with a collective leadership. The Bamrung–Nakon conflict led to the resignation of Bamrung in October 1995; when Nakon was elected secretary-general in March 1996, Bamrung and his group left the SSFAI to join the AOP, which was also in conflict with the SSFAI under Nakon.

The conflict between the SSFAI and the AOP led to the adoption of two different strategies. Under Nakon, the SSFAI experimented with a compromise strategy, while the AOP implemented a confrontation strategy. The two strategies were implemented in a political context very different from those of the SSFAI campaigns in the radical period when the Chuan government was very hostile to grassroots activism. However, when the two strategies were implemented, the Chavalit government adopted policies that tried to incorporate grassroots groups into his political base. Such a policy, while it offered opportunities for the SSFAI and the AOP to win major concessions from the government, also contained dangers of co-optation.

The SSFAI suffered from the co-optation policy of the NAP, Chavalit's party. This co-optation took the form of exchange of interests: in exchange for delivering electoral support to the NAP, the activists-cum-politicians within the SSFAI gained access to the RSFPSP budget. The AOP was very critical of the organizational structure and strategy of the SSFAI. It rejected the centralized structure and adopted a decentralized one in which the highest decision-making body was comprised of representatives from every member group supported by a group of advisors and a secretariat. The decentralized structure of the AOP was designed to prevent the concentration of power in the hands of leaders, and co-optation or destruction by the state. On strategy, the AOP rejected the compromise strategy of the SSFAI. It argued that the campaigns of the SSFAI under Bamrung failed to produce results because they were too weak. To overcome this weakness, the AOP proposed that grassroots movements should hold a protracted protest on a massive scale in Bangkok. This idea was put to the test by the 99-day protest in Bangkok in 1997. The protest won unprecedented concessions from the Chavalit government, yet it failed to secure the achievements that the AOP already attained. In November 1997, when Chuan succeeded Chavalit as prime minister, he reversed all the concessions made by Chavalit.

The organizational structures and strategies adopted by the SSFAI and the AOP contained strengths and weaknesses of their own. In terms of organization, the strong point of decentralization of the AOP was that it overcame the problems created by the centralized structure of the SSFAI. However, this kind of structure faced problems from the lack of unity among member groups. On the issue of decision-making, decisions within the SSFAI were undoubtedly executed along vertical lines. In the case of the AOP, the decision process was more complicated. In principle, the decision of the organization was decided by *pho khrua yai*, but in practice advisors had important influence on the actions of *pho khrua yai*. In terms of strategy, the implementation of the compromise strategy of the SSFAI led to co-optation, conflict and splits in the organization. While the confrontation strategy of the AOP did not contain the danger of co-optation, it suffered from different kinds of problems. The weak point of organizing a protracted protest on a massive scale was that it limited the choice of acceptable outcomes to complete victory. If complete victory was not achieved, its members would be demoralized.

CHAPTER 6

The SSFAI after the Failure of the Compromise Strategy

This chapter looks at the activities of the SSFAI after the failure of the compromise strategy. As shown in the preceding chapter, the implementation of the compromise strategy of the SSFAI led to the organization splitting into two groups: the Auychai and Nakon groups. Although the two groups used the same name – the SSFAI – after the split, their aims and strategies greatly differed. The first two sections of this chapter will examine the activities of the two groups by focusing on aims, strategies and results of their activities. The first section focuses on the Auychai group, the second considers the Nakon group. Section three addresses the reconciliation between the SSFAI and other conflicting groups: the AOP, the SSFAI (1) and the FAI. The final section explores the experiment with land occupation by the SSFAI.

BREAK-UP OF THE AUYCHAI GROUP

The main concern of the Auychai group after the split with the Nakon group was gaining access to the budget from the Readjustment of Farming Structure and Production System Programme (RSFPSP). What were the strategies the Auychai group employed to secure access to such a budget? What was the result of these moves?

Move to Secure Access to the RSFPSP Budget by the Auychai Group

After the split with the Nakon group, the Auychai group still proclaimed the advantages of the compromise strategy. According to Supot Agkrarapram, a close friend of Auychai, if farmers tried to solve their problems by protesting against the government, it would create an unfriendly atmosphere that would make it difficult to settle farmers' woes in the future. Supot compared the success of the compromise strategy with winning a war without a single fight, which he considered the best way to achieve victory (Supot Agkrarapram, interview, 10 September 1997). Another leading figure, Niramit, argued that close cooperation with the government increased the bargaining power of farmers when they negotiated with local officials. Local officials, who branded farmers as troublemakers, made a u-turn when the prime minister ordered them to help farmers. As a result, farmers' problems were solved easily (Niramit Sujaree, interview, 10 September 1997).

Such arguments were used to justify the group's clientelistic relationship with the Chavalit government. The group used this relationship to secure access to the RSFPSP budget. The RSFPSP was a source of wealth for leaders of the Auychai group. They gained fortunes from the programme by collecting fees from farmers, who wanted to participate in the RSFPSP. In some areas, for example, in Khon Kaen, leaflets were distributed to invite farmers to join the RSFPSP. According to the leaflets signed by Somyong Kaewsupan, each farmer had to pay 1,080 baht in fees if he wanted a pond from the RSFPSP (Somyong 1997). Actually, farmers received ponds free under the programme (*Krungthep Thurakit* [Isan section], 22 September 1997: 5).

Collecting fees from farmers was not the only means to gain benefit from the RSFPSP. Another was to obtain 'commissions' from the RSFPSP budget. The Chavalit government, as mentioned above, agreed to allow SSFAI members to join the RSFPSP, and in 1997 it promised to allocate 25,978 SSFAI members a budget under the RSFPSP, amounting to 836 million baht, of which 500 million baht was for digging small ponds and 336 million baht for buying plants and animals. The leaders of the Auychai group saw this as an opportunity to gain wealth for themselves by asking for commissions from contractors. There was a newspaper report that the leaders of the Auychai group, by colluding with some politicians and government officials, would receive commissions amounting to 15 per cent of the total budget (125,400,000 baht), while politicians and government officials who became involved would receive 5 and 10 per cent respectively (*Krungthep Thurakit*, 22 September 1997: 6).

The corrupt practices of the Auychai group, however, faced obstacles when the Nakon group revealed the story to the public. On 25 August 1997, Nakon submitted letters to the Agriculture and Cooperatives Minister, Prime Minister, leader of the opposition and all provincial governors asking them to suspend the programme, and urged the government to allocate the programme through local cooperatives (Nakon Sriwipat 1997). Although Nakon's action did not lead to a suspension of the programme, it drew attention from parliament and he was called to give further details by the House of Representatives' sub-committee on agriculture (Nakon Sriwipat, interview, 28 February 1998). Later, the issue was raised in parliament during a no-confidence debate against Chavalit in late September 1997 (*Krungthep Thurakit*, 26 September 1997: 5).

Another obstacle was that Agriculture and Cooperatives Minister Chucheep Hansawat delayed his approval of the programme. Even though Chavalit promised to allocate the budget from the RSFPSP for the SSFAI no later than 24 August 1997 (*Krungthep Thurakit*, 10 September 1997: 6), it still needed approval from the relevant minister before the government could allocate the budget to local authorities for implementation. As late as September, the last month of the fiscal year, Chucheep still had not approved the programme (*Krungthhep Thurakit*, 11 September 1997: 5).

The Auychai group, however, did not give up its plan. In order to receive the budget on time, it organized a gathering in Mahasarakham from 9 to 11 September 1997. This was designed to create a trade-off between the budget from the RSFPSP and political support for the NAP and Chavalit. Allegedly the gathering was organized to give an opportunity for SSFAI members to offer their opinions on the draft constitution. But during the three days of meetings, those taking part were concerned with other issues. They urged Chavalit to take action that would enable them to obtain the budget from the RSFPSP on time (*Krungthep Thurakit*, 10 September 1997: 5–6), and they used the gathering to show their political support for the NAP and Chavalit. This involved supporting the NAP position towards the draft constitution (*Krungthep Thurakit*, 3 September 1997: 2).

The draft constitution was a product of the political reform process initiated after the May events in 1992. It contained a number of provisions, especially on decentralization and accountability that caused dissatisfaction among holders of institutional power (Prudhisan 1998: 281). As a result, it faced opposition from politicians and ranking officials, including leaders of the NAP such as Interior Minister Sanoh Tientong and Chingchai Mong-koltham (*Krungthep Thurakit* [Isan section], 3 September 1997: 2). Sanoh contended that it would cause havoc if the constitution gave the right to any 50,000 voters to seek the dismissal from office of politicians (Prudhisan 1998: 281). Chingchai criticized the proposal to allow an 'outsider' – a person who did not compete in elections – to become prime minister, which he considered anti-democratic; and he denounced the proposal that prohibited a person who did not have a bachelor's degree from running for parliament, because it violated human rights (*Krungthep Thurakit* [Isan section], 1 September 1997: 3). Even Chavalit, who had declared during the election campaign in November 1996 that 'It's time for political reform' (*Bangkok Post*, 24 November 1996: 4), did not commit himself to the draft. He later reluctantly supported the draft on 5 September 1997, but only when he was under heavy pressure from both outside and inside parliament (Prudhisan 1998: 281, 283).

Leaders of the Auychai group echoed Chingchai's position during the gathering. However, they changed their demand from total rejection of the draft constitution to seeking to amend it on the points made by Chingchai (Auychai Wata, interview, 11 September 1997). The change allowed their demands to accommodate both Chingchai's and Chavalit's positions. Second, the gathering showed its support for Chavalit personally. According to Tawon Lohkam, an executive committee member of the Auychai group, one purpose of the gathering was to oppose the call for Chavalit's resignation. Since Chavalit had agreed to back the draft constitution, the resignation campaign should be ended and Chavalit allowed to run the country and tackle the pressing economic crisis (*Krungthep Thurakit*, 10 September 1997: 6). Chavalit, together with Chingchai and Sanoh, were invited to Mahasarakam, and a *baisri*, a ceremony to encourage and strengthen morale, was held to boost the morale of Chavalit, who was exhausted after facing tough political controversy over the draft constitution (*Krungthep Thurakit*, 11 September 1997: 5; *The Nation*, 11 September 1997: A 6). In return, Chavalit told the gathering that the government had already approved for them the RSFPSP budget worth 836 million baht (*Krungthep Thurakit*, 15 September 1997: 5).

In October 1997, Auychai showed his loyalty to Chavalit once again, this time more boldly. Dissatisfied with the economic crisis, which had worsened since mid-July 1997, and the way the Chavalit government had handled the crisis, a group of businessmen, shopkeepers and labour groups staged a Bangkok protest outside the largest bank in Thailand on 20 October, demanding that Chavalit resign (Prudhisan 1998: 278–280; 284–285). On 22 October, Auychai reacted to the rally by demanding that the protesters stop their anti-Chavalit activities. If they continued to put pressure on the government, he would organize 100,000 farmers to rally in Bangkok on Silom Road, the business centre of Thailand, and close the stock market (*Matichon*, 23 October 1997: 12).

This challenge was the last action of Auychai as chairman of the executive committee of the SSFAI. About one week later, from 31 October to 1 November, Auychai held another gathering in Sri Sa Ket province, which was joined by some 10,000 farmers. At the gathering he announced the change of the name of his group from the SSFAI to the Farmers' Assembly of Isan (FAI) (*Krungthep Thurakit*, 1 November 1997: 1). The change was acknowledged by Chavalit, who travelled to Sri Sa Ket to chair a meeting between the Auychai group and local officials. Chavalit also promised to allocate a budget worth 200 million baht for an additional 10,000 members of the FAI who wanted to join the RSFPSP (*Krungthep Thurakit*, 2 November 1997: 3).

The RSFPSP and the Conflict in the Auychai Group

What was the reason behind this change? According to Sakda Kanjanasen, who was appointed vice-chairman of the executive committee of the FAI, the change was introduced to overcome the confusion created by two groups using the SSFAI name (*Krungthep Thurakit*, 1 November 1997: 2). However, on 5 November, Auychai revealed that the change was not just the adoption of a new name, but actually was the founding of a new organization (*Krungthep Thurakit*, 6 November 1997: 5). Why did Auychai, who acted as sole leader of his group, have to leave the organization? The reasons behind Auychai's departure came from the same source that had caused the conflict between Nakon and Auychai groups, the RSFPSP. However, this time the conflict was about a dispute over quotas from the RSFPSP received by the leaders within the Auychai group.

In many cases, the failure of organizations leads to conflicts and splits. However, in this case, it was success that led to the break-up of the Auychai group. After Chavalit confirmed that the government had approved the budget from the RSFPSP for the Auychai group during the gathering in Mahasarakham, the leaders of the group and a group of Isan MPs speeded up the allocation of pond quotas from the RSFPSP among themselves. Isan politicians to whom pond quotas were allocated were the members of the sub-committee on agriculture of the House of Representatives, who supervised the implementation of the programme (*Krungthep Thurakit*, 15 September 1997: 5; 26 September 1997: 6). There was a report that 3,000 ponds were allocated for Auychai, 2,500 ponds for Somyong and 2,400 ponds for Niramit, while other leaders in Buriram, Nong Bua Lamphu, Mukdahan, Yasothon and Sri Sa Ket provinces also got certain numbers of pond quotas (*Krungthep Thurakit*, 22 September 1998, 6).

The allocation of pond quotas, however, became the source of conflict between Auychai and Kamta Kanbunchan, which led to the split. While Kamta kept quiet about the conflict, Auychai announced the dismissal of Kamta and Chuang Kamlae. They were sacked, explained Auychai, because they were contractors. The FAI wanted to get rid of farmer leaders-cum-contractors, because it wanted to avoid allegations about improper seeking of contracts from the RSFPSP (*Krungthep Thurakit*, 6 November 1997: 6). But if the FAI wanted to get rid of farmer leaders-cum-contractors, why did it not dismiss Niramit and Somyong as well? On the contrary, Sakda came out to defend Niramit when he was accused of seeking contracts from the RSFPSP (*Krungthep Thurakit*, 12 November 1997: 5).

Auychai's statement about the dismissal of Kamta was the opposite of what had happened. Actually, it was Auychai who was expelled from the group. Even though he acted as the highest leader of the group, his power base within the group was small. He did not organize farmers himself. Only a small group of farmers in Mahasarakham organized by Supot belonged to Auychai's circle. However, because of his close relationship with Chingchai he was able to play a prominent role as a group leader during the Chavalit government. Unlike Auychai, Kamta and Chuang had their own areas with considerable numbers of members, and when they won over Niramit and Somyong, they were able to control the majority of group members. Only a small number of group members supported Auychai. As a result, Auychai had no choice but to leave the group. After the split, the Kamta group still called itself the SSFAI until it adopted a new name, the SSFAI (1), in February 1998. So, from February 1998 onwards, only the Nakon group campaigned under the banner of the SSFAI.

After Chavalit resigned on 5 November 1997, Auychai and Kamta's efforts to gain access to the budget from the RSFPSP faced new obstacles. This time objections came from Chalad Kamchuang, a Democrat MP from Roi Et, who asked the new government under Chaun Leekpai to review again the approval of the programme by the Chavalit government (*Krungthep Thurakit*, 11 November 1997: 5). Although Auychai, Kamta, Niramit and Chuang tried to lobby relevant officials, especially the Agriculture and Cooperatives Minister, to approve the programme (*Krungthep Thurakit*, 13 November 1997: 5), the Chuan government did not give a definite answer as to whether they would approve or suspend the programme. Moreover, the government proposed that the programme should employ only villagers, which meant that contractors would be unable to seek benefits from it (Nakon Sriwipat, interview, 8 June 1998).

After the split with the Nakon group, the major concern of the Auychai group was to secure access to the budget from the RSFPSP. The group used clientelistic relationships with the Chavalit government as a means to achieve its objective. However, these moves led to conflict and splits in the Auychai group.

REVISION OF STRATEGY OF THE SSFAI: THE NAKON GROUP

This section looks at the response of the Nakon group to the failure of the compromise strategy. The section is organized into four parts. The first examines the efforts to strengthen the bargaining power of the Nakon group through the building of new allies and the return to street politics. The second considers the revision of its policies towards political parties. The third focuses on the strengthening of cooperative activities by the group. The fourth addresses the campaign for community enterprise and the democratization of agribusiness.

Building New Allies and the Return to Street Politics

After the split with the Auychai group, the Nakon group tried to strengthen its bargaining power by entering into an alliance with other farmers' organizations through the Alliance of Isan Farmers' Organization (AIFO), and turned to political mobilization as a means to pursue its demands. In August 1996, the Thai Farmers' Foundation (TFF) and the Khon Kaen Agricultural Cooperative (KKAC) agreed to form an organization to campaign on debt and the reform of the BAAC (*Phujatkan*, 27 August 1996: 13). Two months later, in October 1996, they agreed to cooperate with the Cooperatives for Isan Sugarcane Planters (CISP), the Federation of Isan Cooperatives (FIC) and the SSFAI, under the banner of the Five Organizations of Isan Farmers. But before any joint action had been taken, the cooperation came to an end. The TFF, the CISP and the KKAC set up a new organization called the Alliance of Isan Farmers Organization (AIFO) (*Phujatkan*, 12–13 April 1997: 5). According to Somkid Singsong, chairman of the CISP, the three organizations gave up their plans to cooperate with the SSFAI because the internal conflicts of the SSFAI made cooperation impossible for the four organizations (*Krungthep Thurakit* [Isan section], 18 April 1997: 4). Asok complained that Auychai wanted to dominate, not cooperate with allies (Asok Prasansorn, interview, 7 December 1997). Nevertheless, the relationship between both sides resumed again on the day that Nakon announced the dismissal of the Auychai group (*Krungthep Thurakit* [Isan section], 18 April 1997: 4).

The AIFO was an alliance of farmers' organizations concerned mainly with 'income issues'. The TFF addressed farmers' debt, while the other two were concerned with credit and better prices for agricultural produce. Before collaborating with the SSFAI, the three organizations did not engage in political protests. They preferred to pursue their objectives by negotiation with the authorities. However, as mentioned in Chapter 5, their efforts failed to make progress. Hence, they considered increasing their bargaining power by cooperating with the SSFAI (Asok Prasansorn, interview, 7 December 1997).

In May 1997, the SSFAI and the AIFO staged a joint protest. According to an organizer of the protest, the joint action plan was for the SSFAI to hold a rally in Sri Sa Ket and then move to join the AIFO, which would organize a simultaneous demonstration in Khon Kaen (Son Roobsung, interview, 10 June 1998). However, the plan failed to materialize because the AIFO called off its protest after only two days. The AIFO staged a protest in Khon Kaen on 26 May, six days after the SSFAI organized a protest in Sri Sa Ket, in which some 17,000 farmers participated. On 27 May, the AIFO moved to block the highway about 10 kilometres from downtown Khon Kaen, and threatened to close down the Nong Khai–Bangkok rail line if the government did not respond to its demands (*The Nation*, 27 May 1997: A 2; *Krungthep Thurakit* [Isan Section], 29 May 1997: 6). Nevertheless, the AIFO abruptly called off the protest that night because of its lack of experience in organizing demonstrations. According to Asok, who called off the protest, the leaders of the AIFO felt uncertain about the situation, since a large number of farmers had joined the protest (about 15,000). Many of them were very angry over the government's inactivity in settling their grievances, while others were unprepared for a long protest (Asok Prasanson, interview, 7 December 1997).

Accordingly, when the SSFAI arrived in Khon Kaen on 28 April, they found that they had to fight alone. The situation, according to Yang Wongkraso, a central committee member of the SSFAI, caused disappointment and confusion among SSFAI members and leaders. More importantly, it weakened the bargaining power of the protest (Yang Wongkraso, interview, 3 March 1998). When the government learned about the situation, it refused to comply with the SSFAI's demands, and local officials began to apply pressure on the protesters, for instance, by cutting off their water supplies. In addition, the food that farmers had brought for consumption during the protests had almost run out (*Krungthep Thurakit* [Isan Section], 30 May 1997: 6). There was also a rumour that the local officials would employ the Village Scouts (see Chapter 4) to end the protest. According to Yang, it was clear that the protest had to end quickly, but how could they end it without severe damage to the organization? To pressure the government to accept all their demands was out of the question. Even a demand to set up a committee separate from the Auychai group was rejected by the authorities. The only choice available was to join the committee that the government agreed to establish to tackle the problems of the AIFO. Such a choice meant humiliation for the organization with a reputation like that of the SSFAI, and was not easy for its members and leaders to accept. For Yang, if the SSFAI was not flexible enough, the organization would face total defeat. He compared the situation with that on a battlefield: a wise commander had to learn to retreat when the situation required. He was successful in persuading Nakon and other leaders to accept the idea of joining the committee that the government set up for the AIFO (Yang Wongkraso, interview, 10 March 1998). As a consequence, the first protest of the SSFAI after the failure of the experiment with the compromise strategy ended with mixed results. On the one hand, the organization failed to organize a strong protest to pressure the government, as it had done in the past; on the other hand, it was able to create a new channel for dialogue with the authorities.

Although the AIFO did not keep its promise, the SSFAI still cooperated with the AIFO because it believed in the sincerity of Asok (Yang Wongkraso, interview, 10 March 1998). However, after the protest, the CISP and the KKAC were not actively involved in joint activities; the alliance later turned into a bilateral form of cooperation between the SSFAI and the TFF (field notes, 24 January 1998).

New Policy towards Political Parties

Their experience with the NAP forced Nakon and other leaders to rethink the relationship between the organization and political parties. After the split with the Auychai group, Nakon adopted a hostile policy towards the NAP. On 20 October 1997, when Chavalit faced protests in Bangkok calling on him to step down, Nakon cooperated with the AIFO and state enterprise unions in Khon Kaen by issuing a press release demanding that Chavalit resign (*Krungthep Thurakit*, 21 October 1997: 6). Such a move and the continuing attacks on Chavalit and Chingchai caused concern among SSFAI leaders. According to Yang, it was not right for the organization to show either its support or its hostility towards a particular political party or politician. It should adopt a policy of keeping a distance from them. To adopt such a policy did not mean that the organization could not criticize the government, but the focus of criticism should be aimed at policies, not individuals. Yang felt that if criticism was aimed at individuals, they would turn against the organization in the future (Yang Wongkraso, interview, 10 March 1998). After some debate, the SSFAI adopted a new policy towards political parties. The core idea was to keep equidistant from both government and opposition parties.

According to the new policy, the idea of building up close relationships with, or campaigning against, any political party was not useful for the efforts to solve farmers' problems, since governments frequently change in Thailand (from 1991–2001, Thailand had nine governments). Opposition parties can become government parties and vice versa in a short period of time. When a party against which an organization campaigned became the government, it would adopt a hostile policy towards that organization, which would cause difficulty in the efforts to tackle farmers' woes (Nakon Sriwipat, interview, 14 December 1997). As a result, the SSFAI stopped its public criticism of the Democrats and the NAP, although it still criticized them at internal meetings of the organization. However, since the Democrats, who now formed the government, had been the main target for criticism of the organization in the past, it was easy to see that the implementation of the new policy could be viewed by outsiders as evidence of co-optation. To avoid such a misunder-standing, argued Yang, the organization carefully had to keep proper distance from all parties (Yang Wongkraso, interview, 10 March 1998). Such a policy was appropriate for the SSFAI, which was weakened significantly after the two major splits. Since it did not single out anyone as friend or foe, it did not become a target of attack, especially from the government and allowed the organization to pursue more flexible policies with more room to manoeuvre.

The equidistant policy of the SSFAI differed from the policy adopted by the AOP in the same period. The AOP, in its early phase, paid no attention to its policy towards political parties, because it emphasized solving the problems of the poor through political mobilization. However, from the last period of the Chavalit government, the AOP began to develop a policy towards political parties. The policy of the AOP was based on the response of parties to its demands. As mentioned above, during the 99-day protest, the NAP made major concessions to the AOP's demands, but when Chuan succeeded Chavalit as prime minister in November 1997, he reversed all such concessions. As a result, the AOP adopted a rather hostile stand towards the Democrats, while its stand towards the NAP was positive. When there was a protest to pressure Chavalit to step down in October 1997, the AOP did not support this move. According to Wanida, 'from the point of view of businessmen, high class people, and some groups of the middle classes the Chavalit government may be bad, but it is not so bad from the point of view of the poor' (*Nation Sudsapda*, 7 November 1997: 14). Bamrung, another leading figure of the AOP, asserted that 'Chavalit talks to the poor much more than other prime ministers and farmers' problems have been solved by his administration more than they were by other governments' (*The Nation*, 19 September 1997: A 3). Such views were shared by an AOP ally. According to Campaign for Popular Democracy leader Pipop Thongchai, Chavalit was 'much better than other prime ministers… At least he listens to the opinions of pro-democracy groups and non-governmental organizations' (*The Nation*, 19 September 1997: A3).

After Chavalit resigned, the AOP still tried to keep its good relationship with him. In December 1997, the AOP and its allies held a *baisri* ceremony called 'Sincerity from the Poor' for Chavalit, attended by some 400 AOP representatives (*Kao Sod*, 31 December 1997: 12). According to Werapon, the ceremony was postponed many times because of differences among AOP allies. Some of them were afraid that such a move would draw criticism from the urban middle classes, while others opposed the plan to hold the ceremony because they disliked Chavalit. However, the AOP finally decided to organize the ceremony to thank Chavalit and his cabinet for their efforts to solve the problems of the urban and rural poor (Werapon Sopa, interview, 5 February 1998). The ceremony was held about one month after Chuan succeeded Chavalit as prime minister. The highlights of the ceremony were speeches by Chavalit and by AOP representative and leading social critic Sulak Sivaraksa. While Chavalit himself promised to work for the poor, Sulak praised the Chavalit government's policies and added that if the Chuan government paid attention to the problems of the poor, it would be honoured in the same way as the Chavalit government (*Kao Sod*, 31 December 1997: 12). Actually, Sulak had lent his support to the Chavalit government before the ceremony. In October 1997, he said that because Chavalit responded to most of the AOP demands during the 99-day protest, his action 'should be put on record in his honour'. Sulak also claimed that businessmen organized a protest against Chavalit because he supported the poor (*Bangkok Post*, 26 October 1997: 3). The move to support Chavalit, according to Term Kotsuno, one of the *pho khrua yai* of the AOP in Khon Kaen, was approved by *pho khrua yai* and AOP members (Term Kotsuno, interview, 9 January 1998). However, for some AOP allies in Bangkok, for example, a fraction of the October Networks, an organization of activists who had participated in the October movements of the 1970s, the ceremony was a betrayal of the people, because the Chavalit government was a 'terrible' government (Amnat Wisuttigo, interview, 15 May 1998).

In contrast to the AOP's relationship with the NAP, the relationship between the AOP and the Democrats was strained because unlike the Chavalit government, the Chuan government did not cooperate with the AOP. According to Suriyan Thongnu-iad, an advisor to the AOP, during the first nine months of the Chuan government, the organization raised 109 problems with the government but only six problems were solved, five of which had been addressed by the Chavalit government. The leaders of the AOP accused the authorities of lacking sincerity in tackling farmers' woes, and of causing disunity among its members. Furthermore, the AOP decided to boycott talks with the government by citing lack of progress in negotiations during the past nine months as a reason for its action (*Bangkok Post*, 24 August 1998: 1). Later, leading AOP advisor Bamrung Kayotha criticized the Chuan government on several grounds, ranging from helping the rich while ignoring the poor, to selling Thailand off to the IMF, and inciting rifts among farmers' organizations; at the same time he praised Chavalit for his role in tackling farmers' problems (*Bangkok Post*, 6 September 1998: 3).

Because of this stand, the AOP was accused of supporting the Chavalit government during the protest against Chavalit in October 1997 (*Nation Sudsapda*, 7 November 1997: 14). The AOP also became the target of government criticism when Chuan became prime minister in November 1997. It was singled out by Chuan's personal secretary, Alongkorn Polabut, as a group that had become involved with a political party (*Matichon*, 27 March 1998: 20). Compared to the 'equidistant' policy of the SSFAI, the 'leaning to one side' policy of the AOP was less flexible, since friends and opponents were determined beforehand. Moreover, in adopting a 'pro Chavalit-anti Chuan' stand during the early period of the Chuan government, the AOP alienated itself from the Bangkok middle classes, who preferred Chuan to Chavalit (*Bangkok Post*, 21 November 1996: 14). Such a move went against the new strategy of the organization proposed by Wanida, in which the middle classes occupied a very special place. The success of the AOP, according to Wanida, depended on the support of the middle classes. Hence, the AOP had to look for ways to encourage the middle classes to become involved in the organization's activities. It 'cannot afford to exclude the middle classes' from its movement. 'Otherwise', argues Wanida, 'it will fail as the communist parties all over the world did'. When the middle classes had not yet decided to back the organization, the AOP had to be patient, avoiding 'any no-win confrontation', and at the same time 'accumulate its strength'. The AOP, had to wait 'for the right moment when the middle classes lend their support to it', before the organization could launch its major protests (Wanida 1999: 50). It should be noted that this statement was a major revision of the AOP strategy by one of its prominent leaders. As has been shown in Chapter 5, the support of the middle classes to the organization was important but did not become a decisive factor in the struggle of the AOP; the most important element in its struggle was the internal strength of the poor themselves. This revision reflected the more sober thinking of a leader of the AOP because of the weakening of the organization. However, in some respects this revision reflected real frustration because, unable to rely on their own strength, the poor had to base their struggle on support from outsiders.

Strengthening Activities of Cooperatives

The SSFAI believed that cooperatives were a means to solve the economic problems of farmers. It was impossible for farmers to solve their economic hardships, argued Nakon, if they still confined their economic activities to individual household economies. So, it was necessary to establish collective economic organizations such as cooperatives to tackle this problem (Nakon 1996: 1–2). This idea, according to Ken Fanglit, was opposed by a group of leaders led by Bamrung on two grounds. First, farmers' cooperatives had no chance of success under the existing law, because they operated under rigid and out-of-date bureaucratic rules. Cooperatives did not have enough freedom to run their own activities. Second, cooperatives discouraged farmers from direct involvement in political mobilization. Members tended to wait for economic benefits from the cooperatives. However, SSFAI cooperatives were set up in many areas (Ken Fanglit, interview, 4 May 1998). After Nakon succeeded Bamrung as general secretary, the SSFAI paid more attention to cooperatives development. Most of the agricultural cooperatives in Thailand were under the Cooperative Promotion Department of the Minister of Agriculture and Cooperatives. They were set up and controlled by the government instead of farmers. The source of funding of cooperatives was the BAAC (Kanoksak 1989: 58–59; field notes, 8 April 1998).

According to Nakon, SSFAI cooperatives had to operate differently from the agricultural ones. Instead of trying incrementally to accumulate small amounts of funds, like most Thai cooperatives, SSFAI cooperatives had to pressure the government to allocate a substantial sum of funds to support them (Nakon 1996: 2). Apart from bargaining for support from the state, the SSFAI emphasized (1) raising the sense of belonging among cooperative members, (2) building economic bargaining power of cooperatives in buying and selling and (3) supporting cooperatives to operate independently from government officials (SSFAI 1996: 5).

Initially, the SSFAI cooperated with its ally the FIC in setting up a committee to take charge of cooperatives projects, but later, the FIC took over the projects. The change was proposed by Son Rubsung, a leader of the FIC and an advisor of the SSFAI. According to Son, political tasks should be separated from economic tasks. While the SSFAI was responsible for political work, which involved political mobilization and contestation with the authorities, the FIC, which was rarely involved in political mobilization, was responsible for cooperatives development. What was the advantage of such a change? For Son, if cooperatives still operated under the SSFAI leadership, they would face opposition from government officials because they would be considered 'political cooperatives'. To avoid official sanctions, cooperatives had to work under an organization that dealt directly with cooperative development, the FIC. However, when the SSFAI organized a protest, cooperative members were still able to join as members of the SSFAI (Son Rubsung, interview, 19 August 1997). Son's idea was implemented after the split with the Auychai group (Ken Fanglit, interview, 28 December 1997).

One important step to develop cooperatives of the SSFAI was to bargain for funds from the government. As mentioned above, the SSFAI anticipated that the most important source of cooperatives funding would be the government. Before the separation of cooperatives and political activities, in 1997, the SSFAI successfully lobbied the Chavalit government to allocate a budget to support 74 SSFAI cooperatives (The Meeting of the Joint Committee between Government Representatives and the SSFAI (supplement 3) 1997). This success was more of a problem than a solution for cooperatives development. It undermined the autonomy of cooperatives because when they accepted funds the cooperatives had to follow rules and procedures set up by the Ministry of Agriculture and Cooperatives. Although the cooperatives were operated by the SSFAI, and later by the FCI, the control was lost on many issues. For example, the cooperatives were unable to make decisions on reinvestment by themselves, but had to get permission from relevant officials. They also could not control cooperative staff, whose salaries were paid by the government. More importantly, because the cooperatives were funded by the government, cooperative members were afraid that if they did not follow the instructions of officials, they would lose this support (Chaluen Chanasongkram, interview, 29 May 1998). As a result, in practice, SSFAI cooperatives were no different from other agricultural cooperatives controlled by the government. According to Ken, in retrospect, Bamrung was right when he pointed out the limitations of cooperatives under the existing law (Ken Fanglit, interview, 4 May 1998). Actually, the SSFAI recognized these limitations and tried to solve the problem by proposing a new Cooperatives

Bill aimed at increasing the power of cooperatives and reducing the role of the authorities in running them. For instance, the SSFAI proposed to change the proportion of officials: cooperative representatives in the National Cooperative Development Committee (NCDM) from 11:8 to 11:15. In addition, the bill proposed that cooperative representatives, who had previously been nominated by the Agriculture and Cooperatives Minister, would be selected by election (SSFAI, 1997: 3). However, the SSFAIS efforts to introduce a new Cooperatives Bill like most of its others demands, failed to materialize.

Community Enterprise and the Democratization of Agribusiness

Community enterprise was another idea for tackling farmers' problems proposed by the SSFAI. The idea represented another point of difference between the SSFAI and the AOP. The AOP believed that commercial agriculture caused more harm than good to farmers. The expansion of commercial agriculture, especially for export, on the one hand, led to bankruptcy and disintegration of rural communities, while on the other hand, it destroyed the environment in the countryside. To overcome such problems, the AOP contended that farmers had to turn to alternative agriculture (Prapas, 1998: 83). In other words, on this issue the AOP shared the same convictions as the community culture school, which also believed that by escaping from commercial agriculture, farmers would be able to overcome their difficulties (see Chapter 3).

While the AOP chose to escape from commercial agriculture as a way to cure farmers' troubles, the SSFAI opted to work within the market economy. As discussed in Chapter 3, the SSFAI believed that efforts to escape from the market were unrealistic. Although from 1998 onwards the SSFAI started its own organic farming project, this kind of farming was envisaged as a supplementary activity to commercial agriculture. For the SSFAI, organic farming would help reduce farmers' expenses. Moreover, the SSFAI engaged in organic farming because it was interested in doing 'green business', which could offer organic products with higher prices than in the general market (field notes, 11 April 1998). Since commercial agriculture was the main type of farming activity, farmers should try to find ways to deal with it. According to Nakon, the best way for farmers to engage in the market was not to confine their activities only to the production of primary produce but to become involved in the processing and marketing of agricultural produce. Because the prices of agricultural produce as raw materials were always low, only by engaging in the processing and marketing stages could farmers increase their incomes (Nakon 1998: 1). Some groups of Isan NGOs already worked in that direction. They engaged in so-called 'community businesses' that produced products from raw materials available in local communities and sold them in the market (Isan NGO-CORD 1997: 107–116). The difference between community business and the SSFAI's economic plan was that while community business advocates did not try to pressure the government for policy changes, the SSFAI aimed at restructuring the agriculture–industry relationship. Such a change, for the SSFAI, would happen only through bargaining with the state. The idea of engaging in the processing business, which meant that farmers had to have their own factories, led to the question of whether farmers had enough funds for such activities. Nakon insisted that farmers had enough money to invest in the processing and marketing of their products, because they had some 300 billion baht in funds accumulated over decades under the so-called rice premium and the Farmers' Support Fund (FSF) (Nakon 1996: 1).

According to Tsujii, the rice premium was 'a policy of heavy taxation of the farmers and results in the unfair transfer of income from the majority of poor farmers to the minority of relatively affluent city dwellers' (Tsujii 1975: 313). The rice premium was introduced in 1949 by the Phibun government (Kanoksak 1989: 64). According to Rangsan, the rice premium played an important role in transferring resources from the agricultural sector to the non-agricultural sector, which led to an imbalance in growth between them (Rangsan 1987: 235). According to Nakon, the funds accumulated under the rice premium amounted to 210 billion baht. In 1991, the Chatchai government replaced the rice premium with the FSF, which accounted for 2 per cent of the government's annual budget. In 1996, these funds together with the fund accumulated under the rice premium, now the FSF, meant that the total sum of funds was some 300 billion baht.

In the past, argued Nakon, the government had spent money from the fund on projects from which farmers gained no benefit. For example, the government lent credits without interest from the FSF for traders to buy agricultural products from farmers with guaranteed prices. But in practice, farmers were never able to sell their products with a guaranteed price, so only capitalists benefitted from the government programme. For Nakon, since the fund was set up to support the agricultural sector, farmers should have the right to participate in the allocation of the FSF to ameliorate farmers' economic hardships. Nakon proposed that the fund should be used to set up the Farmers' Rehabilitation Fund (FRF). The FRF would partly help farmers to solve their debts, and partly help them to set up community enterprises. For Nakon, solving the debt problem was an important step to rescue farmers from bankruptcy. However, it did not guarantee that farmers would not become indebted again if they still acted only as the producers of primary products. In order to survive in the market economy, it was very important for farmers to set up 'community enterprises', to process their agricultural produce into commodities and then either sell them in the domestic market or export them to the international market. According to Nakon, community enterprises must be collectively run by cooperatives, because this would help to increase bargaining power of farmers. Running community enterprises required a financial institution that could provide farmers with low interest credit. Hence, part of the funds from the FSF should be allocated to set up the Cooperatives Bank, which would be run by cooperatives (Nakon 1996: 3).

The idea of community enterprise raised by Nakon led to the problem of democratization of industry, because many industries related to agriculture were monopolized by the state and agribusiness. For example, the tobacco industry was monopolized by the state, and the animal food industry was under the control of agribusiness. The whisky and wine industries were monopolized by the state and private companies, while farmers were legally prohibited from engaging in such industries although they had 'underground' knowledge and skills in making traditional wine and whisky. So, the break-up of the monopoly of such industries was essential to the implementation of community enterprises. The democratization of industry in Thailand comprised two main aspects. First, it involved the abolition of laws that allowed anyone to monopolize a certain industry. Second, it involved processes that introduced changes to create conditions that made it possible for individuals or groups other than large capitalist ones to own and operate industry. The democratization of industry was a process of deepening democracy beyond the political sphere. It was a form of economic democracy, which had never before emerged in Thailand.

The above two sections of this chapter have examined the activities of the SSFAI after the failure of the compromise strategy, which led to the disintegration of the Auychai group and the adjustment of the strategy of the Nakon faction. The Auychai group initially split into the FAI led by Auychai, and the SSFAI led by Kamta. However, in February 1998 Kamta changed the name of his group to the SSFAI (1). As a result, only the Nakon group rallied under the name of the SSFAI. As mentioned above, the Nakon faction of the SSFAI tried to strengthen its bargaining power by making adjustments to its political and economic strategies. The following section looks at another move of the SSFAI under Nakon, in an effort to enhance the bargaining power of the organization: reconciliation with other rival groups.

ATTEMPTED RECONCILIATION BETWEEN THE SSFAI AND OTHER RIVAL GROUPS

This section considers the causes that led to the attempt of reconciliation between the SSFAI and the rival groups the AOP, the SSFAI (1) and the FAI, and the factors that contributed to the failure of this move.

A reconciliation between the SSFAI and other conflicting groups occurred in December 1997. The move that led to cooperation was initiated by the three advisors of the AOP: Bamrung Kayotha, Werapon Sopa and Somkiat Pongpaiboon. According to Nakon, he was contacted by Werapon about joint activities between the SSFAI and the AOP. Nakon had no difficulty in accepting such a gesture because the meeting of the central committee of the SSFAI in December 1997 had also decided to seek cooperation with other grassroots organizations. On 25 December, Nakon and Werapon held talks in Nakon Ratchasima and reached an agreement that the SSFAI, the AOP and the TFF would orchestrate their campaigns by staging protests at the same time to pressure the government (field notes, 20 February 1998). The reconciliation between both sides arose from the weakening of the organizations from internal splits (the SSFAI), or from setbacks in their efforts (the AOP). Moreover, the desire for cooperation between them also arose from the recognition that if they did not form an alliance, the Chuan government would be a formidable opponent. Both Nakon and Werapon reckoned that to pressure Chuan to respond to their demands, the numbers of protesters should not be less than one hundred thousand (field notes, January 26, 1998).

A Network for Reconciliation: The People's Organization of Isan

In preparation for their cooperation, Werapon was invited to speak at the meeting of the central committee of the SSFAI on 25 January 1998. He told the meeting that the AOP would negotiate with the government on 6 February concerning problems that had yet to be solved after the 99-day protest, and if the negotiations failed, the AOP would have no choice but to stage a protest. In view of the record of the Chuan government in dealing with people's organizations, it was more likely than not that the negotiations would fail (field notes, January 25, 1998). A day later, at a meeting between the SSFAI, the AOP and the TFF, Werapon suggested that he would invite the SSFAI (1) and the AIF to participate in the planned joint action. Werapon's proposal was opposed by the SSFAI because it did not want to cooperate with leaders of these two groups, which used farmers for their own interests (field notes, 26 January 1998). However, on 29 January when another meeting was held to set out a common policy and to announce the founding of the People's Organization of Isan (POI), the AOP invited the SSFAI (1) and the AIF to join the POI. The POI was a loose coordination network, consisting of seven grassroots groups. Apart from the AOP, the SSFAI, the SSFAI (1), the AIF and the TFF, the other two groups were the AIFO and the Alliance of Isan People (AIP). The AIP was an organization of former CPT members, who had been promised land by the government for cultivation when they left the jungle in the 1980s, but had still not received it. Later on, four new groups joined the POI. However, most of them were quite weak and were not active in the network.

At a first press conference on 29 January, the POI declared that the government must respond to its demands by the end of February 1998. The demands of the POI concerned two sets of problems. The first set addressed the economic crisis. The POI's demands on this issue included an insistence that the government reveal to the public the agreements that it had made with the IMF, and that while implementing the IMF conditions, the government must not increase burdens on the poor. In addition, the government had to take action against 'economic criminals', who were involved in and had gained benefits from the economic crisis. The second set of problems comprised those that the various groups had previously asked the government to tackle (Manifesto of the POI (press release), 29 January 1998). A week after the meeting, the three main member groups of the POI took action according to the POI's plan. The action to pressure the Chuan government started with a rally of the SSFAI in Nakon Ratchasima on 3 February. The protest of the SSFAI was followed by that of the SSFAI (1), and in late February the AIF organized a protest in Bangkok.

The Conflict in the POI

Coordinating protests under the POI initially seemed promising. However, the POI contained seeds of conflict that undermined its strength. The inclusion of the SSFAI (1) and the AIF undermined the unity of the POI. As mentioned above, Nakon had already expressed his objections to the inclusion of these groups to Werapon. Although this inclusion helped to increase the number of POI member groups, the POI was not able to achieve real cooperation as had been hoped. Another point of conflict related to the failure of the AOP to organize a protest, as the three AOP advisors had promised, after there was no breakthrough in negotiations with the Chuan government. While other POI members held protests in February, the AOP did not organize its own protest. Werapon told Nakon at the SSFAI rally site that the AOP was unable to stage a protest because the result of the negotiations with the Chuan government prevented it from doing so. Since there had been no progress in these negotiations, Werapon's explanation was not convincing at all. The SSFAI regarded the actions of the three AOP advisors as a tactic to borrow the power of other organizations to pressure the government for them. Hence, the SSFAI decided not to join the activities of the POI actively (field notes, 8 February 1998). Not only was the SSFAI alone in believing that the three advisors of the AOP tried to use the strength of other organizations to pursue their objectives; the TFF also felt the same. According to Asok, when the POI planned to organize its activities, the three AOP advisors kept telling other member groups to bring their members to join in. He was very unhappy and disappointed with this tactic. He told Nakon that he wanted to show his disappointment by resigning from the POI and writing a letter to explain his decision. Asok, however, changed his mind after Nakon persuaded him to stay by arguing that the government would ignore farmers' demands if it knew that there was a conflict within the POI. In addition, even if they did not like the POI, it might be useful for their activities (Asok Prasansorn, interview, 10 May 1998).

Why did the AOP fail to organize a protest in February 1998? There were at least two possible answers to this question. The first view was that the three advisors were not authorized by the AOP to cooperate with other organizations, and the move to set up the POI was initiated by the advisors alone. So, the AOP did not acknowledge the agreement made with other POI members. This view was shared by some SSFAI leaders (field notes, 11 February 1998). The idea that the AOP did not become involved with the POI also appears in Nantiya and Pennapa (1998: A 4). It was possible to explain the failure of the AOP to organize a protest by looking at the internal problems of the organization. As mentioned above, the reversal of Chavalit's concessions by Chuan disheartened AOP members. As a result, the AOP was unable to hold a major protest again after the 99-day protest, Not only was the AOP unable to organize a major protest in 1998; it also failed to do so in 1999 and 2000. So, the protest promised by the three advisors was beyond the capacity of the AOP.

Moreover, apart from the issues discussed above, the SSFAI was also dissatisfied with the three AOP advisors over their close relationship with Kamta. When Kamta staged a protest in February 1998, the three advisors played a major role in helping Kamta organize the rally and negotiate with the authorities. The SSFAI was unhappy with this role of the three AOP advisors, because when Kamta first organized the protest, he still called his group the SSFAI before he decided to adopt the new name, SSFAI (1), about three weeks later. Helping Kamta was viewed by Nakon and other leaders as having made efforts to undermine their group. Nakon questioned the real intention of the three AOP advisors by pointing out that Kamta and other leaders of his group in the past were the main opponents of the Bamrung group. Bamrung had severely criticized them as corrupt leaders who joined the organization to pursue their self-interests, so how could he support such people now? There were different views on this issue within the SSFAI. For instance, Wera Rubkom, an advisor from Ubon Ratchatani, urged Nakon and other leaders to forget about 'personal conflicts' with the Kamta group and cooperate with them to increase the pressure on the government. Wera supported his position by arguing that the SSFAI should give priority to farmers' problems rather than 'personal conflicts' (field notes, 20 February 1998). This view was shared by Bamrung. He explained his decision to cooperate with Kamta and Auychai by saying that he would work with anyone if it helped to solve the problems of the poor (Thawan Phuthawan, interview, 24 May 2000).

There were dangers in this kind of logic. First, cooperation with Auychai and Kamta, although it helped to increase the number of member groups, tarnished the image of the POI. It was not surprising that the first question at the first press conference of the POI asked why the organization chose to protest against Chuan, but not against Chavalit (field notes, 29 January 1998). Second, the POI helped to prolong the activities of corrupt leaders, who used farmers for their self-interest. Bamrung pointed out the negative impact of corrupt leaders within farmers' movements. According to Bamrung, one factor that contributed to the weakening of farmers' movements was the existence of 'fake' leaders within the movements. Some farmers' leaders, argued Bamrung, were 'small scale contractors' who could 'easily be bought' by the government (*The Thai Development Newsletter*, July–December 1999, p. 2)

Another point of conflict between the SSFAI and the three AOP advisors was the way the three advisors ran the POI. According to Ken, who represented the SSFAI in the POI, the POI was supposed to be run by all its member groups, but more frequently internal issues were decided beforehand by Somkiat, Bamrung and Werapon. For example, Werapon had become the secretary of the POI and Bamrung and Somkiat had become advisors without the holding of elections or consultation with member groups. Such a style of working discouraged the SSFAI from cooperating with them (Ken Fanglit, interview, 11 May 1998).

The ineffectiveness of the POI

Because of the problems discussed above, the plan to orchestrate the protest of POI member groups in February 1998 did not materialize. Instead of collectively pressuring the government, they bargained with it separately. As a result, their bargaining power decreased considerably. Another protest of the POI four months later also suffered from the same problem. In late May, some 20,000 farmers, mainly from the TFFI, rallied in Khon Kaen for two days under the banner of the POI. They demanded that the government declare a five-year moratorium on debts that farmers owed to the BAAC and approve the Farmers' Rehabilitation Bill, which would help to revive the agricultural sector (field notes, 24–25 May 1998). The protest was organized when the government was preparing to borrow some 700 billion baht to cover the debts of collapsed financial companies. The POI justified its demands by arguing that if the government could help the rich, why could it not support the poor as well? 'If the government', argued Bamrung, 'can borrow money to help the finance companies, why not for the poor?' (*Bangkok Post*, 25 May 1998: 1). Another leader, Nakon, insisted that the government must not discriminate against the poor. Farmers, for him, deserved equal treatment with the financial sector (*Bangkok Post*, 26 May 1998: 1) After negotiating with the authorities, Bamrung revealed that if POI demands were ignored, it would organize another demonstration on 24 June in front of Government House (*Bangkok Post*, 25 May 1998: 1). The POI's plan worried the Chuan government, because when the POI prepared for the June protest, its 'rich versus poor' argument seemed to have gained momentum. As Suthichai Yoon pointed out, such a situation for Chuan was not 'just an economic issue'. The issue 'has been politicized to the point that the perception of his government being "pro rich" and "anti-poor" is beginning to stick – and will end up politically very harmful' (Suthichai, 1998: A4). Another development that worried the government was that the proposed demonstration, in which the POI announced that some 50,000 farmers would participate, was supported by 30 democracy organizations. They declared that they would send their representatives to join the demonstration on 24 June (*Bangkok Post*, 22 June 1998: 3; *The Nation*, 23 June 1998: A1)

Although the plan gathered momentum, its implementation was impeded by the internal problems of the POI. Disappointed with what had happened during the February 1998 protest, the SSFAI determined that it would not 'let history repeat itself again'. It was very cautious about bringing its members to join the POI's demonstration. For the SSFAI, every member group of the POI should share roughly the same burden. It decided that if the three advisors of the AOP did not take large numbers of AOP members to join the demonstration, they would send only a few members to Bangkok. When it learnt that the three advisors of the AOP would go to the capital city with a small group of farmers, the SSFAI adopted the same policy (Nakon Sriwipat, interview, 21 July 1998). Other member groups were not fully committed to the POI's plan either. The SSFAI (1) chose to gather near Lam Takong Dam in Nakon Ratchasima instead of Bangkok. The TFF decided to send only about 100 representatives to Bangkok, after a government representative accepted the demand for a debt moratorium. As a result, only some 3,000 farmers participated in a rally that had been expected to be a major political crisis for the Chaun government (*The Nation*, 25 June 25, 1998: A1).

Participation in the POI did not bring about any significant progress in the struggle of the SSFAI. The idea of strengthening the organization through building up an alliance with the AOP led to new conflicts instead of cooperation. The following section explores another attempt to strengthen the struggle of the organization by a different means: a land occupation strategy.

THE SEARCH FOR A NEW STRATEGY: LAND OCCUPATION

Land occupation was a new alternative with which the SSFAI experimented to solve land rights problems. This experimentation differed from other measures implemented by the organization to bargain with the state. It involved a high risk of violent suppression by the state, but also had the potential to be very effective if the occupiers were well organized. This section examines the debate within the SSFAI on the implementation and outcome of this strategy.

The Debate on a Land Occupation Strategy

Land occupation was first seriously considered after the major protest in February 1998 failed to make significant progress. The SSFAI organized the protest by adopting an old strategy that the organization had employed from 1993–95. Protestors started gathering on 3 February, in the same area in Si Khiu, Nakon Ratchasima, as previous major protests. After camping for a few days, the SSFAI marched along the Friendship Highway towards Bangkok. Such a strategy did not produce strong pressure on the government. The ineffectiveness of the march mainly resulted from a change in the government policy towards the protest. Instead of employing large forces to threaten the marchers as in the past, the Chuan government did not interfere. As discussed in Chapter 4, one condition for the success of the 'march to Bangkok' strategy was government hostility. Without the threat of government force, the march along the highway became an isolated and quiet event. At the meeting of the central committee before the dispersal of the protest, the leaders of the SSFAI reached the conclusion that old style protest was out-of-date. It was inadequate for solving problems raised by the organization. A new approach was needed if progress was to be achieved. But the meeting was still unable to answer what new approach the SSFAI needed (field notes, 20 February 1998).

In April 1998, the SSFAI organized a political school in Nakon Ratchasima province. Among the topics discussed at the school was the land occupation of the Landless Worker Movement (MST) in Brazil. The success of the MST impressed all those taking part in the school. 'Could we solve our problems by the Brazilian approach?' was a question that led to lively debate in the classroom. Although they were aware that Thai law did not allow landless farmers to occupy unproductive land, as did Brazilian law, the participants still regarded land occupation as a strategy worth trying. After a long debate, they reached the conclusion that if any area wanted to experiment with the land occupation strategy, it had to be aware of the dangers of a strong reaction from the state. Therefore, such a move needed a high level of commitment and had to be well planned and organized to counter state action (field notes, April 14–15, 1998).

The Experiment with a Land Occupation Strategy

SSFAI members in Kon Kaen were the first group that decided to implement the land occupation strategy. In June 1998, more than 1,000 SSFAI members from 643 families moved to occupy part of the Dong Lan forest, which covers parts of Loei and Khon Kaen provinces (Onnucha 1999). The reason why this group of SSFAI members decided to take such a high-risk action is readily apparent if this group's background is examined. It comprised villagers from eight villages who were forced to relocate their farms in Chaiyaphum and Khon Kaen to two villages, Pakam and Aungtong, in Si Chomphu district, Khon Kaen, between 1983 and 1986. Initially, farmers tried to oppose the evictions, but their efforts failed because the government employed the military to suppress their resistance. Some of their leaders were brutally beaten and arrested by the officials. To defuse opposition from farmers, the authorities pledged 15 rai of land for every family and promised to provide them with a free electricity and water supply, reservoirs, credit and to help them find markets for their produce. But after the evictions, some of them received nothing the officials promised, while some obtained only 7.5 rai of arid land on which almost nothing could grow. As a result, most of the evicted farmers were unable even to grow enough rice for family consumption, and managed to survive only by working as labourers outside their villages.

Disillusioned with government promises, they travelled to Bangkok to petition various government agencies. Nevertheless, their efforts gained nothing but empty promises. When the anti-*Kho Jo Kho* projects broke out in 1993, the state's forced evictions faced a major challenge for the first time (see Chapter 3). However, this group of evicted farmers missed the chance to return to their villages, because they decided not to join the anti-*Kho Jo Kho* movement. In 1996, they reached the conclusion that if they wanted to solve their problems, they had to join a farmers' organization. The AOP, active in the area, was the first organization they approached. But the AOP refused to help them because it disagreed with their demands. Realizing that it was impossible for them to return to their villages, the evicted farmers demanded land, which the government failed to deliver, in the area (SSFAI Dong Lan committee, interview, 14 June 1998). The AOP, however, had a policy to protect only those farmers who originally lived in their areas from state evictions. For farmers who had been evicted from other areas, the AOP told them to return to their villages (Term Kotsuno, interview, 9 January 1998). Disappointed with the AOP, they joined the SSFAI.

From 1996 onwards, SSFAI members in Dong Lan organized protests and negotiated with local officials several times, but with little progress. After two years of negotiations, they came to believe that local officials were insincere in dealing with their problems, only using negotiations as a tactic to prolong the problem. Since negotiations with the authorities were useless, they considered experimenting with the land occupation strategy. According to Prachuab Klangnog, a leader of the SSFAI in Dong Lan, after two years of negotiations failed to make significant progress, there were two choices available to them. The first choice was to give up their struggle. The second was to take a risk by implementing the land occupation strategy. They were ready to take any kind of risk, including being imprisoned or even killed, rather than starving because of shortage of land for cultivation. They believed that they had to take action before it was too late for the farming season in June (Prachuab Klangnog, interview, 14 June 1998).

In early June 1998, SSFAI members moved into the Dong Lan forest to start their land occupation. They set up shelters in Sum Noknoi, the area in which some of them had lived until the mid-1980s. After occupying the area, they demanded the opportunity to negotiate with the authorities, saying that if their demand was refused, they would clear the forest (SSFAI Dong Lan committee, interview, 14 February 1998). From the mid-1980s, Forestry Department officials had used the area to plant trek, eucalyptus and other commercial trees. The land occupation strategy did not involve refusal to negotiate with the authorities, but within its scheme, negotiation came after occupation. According to Nakon, the aim of such a move was to gain the upper hand in negotiation. In other words, land occupation was a form of taking land 'hostage', which was designed to boost the bargaining power of poor farmers (Onnucha 1999).

The success of the occupation, however, depended on the tactics, unity and discipline of the occupiers. Since the action was likely to be viewed as forest encroachment, the Dong Lan committee instructed farmers to refrain from cutting trees before an agreement had been reached. They also chose to settle in an area that had only a few trees (in some parts of the forest most of the trees had died because of fire). The safety of the settlers was another important issue. A security unit was formed to prevent outside intervention and surprise attacks from the authorities. Internal discipline was imposed (field notes, 8, 14 June 1998). Since the evicted farmers in Dong Lan came from different villages, no one was able to act as a sole leader of the group. Such a situation sometimes led to disunity among members. However, in the case of Dong Lan, the opposite was true. Differences among them did lead to differences in opinions, and representatives from each village always engaged in heated debates among themselves, but their differences did not develop into conflicts. As a result, instead of leading to disunity, they created a genuine collective leadership system, which helped to strengthen their unity. The unity among them was an important factor behind the success of their resistance against state pressure.

Initially, local officials did not show their hostility towards the occupation. Some acted in the opposite way than before the occupation took place. For example, a village headman who had opposed the SSFAI in Dong Lan from the beginning, expressed his sympathy with the occupation, while the rangers, who were supposed to order SSFAI members to withdraw from the forest, encouraged farmers to settle in an area full of big trees. SSFAI members, however, refused, because they were aware that it would make them more vulnerable to the 'forest destroyer' accusation (SSFAI Dong Lan committee, interview, 14 June 1998). The local officials changed their policies towards the occupation after it had taken place for seven months. In January 1999, the Khon Kaen provincial governor instructed the military, rangers and police to blockade the occupation in order to cut off farmers' food supply from nearby villages. They ordered SSFAI members to end their occupation within three days. A senior police officer told the occupiers that prison was already prepared for them all. The authorities threatened the farmers verbally and physically. Rangers tried to intimidate the occupiers by opening fire when confronted with their security guards (*Matichon Sudsapda*, 2 February, 1999: 9). Instead of being scared by the officials' pressure, the occupiers stood firm against the threats. The confrontation led to a stalemate (*Matichon Sudsapda*, 9 February, 1999: 12). The determination of the SSFAI members finally paid off. When hostility proved ineffective, the officials changed their policy. They knew that this time empty promises were not enough. To reach an agreement with the occupiers, they had to come up with a concrete solution. The Forestry Department agreed to provide land near Dong Lan in Nong Ya Plong village for them (Onnucha 1999). However, after farmers called off their occupation, eight of their leaders were arrested and imprisoned for two years (field notes, 15 October 2002).

The Dong Lan occupation had an immediate impact on farmers in other areas in Isan. In Somdej district, Kalasin province, farmers from Khamin, Dong Bao and Kaeng Ka Am villages moved to occupy part of Phu Pan national park. The area farmers moved into had belonged to them before the state drove them out in 1982 to make way for the national park. After being driven out from their lands, some went to Bangkok to work in factories or on construction sites. However, they were forced to return home again because of the economic crisis that started in 1997. When they returned to their villages, they found themselves in a situation with no jobs and no lands for cultivation. When they heard about the Dong Lan incident, they decided to follow its example, reasoning: 'If those who trespassed into the Dong Lan forest finally got the land, why can't we do the same?' Their efforts, nevertheless, failed to materialize because they were too weak to resist state pressure. Before holding talks with the relevant officials, they were moved out of the occupation area by the Forestry Department (Onnucha 1999).

The experiment with the land occupation strategy at Dong Lan provided a valuable lesson for the struggle for land of the SSFAI and other grassroots movements in Thailand. It helped to raise expectations concerning the possibility of applying such a strategy to the struggle for land in the Thai countryside. However, the Kalasin case showed that land occupation was not easy to duplicate. It is an adventurous action; its success needs a very high level of commitment, unity and discipline, which is not easy to achieve.

SUMMARY

This chapter has looked at the activities of the SSFAI after the failure of the experimentation with the compromise strategy in 1997. The experiment led the SSFAI to split into two groups: the Auychai and the Nakon groups. After the split, the Auychai group concentrated its activities on securing access to the budget from the RSFPSP. For that purpose, the Auychai group created a trade-off between the budget from the RSFPSP and political support for the NAP and Chavalit. The move was successful, although conflict over the quotas from the RSFPSP among its leaders led to splits within the group.

The aims of the Nakon group were quite different from those of the Auychai group. The main concern was to regain its strength. For this purpose, it entered into an alliance with other farmers' organizations through the AIFO. Another important issue for the Nakon group was the relationship between the organization and political parties. The experience with the NAP forced the group to revise its policy towards political parties. The new policy towards political parties was to keep its distance from such parties. Such a policy was appropriate for the SSFAI, which was weakened considerably after the two major splits. It provided the organization more room to manoeuvre. The equidistant policy of the SSFAI adopted by the Nakon group was almost opposite to the policy of the AOP in the same period. Unlike the SSFAI, the AOP chose to pursue a policy of leaning towards one political party. After the 99-day protest, the organization showed its support for Chavalit and became very critical of the Chuan government.

Besides the above activities, the SSFAI tried to strengthen its bargaining power by joining the POI. This move, although promising, contained the seeds of conflict. The main conflict was between the SSFAI and the AOP advisors. Because of its internal conflicts, the POI was not as effective as it should have been. A plan to coordinate the campaign of its member groups in February 1998 did not materialize, and the plan to stage a massive protest in Bangkok in May also suffered from the same problem. Although the effort to strengthen its bargaining power through participation in the POI was unsuccessful, the failure of the February 1998 protest, which the SSFAI organized under the plan of the POI, stimulated the organization to experiment with a land occupation strategy. The experiment was inspired by the success of the land occupation of the MST in Brazil. In June 1998, more than 1,000 SSFAI members moved to occupy part of the Dong Lan forest in Khon Kaen for seven months. This group of farmers had been evicted from their land by the state in the 1980s, and demanded land in the Dong Lan forest. After successfully enduring pressure from local officials, the SSFAI members finally won concessions from the Forestry Department.

CHAPTER 7

From Regional to National Organization

After experiencing conflict, split and decline, the SSFAI entered a new period of rapid expansion. From 1999 onwards the organization grew steadily, and in 2001 the Assembly expanded its activities beyond Isan's boundary into the North, the Central plain and the South. The organization transformed itself from a regional organization into a national one. The reasons behind the success of the Assembly in this period are the first questions to be addressed. After examining the cause of the SSFAI's expansion, the chapter will look at a new strategy that the Assembly implemented in this period.

THE EXPANSION OF THE SSFAI IN THE 1999–2002 PERIOD

The expansion of the SSFAI in 1999–2002 was influenced by changes outside and inside the organization. The first factor that contributed to the expansion of the Assembly in this period was the establishment of the Farmers' Rehabilitation Fund (FRF) in 1999. Another factor that boosted the expansion of the SSFAI was the decision of the organization to shift the priority of its work from campaigning for land rights to campaigning to solve farmers' economic problem. This section will examine the impact of those two factors on the development of the SSFAI during 1999 to 2002.

The Farmers' Rehabilitation Fund and the Expansion of the SSFAI

The FRF developed from the idea of community enterprise proposed by the SSFAI in 1996. From 1997 onwards, community enterprises became a major issue of discussion at the internal meetings of the SSFAI. However, when it campaigned for the FRF, the SSFAI had to emphasize the debt problem because this helped to expand the support base of the campaign. Initially, the SSFAI cooperated with the AIFO in campaigning for the FRF; later, when the SSFAI and other major Isan farmer organizations cooperated under the name of the People's Organization of Isan (POI), the FRF became one of their common campaign points. In 19987, The POI rallied in Bangkok demanding the government to pass the Farmers' Rehabilitation Bill. Because of the conflict within the POI the campaign did not win concession from the government (see Chapter 6). But in 1999, the government changed unexpectedly the policy towards the FRF: even political parties recognized the popularity of the FRF among farmers. The FRF was approved by the parliament and became a law in May 1999. The government's move surprised the leaders of the SSFAI because they did not expect an easy approval (Yang Wongkraso, interview, 20 February 2005). What were the reasons behind this change of mind? For some, the FRF was approved because of the competition among politicians to win over the farmers. Some political parties, e.g. Thai Rak Thai – the present ruling party in Thailand – incorporated ideas concerning the FRF into heir party policies in order to increase their popularity (*Matichon Sudsapda*, 18–24 September, 2000: 12; 16 October 2000; 22). However, the approval also derived from a compromise between farmers and the authorities. According to Nakon, who drafted the Farmers Rehabilitation Bill on behalf of farmers' organizations, compromise with the Agriculture and Cooperatives Ministry's officials was unavoidable, because farmers were not strong enough to pressure the government to comply fully with their demands. As a result, the Bill allowed the authorities to play a bigger role than was originally envisaged. For Nakon, such a compromise was a realistic option to enable the bill to be approved. Problems that might arise would have to be tackled in the future (Nakon Sriwipat, interview, 15 April 1998).

The approval of the Bill offered the SSFAI an opportunity to recruit new members. Under the Bill, the government would allocate funds for agriculture projects. For the first year, the government approved a budget worth 1.8 billion to the FRF (*Bangkok Post*, 29 March 2000). However, farmers could apply for funds from the FRF only when they were members of a farmer group with at least 50 members. A well-known organization like the SSFAI was in a position to take most advantage of such a rule. There were three reasons for farmers to join the SSFAI. First, they wanted to join because, as SSFAI members, they were able to access credit from the FRF. Second, the FRF would help them to solve their debt problem, which they borrowed from financial institutions. Third, apart from material benefits, farmers joined the Assembly because they believed that in the long run the FRF would help to solve their economic problems (Nakon Sriwipat, interview, 10 October 2002).

New Perspectives on Farmers Economy and the Expansion of the SSFAI

The reassessment of the main task of the SFAI was the second factor that contributed to the expansion of the organization. Generally, the left in Thailand believed that land right was the most important issue for farmers. If the Assembly still clung to the orthodox view, it could never experience high growth during 1999 to 2002. Because the organization understood the nature of 'postpeasant society', it managed to expand its political base into new groups of farmers.

As we saw in Chapter 6, after the major protest of the SSFAI in February 1998 the organization reached the conclusion that the old strategy was inadequate for solving problems raised by the Assembly. At the political school organized by the Assembly in Nakhon Ratchasima province in April that year, the SSFAI reviewed and assessed its work. Apart from the strategy of the organization, the Assembly also debated what the most important problem of farmers was. In the past, the SSFAI campaigned on two main issues, land rights and price and debt issues, by singling out the lack of land rights as the major problem. As a result, the organization devoted most of its energy to tackling the land rights problem. This priority was questioned at the school but no clear answer was found. In the course of struggle, the SSFAI reached the conclusion that the emphasis of its work had to be changed. The Assembly decided that its main activity had to shift from the struggle for land rights to the campaign to solve farmers' problems, which arose from the commercialization of agriculture. Why? Because to single out land rights meant that the organization confused the problems of cultivators in pre-capitalist society with the capitalist ones. Land ownership was the most important problem for peasants in pre-capitalist society since their survival depended on land. But crucial to cultivators in capitalist society were prices and capital. Because of the commercialization of agriculture, the farmers were still unable to survive if the price of agricultural produce was very low, or if they did not have enough capital for production, even if they had land rights (Nakon Sriwipat, interview, 10 October 2002). The conclusion of the SSFAI captured the nature of post-peasant society. As shown in Chapter 4, in Thailand capitalism had transformed a traditional peasant society into a post-peasant society. In such a society, land tenure was a problem of just one type of farmer, while the 'income issue' was a common problem of most rural dwellers. Therefore, the decision to concentrate its campaign on the 'income issue' meant that the SSFAI addressed the problem of the majority of the rural populations. As a result, it enabled the organization to recruit new groups of farmers other than those who had land rights problem.

However, tackling farmers' problems that arose from the commercialization of agriculture did not mean that the campaign for remunerative price and debt issues would become the main concern of the SSFAI. The Assembly believed that the campaign on those issues in the past did not tackle the roots of farmers' economic problem. Even though the government agreed to subsidize agricultural prices and get rid of farmers' debts, the problems would reappear again in the future because they did not touch the roots of the problem. According to the SSFAI, low price and debt were the result of unequal relations of production in which farmers had no power to control the agriculture sector. Therefore, a long-term solution to farmers' economic problems was to strengthen farmer control over that sector. The Assembly saw the set-up of the FRF as a first step to address the cause of farmers' economic problem, and the organization decided to concentrate its activity on the FRF.

The combination of the two factors led to the most rapid expansion period of the SSFAI. Within three years (1999–2001), the Assembly succeeded in expanding its political base from Isan into other regions of Thailand. Because of this, the Assembly decided to change the name of the organization to the Assembly of Small Scale Farmers (ASSF). In December 2001, the ASSF organized a meeting in Nakhon Sawan province to set up a new branch in the North. In the same month, ASSF members from 15 provinces in the Central plain founded the Central plain branch of the ASSF in Nakhon Nayok province. And in the South, an ASSF branch was founded in January 2002. In March 2002, the ASSF operated in 43 provinces, with 3 in the North, 18 in Isan, 17 in the Central plain and 5 in the South (ASSF 2002: 6). The number of farmers involved in the activities of the Assembly reached a new high of some 300,000, with 200,000 in Isan, 50,000 in the Central plain, 40,000 in the North and 10,000 in the South. However, not all of the newcomers were ASSF members. Among 300,000 only 10,000 were ASSF members, because the rapid expansion of the organization caused concern within the Assembly. It was afraid that the influx of hundreds of thousands of farmers into the Assembly within a short period of time would cause problems, such as lack of discipline and lack of commitment to long-term objectives. To prevent such tendencies, the ASSF set up a new rule for member recruitment; any small-scale farmer could join the activities of the Assembly, but only a person who committed to the organization's objectives would be accepted (Nakon Sriwipat, interview, 10 October 2002).

THE ASSF AND THE ETHNIC LAO OUTSIDE ISAN

When the ASSF expanded its activities into other regions, it was expected that the recruited farmers would be Thai or other ethnic groups, rather than

Lao. However, that was not the case. The majority of farmers recruited from the North, the Central plain and the South were Lao. Where did the Lao in those regions come from? Like in Isan, Lao settlement in the North had a long history. Before the Chakri Reformation, Siam classified people who lived in the two regions as Lao (Bung-on 1998: 1–4). However, the development of the two regions took different routes. While Isan maintained its Lao culture, the North developed its own culture, which differed from Isan. As a result, we find Lao only in certain areas of the North today. In the Central plain, Lao settlement was the result of war. In the Ayutthaya period (1350–1767), Lao war captives from the North, for example from Chiang Mai, were forced to resettle in areas around Ayutthaya. In the Thonburi period (1767–1782), after the capture of Vientiane in 1779, the Siamese army relocated several tens of thousands of war captives in various parts of the Central plain, such as Ratchaburi, Phetchaburi and Chanthaburi (Bang-on 1998: 7–14, 30–32). Major Lao settlement in the Central plain occurred in the early Bangkok (Rattanakosin) period. In 1827, Vientiane, then a vassal of Siam, rebelled against Bangkok domination. The rebellion was suppressed by the Siamese a year later. After the war, the Siamese army completely destroyed Vientiane and depopulated the city and its hinterland. Moreover, Lao populations were deported to Isan and the Central plain. It was estimated that at least 100,000 Lao were resettled in Isan, and up to 50,000 were resettled in the Central plain (e.g. in Suphanburi, Chachoengsao, Prachinburi and Chonburi) by the mid-nineteenth century (Bang-on 1998: 52–68; Grabowsky 1995: 120–121). According to Grabowsky, the resettlements in the aftermath of the rebellion were 'without precedent, at least in the Siamese and Lao world, both in terms of territories devastated and the number of people deported' (Grabowsky 1995: 121). Lao settlements in the South took place in the Ayutthaya period. Lao war captives from Chiang Mai were deported to Phatthalung, Songkhla and Nakhon Si Thammarat (Bang-on 1998: 9–10). Another settlement occurred in the early Bangkok period. The Holy Men revolt, the biggest millenarian uprising, broke out in Isan in 1902. The uprising was crushed by the Siamese army (see Chapter 2). After the defeat of the rebellion, some of rebels, who were arrested by Siamese troops, were deported to the South (Tweesilp, interview, 5 November 2002). And because of political dissent, Lao settlement has also taken place in the South in more recent times. In the 1960s, the government tried to isolate CPT armed forces in the jungle by relocating villagers from the CPT stronghold in Northern Isan to the South (field notes, 1 November 2002).

Besides political reasons, settlement of the Lao ethnic group in the North, the Central plain and the South was caused by economic reasons. This kind of settlement was a recent phenomenon related to the modernization process in Thailand. Most people who settled in the three regions in the modern period were Lao of Isan. As we saw in Chapter 3, agricultural exports were the main source of financing Thailand's industrialization. During the 1960s and 1970s, areas for cash crops expanded rapidly. Although government passed the Protection and Reservation Act, in practice it allowed people to clear forests for cash crops. The situation provided an opportunity for Isan farmers who did not have enough land for their family members, and for those who wanted to earn their living through a new source of income, cash crops. Apart from searching for new lands in Isan (see Chapter 3), they emigrated to other regions. Some of them bought land from local people, others cleared forests for cash crops. They set up their own villages, which local people dubbed 'Lao village'. This type of settlement now exists in the North, the Central plain and the South. However, another type of Lao settlement appeared in the South. Instead of searching for new lands, some groups of Isan farmers worked as wage-labourers in rubber plantations (field notes, 6 October 2002). For the moment there is no official data on the number of Lao in the three regions. However, it is certainly considerable. In some places, for example in Sra Kaeo province in the Central plain, it seems that the majority of the population is Lao (field notes, 7 October 2002). The existence of these groups of Lao proves that it is incorrect to believe that today Lao communities in Thailand exist only in Isan. Moreover, the numbers of Lao in Thailand far more exceed what was generally believed.

Why were Lao outside Isan more susceptible to ASSF recruitment than other ethnic groups? Because of the ethnic bond between them and the ASSF. Lao in the three regions trusted the ASSF because they viewed the Assembly as the organization of ethnic Lao. ASSF members, in their view, were their 'brothers and sisters' from Isan. This brotherly solidarity contrasted with the skeptical view of some Thais in the Central plain who did not believe that the 'inferior Lao' would be able to solve their problems (field notes, 7 October 2002). The persistence of Lao identity among Lao outside Isan, especially among those groups resettled before the twentieth century, was astonishing. It related to the pattern of their settlements. If we compare this pattern with those of other ethnic groups, we see its distinctiveness clearly. For example, local people in the South tended to live on their farms separated from each other. Lao, on the contrary, always live in clusters of houses close to each other. Close relationship among villagers nurtures strong community life and enables them to maintain their identity.

NEW FORM OF STRUGGLE

Apart from the expansion of the organization, another important change within the Assembly was the implementation of a new strategy. In the past the Assembly either adopted the confrontation strategy, which relied on political mobilization, or the compromise strategy, which emphasized cooperation with the state. After the approval of the FRF in 1999, the Assembly embarked in a new strategy comprised of three elements. First, it used state resources for farmers' objectives. As mentioned above, the Assembly viewed the set-up of the FRF as the first step to tackle farmers' economic problems. The organization aimed at using funds from the FRF to solve farmers' debts and start new agriculture projects. Second, to achieve such an aim, the Assembly had to work within the FRF, an organization set up by the state. The Assembly worked within the FRF both to cooperate with state authorities and, more importantly, to build farmers' control over the FRF. Third, although the Assembly concentrated on economic issues and work within the FRF, political mobilization was still an important element of the organization. When works within the FRF faced an obstacle, the Assembly turned to street politics to increase its bargaining power. The new strategy of the Assembly shed some light on the complexity of state–civil society relationships. As argued in Chapter 1, the relationship between the state and civil society was complex and interaction took various forms. The new strategy of the Assembly was an example of another mode of state-civil society interaction, which was more complex than the relationship between the two sides under the confrontation and compromise strategies. The following sections will examine the implementation of the new Assembly strategy.

The FRF and the New Strategy

After the FRF was approved by the parliament, the Assembly became active within the FRF. According to Nakon, the Farmers' Rehabilitation Bill was drafted and proposed by farmers, so it had to serve farmers' interests (Nakon Sriwipat, 5 October 2002). Working within the FRF, an organization set up and funded by the state, revealed an important difference between the new and previous strategies. Such a move seemed to increase the danger of being co-opted by the state. However, the Assembly planned to achieve an opposite outcome by using the FRF to help farmers to organize themselves and develop into independent, strong farmer organizations. To attain this goal, the Assembly had to establish farmer control over the FRF. Because the Bill, as mentioned above, was the result of compromise between farmers and the state, to build farmer control over the FRF was not easy. Any effort to consolidate farmers' domination would face resistance from the state, since the state was allowed to hold considerable power within the FRF. The compromise between the two sides showed in the contradictory nature of the Bill, which asserted that in the past Thailand's agriculture policy was decided solely by the state, yet farmers were excluded from the decision-making process. As a consequence, such a policy failed to solve farmers' problems. Because of that it was necessary to set up an organization free from state control to take care of farmers' welfare. On the other hand, the Bill assigned state officials power that enabled them to interfere in the FRF. Among the 41 members of the oversight committee, only 20 were farmers, the rest comprised of 12 bureaucrats, 6 private sector representatives, FRF secretary-general, vice-chairman (Agriculture and Cooperatives minister) and chairman (prime minister or deputy prime minister). In addition, the power of the state within the FRF was also enhanced by the provisional clause of the Bill, which authorized the Agriculture and Cooperatives ministry to oversee the set-up of the FRF (Terapon 2002: 16, 40–41).

Because they held such power, state officials tried to control the FRF from the beginning. However, their efforts were not so effective. To control the FRF it was necessary to marginalize the Assembly and its allies, such as the TFF and the Organic Farming Club of Thailand (OFCT), within the FRF. The most effective way to achieve that goal was to prevent them from representing farmers on the committee of the FRF. According to the Bill, during the provisional period (the first 120 days) the FRF was under the supervision of a contemporary committee, and farmer representatives within this committee were appointed by the Ministry of Agriculture and Cooperatives. However, the ministry chose to hold an election instead. Why? Because if it chose to appoint farmer representatives, the ministry had to choose from farmer groups participating in drafting the Bill, which meant that farmer representatives would dominate through the Assembly and its allies. On 8 July 1999, the deputy Agriculture and Cooperatives Minister Newin Chidchob, who was authorised by the Agriculture and Cooperatives Minister to oversee the FRF, issued an order to hold the election for farmer representatives in the contemporary committee of the FRF within 12 days. Moreover, the election had to be held in Bangkok and farmers had to register from 7 to 10 am on 19 July (Newin 1999). The order, in practice, would effectively undermine the competitiveness of the Assembly and its allies in the election, as it was very difficult for their members to go to Bangkok to cast their votes due to high travel costs. Even if they managed to travel to Bangkok it was still very doubtful whether all of them would be able to register within three hours. The time for campaigning was also too short, about two weeks, for any meaningful campaign. The difficulties would help the state-sponsored agriculture cooperatives to have an edge over the Assembly. However, Newin's plan did not materialize; it was opposed by the Assembly and its allies, and the election was held at the regional level instead. The Assembly sponsored one candidate and won a seat at the Khon Kaen constituency.

The conflict between the two sides intensified in 2000. The Assembly grew dissatisfied with Newin and the Ministry of Agriculture and Cooperatives on a numbers of issues. In May 2000, Newin made another move to control the FRF by sponsoring his friend Nathee Klibthong to become secretary-general of the FRF. Nevertheless, Newin did not plan to dominate the FRF only through the secretary-general, but he aimed at total control. He instructed Agriculture and Cooperatives' bureaucrats to mobilize the state-sponsored agriculture cooperatives in every province to compete with the Assembly and other farmer groups in order to win all seats in the elections for the committee and the provincial sub-committees of the FRF. Moreover, Newin tried to centralize the FRF by planning to transfer power from the provincial sub-committees to the secretary-general. The Assembly was also dissatisfied with the way the Ministry of Agriculture and Cooperatives handled the budget of the FRF. When the government allocated money to the FRF, the ministry did not transfer the budget to the FRF. As a result, it caused great difficulty to the works of the FRF. Apart from the financial issue, the Ministry of Agriculture and Cooperatives hindered the progress of the FRF by ordering the provincial Agriculture and Cooperatives offices, which temporarily oversaw FRF provincial offices, to hold back the meeting of FRF provincial sub-committees. Such a move almost paralysed the activities of the FRF (Nakon Sriwipat, interview, 5 October 2002). To counter such interference, the Assembly turned to street politics. In early August 2000, it organized some 3,000 farmers to stage a protest outside the Agriculture and Cooperatives ministry. It demanded that Newin and Nathee be dismissed as FRF vice-chairman and secretary-general, the Ministry of Agriculture and Cooperatives must not interfere in the FRF's affairs and the budget of the FRF had to be passed onto the FRF. In addition, the Assembly pressed for the drafting of the second Farmers' Rehabilitation Bill, which dealt with farmers' debt. After the Assembly rallied for one week, the government finally responded to all of its demands except the first (Nakon Sriwipat, interview, 5 October 2002). Newin's interference in the FRF was ended when Thaksin succeeded Chuan as the prime minister after the elections in January 2001 (see Chapter 1). Under the new government, Thaksin did not appoint Newin into the new cabinet, and Nathee resigned as secretary-general of the FRF to become the deputy minister of Agriculture and Cooperatives. In this period the site of protest of the Assembly moved away from Isan to Bangkok, because of the inefficiency of the march along the highway (see Chapter 6). In addition, the advantage of organizing protests in Bangkok increased in the later period when the Assembly was able to recruit farmers in the provinces in the Central plain and organize them to support the rally in Bangkok.

In order to enhance farmers' influence in the FRF, the Assembly also played an important role in drafting the regulations of the FRF. The success of the Assembly on this front happened partly by chance. When Nathee resigned, Trirat Soonthornprapat was made acting secretary-general in March 2001 (*Bangkok Post*, 1 March 2001). Trirat made a change in the seven-member executive committee by appointing Nakon Sriwipat, the Assembly's representative within the FRF, and his allies Asok Prasansorn from the TFF and Uthai Sornlaksap from the Federation of Rubber Planters of Thailand (FRPT) to the committee. The change enabled the Assembly and its allies to make progress in terms of passing new regulations, and training the sub-committee for the implementation of the FRF. The progress was interrupted by the appointment of a new secretary-general, Suriyan Boonnagkha, in August 2001. However, Suriyan was sacked a month later by the executive committee and Asok was appointed acting secretary-general. Asok's appointment showed the growing power of farmers within the FRF.

Although some successes came through work within the executive committee, political mobilization was still the most effective way to pursue the objectives of the Assembly. During 3–10 September 2001, the Assembly organized another protest outside the parliament, demanding the senate to pass the second Farmers' Rehabilitation Bill. The Bill, which dealt with debts that farmers owed to financial institutions, private lenders and debts caused by state projects, was drafted after the protest of the Assembly in August 2000. When the Bill was sent to the senate for approval, the sub-committee of the senate proposed that the Bill should cover only debts caused by state projects. The Assembly saw such revision as a move to 'kill' the Bill, and decided to organize farmers from Isan, the Central plain and the South against the revision. Isan farmers, the main force of the protest, mobilized outside the parliament in Bangkok, supported by farmers from the Central plain, who joined the rally and supplied food for the campaign. Farmers in the South organized protests in various provinces of the region to support the protest in Bangkok. The rally forced the senate to pass the Bill, though farmers' debts borrowed from private lenders were still omitted from the Bill (*Bangkok Post*, 11 September 2001). The protest marked a new stage of the struggle of the Assembly. From now on its campaign was not confined to the struggle of Isan farmers but the common effort of farmers from different regions of Thailand. The campaign for a new law was central to the struggle of the Assembly in this period. As mentioned above, the goal was to tackle farmers' economic problems systemically. According to Nakon, campaigning for a new law was crucial to that objective, because if the Assembly was able to press the government to pass a law that addressed farmers' economic problems at the policy level, it would significantly facilitate the struggle of the Assembly.

In late 2001 the conflict between the Assembly and the Agriculture and Cooperatives ministry intensified when the executive committee of the FRF, which was dominated by the Assembly and its allies, moved to enhance the independence of the FRF from the ministry. Under the provisional clause of the Farmers Rehabilitation Bill, the setting up of the FRF was under the supervision of the Ministry of Agriculture and Cooperatives. In the provinces, the ministry authorized the provincial Agriculture and Cooperatives offices to oversee the activities of the FRF. According to the Assembly, the ministry used that power to hinder the progress of the FRF. The ministry's officials in the provinces, for example, held back training that was necessary for farmers before they were able to register with the FRF, and refused to hold registration for farmers who wanted to join the FRF. To solve this problem, it was necessary to take the whole works of the FRF in the provinces out of the hands of the ministry. In November 2001 the executive committee of the FRF appointed new staff to replace the officials of the Ministry of Agriculture and Cooperatives as the heads of FRF provincial offices, to take charge of FRF activities in the provinces. The move faced resistance from the officials of the ministry. In many provinces, they refused to pass the work over to FRF staff. According to the Assembly, the ministry's officials wanted to hold on to power to control the FRF and also to spend the FRF budget lavishly and with 'unexplainable expenses' (ASSF 2001: 3).

In December 2001, the conflict between the two sides developed to a new stage after Asok resigned as acting secretary-general of the FRF. The reason behind this resignation is not clear. According to Nakon, Asok was forced to resign by the government (Nakon Sriwipat, interview, 5 October 2002). Asok was replaced by Samarn Lertwongrat, a staff member of the ruling party, Thai Rak Thai. His first move was to take power back to the Ministry of Agriculture and Cooperatives by sacking the heads of FRF provincial offices on the ground that they were wrongfully employed, and replaced them with officials from the provincial Agriculture and Cooperatives office. The Assembly reacted by organizing protests against such a move on 27 January 2002. It demanded that the head of FRF provincial offices had to be re-employed. Moreover, the organization also demanded that the government to implement the second Farmers Rehabilitation Bill by setting up a debt management office to tackle farmers' debt within 30 days. This time the Assembly combined the rally in Bangkok with the old tactic, the march along the highway. Although the Assembly organized protest by the same highway, it moved the rally site from Isan to the Central plain. The reason for such a change, as mentioned above, was that the main reserve force of the organization came from the provinces in the Central region. The Assembly mobilized its main forces in Nong Khae district, Sara Buri province, and dispatched some of its members to gather in front of the parliament in Bangkok. After rallying at Nong Khae for three days, farmers marched along the Friendship Highway towards Bangkok. On the same day, the government moved to defuse the protest by opening talks with the Assembly and its allies at Government House, and they reached a tentative agreement on 31 January. The government agreed to set up a debt management office within the FRF. In addition, it also agreed to set up a committee to investigate the employment heads of FRF provincial offices, and to make a decision within one week.

After the negotiation, the Assembly continued its protest to keep pressure on the government and called off its protest on 6 February after the committee decided that the heads of FRF provincial offices would be able to work until the end of May 2002 (ASSF 2002: 4–5). However, on 22 February 2002 the Agriculture and Cooperatives ministry made a u-turn on the issue by sacking all heads of FRF provincial offices (Chucheep 2002). Moreover, the government did not establish the debt management office, which it had promised to set up within 30 days. In April 2002, the Assembly decided to hold another protest in Bangkok. Although the organization raised the same issues as the previous protest, it gave priority to debt issues. It demanded a debt moratorium for farmers who registered with the FRF, because when the government failed to set up the debt management office those farmers were unable to transfer their debts to the FRF. The Assembly called off the protest when the government agreed on a debt moratorium (Nakon Sriwipat, interview, 5 October 2002). The protest was the last rally of the Assembly in the period that the FRF was run under the provisional clause. According to the Farmers Rehabilitation Bill, as mentioned above, the FRF would run under the provisional clause for only three months. Nevertheless, it took three years before elections for the 20 farmer representatives were held on 2 June 2002.

The elections were a crucial test for the Assembly. So far, the strength of the organization was shown only through street politics, but how strong it would be when the Assembly had to compete without political mobilization. The campaign of the Assembly shed some light on the debate on vote-buying in Thailand. The Assembly campaign in the election was different from those of political parties. As we saw in Chapter 1, to win elections, politicians spent large sums of money on vote-buying. In return, villagers supported them at the ballot box. In the case of the Assembly, the relationship between candidates and voters was the other way round. Farmers did not only vote for the Assembly, but also helped the organization to raise funds for the election campaign (field notes, 6 October 2002). This evidence proved that vote-buying can be avoided. Vote-buying, as Callahan has pointed out, 'is not natural or "culturally Thai", but has developed because of specific historical forces' (Callahan 2000: 134). However, voters supporting candidates without seeking rewards, such as money or material benefits was not new in Thailand. For example, in the 1970s, the socialist parties won wide support from Isan farmers because of the attractiveness of their policies (see Chapter 2).

The elections were very competitive. As mentioned above, any farmers' group that had at least 50 members could register with the FRF and could compete in the elections. There were 5.6 million farmers from 47,602 groups in 51 provinces eligible to compete for 7 seats in Isan, 5 seats in the North, 4 seats in the Central plains and 4 seats in the South. The Assembly's goal in the elections was to win the seats in every region. To achieve that goal, apart from relying on its supporters, the Assembly also tried to win over farmers from smaller groups that did not compete in the elections. Before the elections there was a rumour that the Thai Rak Thai Party planned to turn the FRF into its political base by preventing the Assembly and its allies from wining the elections (Somkiat 2002: 24, Nakon Sriwipat, interview, 5 October 2002). However, if that rumour was true, the Party's effort was somewhat inefficient, because the Assembly was still able to win more seats than other groups. It won 2 seats in Isan, 2 seats in the South, and 1 seat in the Central plain. Moreover, the Assembly was the only organization to win seats in more than one region. The result of the elections showed that the organization was not only capable in organizing political protests, but could also compete at the ballot box. Nevertheless, at the same time it indicated the complicated task for the Assembly. To pursue its goal, the Assembly had to be very good at building alliances with other farmers' groups, because the organization controlled only one-fourth of farmer representatives within the FRF. The elections were just the beginning of the new period of the Assembly's struggle within the FRF. More difficult tasks lay ahead.

SUMMARY

This chapter has looked at the struggle of the SSFAI in the 1999–2002 period, when the Assembly expanded rapidly from a regional organization into a national movement. In 2002, the Assembly operated in 43 provinces with 3 in the North, 18 in Isan, 17 in the Central plain and 5 in the South. The number of farmers who got involved in the activities of the Assembly reached a new high of some 300,000 with 200,000 in Isan, 50,000 in the Central Plain, 40,000 in the North and 10,000 in the South. What were the reasons behind the expansion of the Assembly? The expansion derived from the availability of new political opportunity, that is, the founding of the FRF, and the shift in priority of its work from campaigning for land rights to solving farmers' economic problem. The struggle of the Assembly in this period shed light on the relationship between a social movement and political opportunity. It showed a movement able to create new political opportunity for itself. However, to take advantage of political opportunity, a movement had to re-orient its strategy and goals.

During the 1999–2002 period, the Assembly adopted a new strategy, which was more complex than previous strategies. It comprised of three elements. The first was political mobilization. When the Assembly decided to concentrate its activities on solving farmers' economic problems through the FRF, it seems that the organization distanced itself from political struggle. However, in practice such a move drew the organization into a new kind of conflict with the government. As a result, political mobilization was needed for increasing its bargaining power. The second element was concerned with cooperation with state authorities. Since the Assembly tried to solve farmers' economic problems through the FRF, it was impossible to ignore state authorities. The last element of the new strategy involved using state resources for farmers' objectives. The new strategy of the Assembly highlighted the complex relationship between the state and civil society.

For the moment, it is too early to make a conclusive judgement on the new strategy. Here we can only draw some preliminary observations. The positive element of the new strategy was that it opened up new opportunities for the Assembly to recruit new supporters. The numbers of farmers recruited far exceeded those of other periods in the history of the Assembly. Another positive element of the new strategy derived from the combination of political mobilization and cooperation with state authorities. Although under the new strategy the main activities of the Assembly were centered around the FRF, the organization did not confine its activities only to cooperation with state authorities. When necessary the Assembly resorted to political mobilization to enhance its bargaining power. In so doing, the organization was able to maintain its political autonomy against the state. However, the new strategy also contained a negative element. Its success depended on the domination of the Assembly over the FRF. To attain such a position was not easy because about half of the committee of the FRF was government officials. Moreover, although farmers' representatives formed another half of the committee, if the Assembly failed to win over farmers' representatives from other groups, its position against the state would be weakened. And in this case, it would open the way for the state to marginalize the Assembly within the FRF. In sum, while the new strategy of the Assembly offered a new channel for the organization to strengthen its struggle, it contained the seed of failure.

CHAPTER 8

Conclusion

This book has sought to examine the struggle of an important grassroots organization, the SSFAI, informed by the conceptual advances of civil society, social movements and class theory. At the same time it has also sought to test and verify this body of theory. The usefulness of the theory of civil society is derived from its general hypothesis about the importance of associational life for democratization, that is, the capacity for self-organization independent of the state. If there are no independent social organizations, there are no channels to resist dictatorial rule and deepen democracy. This thesis employs the idea of civil society as an umbrella concept complemented by the concepts of social movement and class agency. The two concepts provide insights into the role of collective action and class on democratization. This final chapter attempts to situate the findings of the empirical study within a wider perspective on the following themes: the relationship between civil society, class and democracy, the nature of Thai civil society, the strategy and tactics of the struggle for the right to have rights and the organizational structure of the struggle for the right to have rights.

CIVIL SOCIETY, CLASS AND DEMOCRACY

This section evaluates the claims concerning positive relationships between civil society, class and democracy reviewed in Chapter 1. Civil society theorists point out the crucial role of civil society on democracy, and Rueschemeyer et al. (Rueschemeyer et al. 1996: 49) contend that democracy may be pushed forward by the underprivileged classes, and that the underprivileged classes can strengthen their democratic struggle by organizing themselves autonomously within civil society. Evidence found during this study supported this claim, albeit with reservations. The strong point of civil society theory lies in its emphasis on the importance of associational life for democratization. As has been shown in the present book, civil society became an important channel for the underprivileged classes who were excluded from meaningful participation in electoral politics to organize themselves to defend their basic rights, and to further their campaigns for democratic deepening. Without social space, which enabled them to act independently, it would have been impossible for the sub-ordinated classes to protect themselves from state arbitrariness. However, civil society theory lacked sophistication in analysing the complex inter-relationship between state and society. It emphasized only the role of civil society in counter-balancing state power, but did not pay enough attention to the way in which the state sought to influence civil society. The state was not always 'rolled back' by civil society, but could also find ways to marginalize or co-opt civil society organizations. The outcome of state-civil society contestation is uncertain, since it depends largely on the relative strength of the two sides.

As shown in Chapters 3 and 4, there were moments when civil society organizations were able to force the state to comply to their demands; yet in other circumstances the state could influence, or even co-opt civil society (Chapter 5). Although the co-optation of civil society by the state was the result of the cooperation between state and civil society, it does not mean that co-optation is an inevitable result of cooperation. As we saw in Chapter 7, civil society organizations were still able to maintain their autonomy although they worked within the organization set up by the state. Those outcomes were evidence of the complex relationships between civil society and the state. Generally, the outcome of state–civil society contestation is a combination of success and failure. The two sides gain strength and make concessions in the process of contestation. The achievements and limitations of the SSFAI during the radical period illustrate this point (Chapter 4).

Regarding class–democracy relationships, to claim that the under-privileged classes play a major role in the process of democratization runs counter to most other research on Thai politics. The underprivileged classes, especially the rural poor, have been singled out as the political base of corrupt politicians (Anek 1995). It is true that farmers undermined the progress of democracy by supporting corrupt politicians in exchange for money and other rewards (see Callahan and McCargo 1996: 376–392). However, this is only half of the story. The most significant role of the subordinated classes in the democratization process took place in another area, the struggle for citizenship rights. As argued in Chapter 1, Thai electoral politics is a form of minimal democracy in which democracy simply means elections. The struggle for the right to participate in the decision-making process, the right to compensation, and demands for community rights and the democrati-zation of agro-industry by the SSFAI (Chapters 4 and 6) are examples of the role of the subordinated classes in democratic deepening. On these issues, the SSFAI pushed democracy beyond electoralism. The struggle to deepen democracy of the underprivileged classes is a form of 'strong democracy' (Barber 1984), which aims at intensifying popular sovereignty through increasing popular direct participation in the decision-making process, which in effect would help transform a political system 'from hierarchical forms of elitist or bureaucratic control to forms of popular self-determination' (Roberts 1998: 30). It is important to understand that the significance of this struggle for democratization does not lie in the success of its demands, but in raising issues concerning citizenship rights, which are crucial to democracy, and turning them into public issues to prevent the state from ignoring them.

THE NATURE OF THAI CIVIL SOCIETY

Based on an examination of the struggle of the SSFAI in the previous chapters, this section tries to assess the nature of Thai civil society through the liberal-critical debate discussed in Chapter 1. In this debate, both perspectives agreed that civil society is a social sphere that exists independently from the state. The difference between them was centred around the role of market economy, or 'economic society' in Cohen and Arato's usage (Cohen and Arato 1997: ix). The liberal perspective regards the market economy as an indispensable component of civil society, while the critical perspective excludes 'economic society' from civil society. However, this debate was not only based on two different political perspectives, but also on two different models of democratization. For the liberal model, the key to democratization was the development of a market economy (see, for example, Perez-Dias 1993), while the critical paradigm emphasized the importance of grassroots social movements (see e.g. Cohen and Arato 1997). Which paradigm applies best to Thai civil society? Evidence from the present book supports the critical paradigm. It shows that the efforts of the liberal perspective to include 'economic society' in civil society ignored the role of the actors of 'economic society' in state institutions and the close relationship between the business sector and the state; at the same time it confirms the important role of social movements in democratic deepening. As has been shown in Chapter 1, economic growth in the last three decades in Thailand led to the domination of business people in Thai electoral politics while it excluded the popular masses from meaningful political participation. This domination led to the merger of economic and political power; business people, the actors of economic society, acted at the same time as the actors of political society. They controlled the key institutions of the state, such as parliament and government. The domination of business people in Thai electoral politics also led to close cooperation between the state and the economic sector, which naturally led to pro-business policies by the government. In many cases, the government's policies aimed at promoting capitalist development violated the basic rights of the population and led to conflict between state–business partnership and grassroots social organizations, such as in the case of the *Kho Jo Ko* and the quadripartite agricultural projects (see Chapters 3 and 4). To protect themselves from the intrusions of the state–business coalition, civil society organizations campaigned for democratic rights, such as the right to participation in decision-making, and community rights. However, the critical paradigm of civil society, although useful, provides only the big picture of the relationship between the main components of society. It is unable to explain the success or failure of the struggle of individual civil society organizations, which are many and complex in nature. There are undoubtedly a variety of conditions that influence the outcome of the struggle of civil society organizations. Based on the experience of the SSFAI and the AOP, the next section analyses the factors that are critical to the success or failure of this struggle, that is, the strategy and tactics of civil society organizations.

THE STRATEGY AND TACTIC OF THE STRUGGLE FOR THE RIGHT TO HAVE RIGHTS

In their review on the research on the consequences of social movements, Giugni et al. pointed out that the prevailing themes in the research is 'whether disruptive tactics are more likely to have an impact or, on the contrary, whether moderate actions are more effective' (Giugni et al. 1999: xvi). According to Giugni et al., the responses from movement scholars were divided into two groups. The first group confirmed the positive impact of disruptive tactics on movements' goals. For them, 'disruption is the most powerful resource that movements have at their disposal to reach their goals', because 'they lack the institutional resources processed by other actors, such as political parties and interest groups'. The second group believed that moderation in politics was more effective than confrontation. Only under specific circumstances and conditions did confrontation lead to success (Giugni et al. 1999: xvii). The differences between the two sides 'might be more apparent than real'. Because 'the effectiveness of disruptive tactics and violence is likely to vary according to circumstance under which they are adopted by social movements' (Giugni et al. 1999: xviii).

The debate discussed above is also central to the struggle of social movements in Thailand. We have devoted considerable attention to this issue in the preceding pages. Based on the experience of the SSFAI and other grassroots movements, we can conclude that political mobilizations are crucial to the struggle of social movements. Only through political mobilizations can movements build their bargaining powers and force the state to recognize them as political forces unable to be ignored (Chapters 3, 4 and 5). However, it is very difficult, if not impossible, for the struggle for the right to have rights of social movements to avoid negotiation with the state. As shown in the previous chapters, while it challenges traditional forms of representation by offering grassroots movements as an alternative to representative democracy, the struggle for the right to have rights does not seek a total transformation of the existing political system. Instead, it searches for changes within the framework of the existing political system. As a consequence, the objectives of the movements have to be realized through state concessions. Therefore, although mobilizations help enhance the bargaining power of organizations, they need to be supplemented by negotiation. In sum, protest (disruption) and negotiation (moderation) are integral components of the same strategy, and cannot be separated from each other. From this perspective, we believe that the usefulness of the two tactics depends on the context in which movements operate. If they want to be successful, it is very important for movements to set out the proper relationship between protest and negotiation. It is not right to determine in advance that protest or negotiation is the effective means of dealing with the state.

Unquestionably, political mobilization is the main 'weapon' of grassroots movements in establishing their bargaining power. Without the ability to mobilize strong mass protests, the negotiations of grassroots movements with the state would achieve nothing. However, movements cannot rely only on protests all the time. In certain circumstances, negotiations are required for the struggle of movements. Negotiations are necessary in a number of contexts, for example, when movements need breathing space because they are exhausted, or preoccupied with internal problems, when negotiations might help resist counter-moves by the state, and when movements move forward to pursue further progress after successful protests. If negotiation is necessary for the success of the struggle for the right to have rights, movements face the question of how to maintain their autonomy while dealing with the state and politicians. In other words, how do the movements handle 'the complex interplay of ideological autonomy and political pragmatism, resistance and accommodation, protest and negotiation' (Alvarez and Escobar 1992: 323)? To engage in negotiations with the state, civil society organizations move into a dangerous zone, because such organizations can no longer be politically effective when they have been drawn into 'normal' political channels (Foweraker 1995: 64). Moreover, negotiations open the door for co-optation by the state, which could result in the disintegration of organizations. To avoid co-optation, as Stedile, a leader of the Landless Rural Workers' Movement (MST) has pointed out, when engaging in negotiations with the state, it is important to keep in mind that: 'It is necessary to negotiate but never at the price of demobilizing the movement. Otherwise you have nothing to negotiate in the future' (Meszaros 2000: 10). In other words, the danger of co-optation by the state, which derives from the political nature of the struggle for the right to have rights, has to be overcome not by avoiding negotiations with the state, but by negotiating from a position of strength.

THE ORGANIZATIONAL STRUCTURE OF THE STRUGGLE FOR THE RIGHT TO HAVE RIGHTS

Another important debate concerning the struggle of social movements centred on the effects of organizational structures on goals and activities. As we saw in Chapter 4, the Resource Mobilization theory argued for a centralized form of organization. For them, formal Social Movement Organizations were vital to the success of movements. Such a view was contrary to those of Castells and Touraine, who believed that organization and formal leadership structures may lead to the disintegration of movements (Foweraker 1995: 70). In Chapter 5 we examined this issue by comparing the centralized form of organization of the SSFAI with the decentralized structure of the AOP. The SSFAI decided to replace a decentralized form of organization with a more centralized one because the organization wanted to improve its efficiency. The implementation of a centralized organization of the SSFAI, although it helped to enhance the performance of the organization, generated dependency among members and led to conflict among leaders. The AOP tried to overcome the problems that arose from a centralized form of organization by implementing a decentralized network. This measure appeared successful in preventing split and increasing participation within the network. However, it weakened the group because of lack of unity. From this evidence, it is clear that movements need both centralized and decentralized elements to enhance their efficiency and internal democracy. The problem is how to find the balance between these two opposite tendencies. Efforts to solve this problem by concentrating only on structural issues are insufficient and misleading. The structure of an organization undoubtedly has significant impacts on its performances and its internal democracy. However, it is not sufficient in itself. Structures need support from strong political integrity, which derives from high political consciousness on the part of an organization's members. Efforts to balance efficiency and participation without taking political consciousness into account are more likely to fail. The experience of the SSFAI illustrated this point clearly. As shown in Chapter 4, after the first split the SSFAI tried to overcome the concentration of power in the hands of leaders, especially the secretary general, by implementing a collective leadership system. Although in the new system the power of members compared to leaders at all levels was supposed to increase, in practice only a small degree of change occurred. Large numbers of members were not active in exercising their power to control leaders. As a result, when rules of the organization were violated by leaders, they did not make strong protests, or they simply ignored the abuses. One lesson from this example is that proper relationships between efficiency and participation are more likely to be achieved only when movements can strike the right balance between structure and consciousness.

Epilogue

This study originally ended in 2002, that is, shortly after the landslide electoral victory of Thaksin Shinawatra's Thai Rak Thai (TRT) Party in January 2001. One of the most important impacts of SSFA's activities on the grassroots movements in Thailand after 2002 was that they helped to expand political opportunities for other farmer groups. They stimulated farmers to form new organizations to rally on issues raised by the SSFA. Prominence among these new groups was the Network of Indebted Farmers of Thailand (NIFT). The NIFT operated in 21 provinces of Thailand with some 100,000 members (Fa Diew Kan, 2004: 138).

While the creation of new farmer organizations helped to strengthen the bargaining power of small farmers, opposition from the new TRT government soon began to be felt. Indeed, the entire the relationship between civil society and the state in Thailand entered a new period with the Thaksin government adopting a hostile policy towards grassroots social movements. The roots of this situation lie in Thaksin's past and the way in which he came to power.

Thaksin Shinawatra, a billionaire tycoon, was the owner of a communications conglomerate Shin Corporation. Throughout the late 1980s and 1990s, Thaksin made much of his fortune through various computer and telecommunications ventures. His major successes were based on government concessions. Such concessions, according to Simpson, 'were all monopolies or oligopolies protected by government power and were therefore extremely lucrative' (Simpson, 2005: 1).

Thaksin started his political career in 1994 when he was appointed foreign minister under the cabinet quota of the Palang Dharma Party (PDP). After Chuan Leekpai dissolved the parliament in May 1995, Thaksin assumed the leadership of the PDP. He later became a deputy prime minister under the premiership of Banharn Silpa-archa. In the November 1996 election, the PDP under Thaksin leadership won only one seat in parliament. As a result, Thaksin left the party (McCargo and Ukrit, 2005: 8–10) and spent the following months searching for a new political paradigm. In July 1998 he founded the Thai Rak Thai Party (Pasuk and Baker, 2004: 63–64). TRT was a party of the capitalist class. Most of its leaders were leading Bangkok businessmen from various sectors: telecommunications, banking, real estate, petrochemicals/steel, and entertainments (McCargo and Ukrit, 2005: 219–224). This is an exceptional phenomenon in Thai politics. According to Pasuk and Baker, 'There had not been such a concentration of leading Bangkok businessmen involved directly and openly in party politics (and later in the Cabinet) since the early 1980s' (Pasuk and Baker, 2004: 71). It should be noted that TRT leaders were not solely composed of leading Bangkok businessmen; they also included some provincial political godfathers (Pasuk and Baker, 2004: 71).

Although TRT was a party of big businessmen, its success was based on populist policies that had a strong appeal to the poor. However, such policies in a sense were opportunist in nature. Initially, Thaksin did not have a rural policy; his early campaign focused on city dwellers (Pasuk and Baker, 2004: 81). In mid-1998 – about the time that Thaksin launched TRT – the rural protests described earlier in this volume gained some momentum. Farmers demanded that the government must help them by declaring a moratorium on farmers' debts (see Chapter 6). Various kinds of rural protests – concerning land rights, rural debt and agricultural prices, for instance – occurred throughout 1998 and reached a peak in early 1999. Thaksin tried to capitalize on the situation by consulting with both farmers' leaders and NGO activists. In early 2000, Thaksin announced his first populist policy: a moratorium on rural debts. Later, in August, he added other two populist policies into TRT's programme: a revolving fund of one million baht for every village, and a 30-baht-per-visit scheme of health care (Pasuk and Baker, 2004: 81).

Apart from such populist policies, Thaksin tried to win over farmers by portraying himself as someone who sympathized with their cause. As it has been shown in the previous chapters, the Democrat government had adopted a hostile stance towards farmers' movements. In the 2001 elections, the movements planned to revenge themselves against the Democrats at the polls. Thaksin moved to take advantage of the situation by adopting a progressive rhetoric and echoing the movements' demands. He also organized a meeting with the leaders of the AOP and promised them a sympathetic government response to their demands if TRT won the election. His move proved successful when NGO leaders and AOP advisors publicly supported him (Pasuk and Baker, 2004: 82; Simpson, 2005: 8).

However, it would be wrong if we believed that Thaksin relied solely on his populist policies. To compete with other political parties, throughout the election campaign TRT also adopted the common practice of vote buying (Simpson, 2005: 8). This combination of populist policies and money politics resulted in a landslide victory for TRT in the 2001 elections (see Chapter 1).

The party's victory, as Pasuk and Baker had pointed out, 'was a logical extension' of money politics. However, it was not just the continuity of such politics, 'but also a dramatic change of scale'. Thaksin's victory 'superseded "money politics" with "big money politics"' (Pasuk and Baker, 2004: 97). Equally important was that the victory of Thaksin signalled the defeat of the reformist spirit that had helped shape the 1997 constitution. The underlying themes of the reforms were the separation of money from politics, strengthening of civil society and enhancing popular participation in politics; helping good and competent people to participate in the political process; and the creation of new institutions and rules to control political actors and prevent abuses of power. But Thaksin believed in an opposite set of ideas. As McCargo and Ukrist point out, Thaksin believed that:

> Wealthy entrepreneurs, the most successful element of Thai society, should play the leading role in running the country. Other actors in the political process should be subordinated to a 'vision', an overall business plan devised by a CEO leadership. Popular participation was limited to a 'consumption' mode: voters and citizens would be the end users of products developed by a technocratic and entrepreneurial elite. Dynamic leadership should not be hemmed in by institutions or regulations, which should be subordinated to the will of the executive (McCargo and Ukrit, 2005: 14).

On his first day as prime minister, Thaksin had lunch with leaders among the crowd of AOP members who rallied in the front of Government House; he promised to solve their problems. The main demand of the AOP was that the sluice gates of the Pak Moon Dam should be permanently opened (this dam is discussed in detail in Chapter 3). Thaksin responded by ordered a temporary opening of the sluice gates of the dam. According to Simpson, 'Thaksin's action created optimism that this was indeed a different type of politician with a new, accommodating approach towards activists' (Simpson, 2005: 8). However, as Pasuk and Baker have pointed out, Thaksin's sympathy for farmer protest was 'entirely tactical. His real agenda … was to suppress rural protest and the organizations behind them' (Pasuk and Baker 2004: 144). It was believed that Thaksin's apparent sympathy was partly designed to engender support during his upcoming court case (Simpson, 2005: 9). A month before the 2001 election, Thaksin was accused by the National Counter Corruption Commission of failing to properly declare his assets at the time back in 1997 when he served as deputy prime minister in the Chavalit government. If found guilty, he faced a five-year ban from politics. However, in August 2001 he was cleared of the charge (McCargo and Ukrist 2005: 15–16).

After the trial, according to Pasuk and Baker, 'Thaksin found himself in a more powerful position than any previous elected Thai premier' (Pasuk and Baker 2004: 94). There were a variety of factors that contributed to the consolidation of Thaksin's political power. Apart from a landslide victory in the 2001 elections, which his party had won just short of an absolute majority (see Chapter 1), there were other factors contributing to Thaksin's ascendancy. First was the new 1997 constitution, which enhanced the prime minister's position by requiring agreement of 40 per cent of MPs before a no-confidence vote could be initiated against him. The second factor was Thaksin's personal popularity (Pasuk and Baker 2004: 94–95). He was viewed as one of the very few people who understood the complexity of Thailand's problems (McCargo and Ukrist 2005: 15). The economic recovery also helped to strengthen his legitimacy. In 1997, Thailand experienced a severe economic crisis. The long boom of the 1987–96 suddenly come to an end (Hewison 1999: 22). In 1998, the country's GDP shrank 11 per cent (Pasuk and Baker 2004: 15, 16). However, three years after Thaksin came to power, Thailand's economic growth had reached 6.9 percent (www.bangkokpost.net). Another factor that contributed to Thaksin's ascendancy were his populist policies (McCargo and Ukrist 2005: 89). The combinations of factors mentioned above helped to turn Thaksin into a very popular and powerful prime minister.

Once his political power was strengthened, Thaksin gradually changed his policy towards the popular movements. He branded NGOs as people working for foreign organizations to undermine Thailand's economic development (Chang Noi, 2003). In early 2002, the government tried to discredit NGOs by linking them to organized crime through a dubious asset investigation undertaken by the Anti-Money Laundering Office. In addition, Thaksin did not honour the promises he made with the AOP. When the movement organized a series of protests across the country to put pressure on the government, he responded by passing a resolution authorizing the use of force to suppress any protest that violated the law (Simpson, 2005: 10). Violence against grassroots protests began occurring more frequently. On 5 December 2002 a protest site of Pak Moon Dam villagers near Government House was raided and vandalized. Ten days later, about 40 hooded men raided the village of Pak Moon Dam protesters near the dam in Ubon Ratchathani and destroyed more than 250 shelters (The Nation, 16 December 2002). Thaksin responded to the violence by suggesting that the incident was a ploy because the media learned about the attack before it broke out (The Nation, 17 December 2002). Later the officials dismantled the protesters' site in Bangkok and forced them to return home. The actions were taken after Thaksin had decided to ignore protesters' demand in favor of the electricity authority that operated the dam (Pasuk and Baker, 2004: 146).

Another case that helps to illustrate the authoritarian nature of Thaksin's policy towards social movements was the protest against the Trans Thai-Malaysian gas pipeline project. In 1994 the Petroleum Authority of Thailand and Petronas of Malaysia signed an agreement for an offshore natural gas pipeline and gas separation plant at Jana district in the southern Thai province of Songkla. Since the late 1990s local villagers have protested against the project because they believed it would adversely affect their traditional way of life and pollute the Gulf of Thailand (Amnesty International, 2003: 10). In October 2000 anti-pipeline protesters clashed with police resulting in 28 injured during a public hearing at the Hat Yai stadium (Albritton and Thawilwadee, 2003: 12). More serious violence against anti-pipeline protesters occurred in December 2002, when the protesters tried to hand over a petition to Thaksin who was attending a joint cabinet meeting of Thai and Malaysian officials in Hat Yai. A peaceful demonstration turned violent when police tried to disperse the demonstrators. Thirty-eight demonstrators and 15 policemen were injured, and 12 NGOs activists were arrested as a result of the clash (Simpson, 2005: 21). The National Human Rights Commission, which investigated the incident, concluded that 'the use of force by police officers failed to provide reasonable evidence to proof the protesters' attempt to force their way through in order to cause troubles' (sic). As a result, 'the dispersal of the peaceful and unarmed assembly is considered disproportionate, exceeding to the minimum extent necessary and unjust' (sic) (NHRC, 2005: 17). While the Commission and the Senate blamed the violence on the interior minister and police, Thaksin condemned the protesters as anarchists who had evil intentions (Pasuk and Baker 2004: 146-147; Supara 2003). He accused demonstrators as promoting violence and as dishonest recipients of foreign funding. As Simpson points out, Thaksin's verbal attacks on the integrity of protesters were part of his tactic employed to undermine public support for their cause (Simpson 2005: 21).

Apart from the cases discussed above, there were numbers of harassments against social activists. Between 2001 and 2005 at least 17 community leaders, community rights activists and environmentalists were killed by non-uniformed assassins. More interesting, in most of the cases the victim was opposing a development project on social and environmental grounds or attempting to protect a public environmental area from encroaching private interests (Simpson 2005: 15). In January 2001 an environmentalist who organized protests against the destruction of mangrove forests for prawn farming was killed in Phuket. Four months later, a leader of the Environment Conservation Student's Club at Ramkhamhaeng University was shot dead for leading the villagers against a rock-grinding plant owned by a national-level politician in a forest reserve in Phitsanulok. In July of that year a leader of the Environmental Conservation Group of the Kratae river basin in Surat Thani was murdered after he resisted the building of a dam. Four community leaders, who opposed illegal logging, the construction of local water treatment facility, mineral separation plant and rock quarry, were killed in late 2002. On 21 June 2004 Charoen Wat-akson, a prominent environmentalist who led the Love Bo Nok Group against construction of two coal-fired power plants in Prachuap Khiri Khan for nearly a decade, was murdered by gunmen. Charoen was gunned down on his way home after testifying to a parliamentary committee against influential figures involved in community land grabs. He told senators how local officials were trying to issue title deeds covering 53 rai of public land in Bo Nok to a local powerful person (Asian Center for Human Rights 2004).

The killing of Charoen highlights a systemic killing of grassroots activists since the Thaksin government came to power. However, Charoen was not the last conservationist to become a victim of violence. A year later, a Buddhist conservationist monk Phra Supoj Suwachano was stabbed to death in Chiang Mai. It was believed that the motives for the murder were his conservation of 700 rai of forestland that was wanted by an influential figure and his discovery of illegal logging (Chiangmai Mail 2005). It should be noted that although the murders in almost every case indicated some form of collusion between local authorities and capital interests, the authorities tended to treat the murders as normal crimes, and their motive portrayed by police as due to personal conflict (Simpson 2005: 15; NHRC 2005: 14). Here, international human rights groups have expressed concern, with Amnesty International observing that 'the Thai government … is not providing adequate protection to the protesters, nor does it appear to be initiating proper investigations into the abuses they have suffered' (Amnesty International 2003: 10). According to Hina Jilani, the United Nations Special Envoy for Human Rights, social activists who struggled for socio-economic and cultural rights have been "killed, attacked, sent death threats, intimidated, placed under surveillance, arrested and detained by the police, and had civil and criminal court cases filed against them by both private actors and the State" (cited in Asian Center for Human Rights 2004). Such systemic violence against social activists led Jilani to describe the situation facing Thai civil society as one encouraging a climate of fear (Simpson 2005: 22).

To date, the most violent action against grassroots protests under the Thaksin government occurred in the southern border province of Narathiwat. In October 2004, thousands of villagers rallied in front of Tak Bai police station to protest against the arrest of six villagers. The military opened fire on the demonstrators, which resulted in 6 deaths, 11 wounded and more than 1,300 arrested. The arrested protesters were then forced, bound and in some cases gagged, into trucks. They were stacked four or five deep on top of one another. As a result, 78 of them died on military trucks while they were transported to military camps. Of the survivors, 300 of them would face criminal charges (Roberts 2004; Chaiwat 2004: 7). The hasty and reckless manner of the transfer of protesters was severely criticized by the editorial of the Nation: 'It is not an exaggeration to say that cattle being delivered to the slaughterhouse are provided better conditions and more humane treatment' (cited in Robert 2004). The investigation of the National Human Rights Commission founded that the military was guilty of violent breaches of human rights. They mistreated the demonstrators when they dispersed the protest and failed to exercise enough restraint in firing live ammunition into the protesters (BBC News, 2004). Thaksin responded to the criticism by ordering the military to intensify its campaign (Robert 2004).

In addition to its use of physical means, the Thaksin government adopted strong legal methods to control grassroots political activities. An anti-terrorist law was implemented by executive decree in August 2003. Under the new law, terrorism was defined broadly enough to cover most dissent (Pasuk and Baker 2004: 148–149). Because of these and other essentially anti-democratic responses to opposition, Thaksin's rule has been dubbed as 'democratic authoritarianism' and 'elected capitalist absolutism' (Chaiwat 2004: 9-10).

Thaksin's offensive against them has forced grassroots social movements to rethink their strategies and tactics. In early 2005 the leaders of various movements, including the SSFA, organized a series of meetings to find a way to counter this offensive. Several groups previously in conflict with each other (see the previous chapters) agreed to settle their differences and work together, but apart from that no other solution was reached. On the question of strategies and tactics, some groups proposed that the movements should set up a political party to voice their demands through political institutions. However, the idea to set up a party was rejected by the majority of social activists. Yet the question remains, if the route of parliamentary politics is to be rejected, what is the alternative to it?

For the SSFA, extra-parliamentary politics is still the most important channel to pursue their popular demands. Nevertheless, since differences are so great between the social movements in terms of strategies and tactics, it is necessary for them to set up a forum to exchange ideas. Debate within such a forum would help to reduce differences, which in return would help to build unity among the movements (Yang Wongkraso, interview, 10 August 2005). Even if unity among the movements were obtained, their campaign against the Thaksin government would still be complicated. This is because Thaksin's anti-movement policy has been designed by former activists who know the movements very well. To make effective countermoves, social movements will have to make thoroughgoing changes in their existing strategies and tactics.

Bibliography

PRIMARY SOURCES

Newspapers

Bangkok Post
Daily News (เดลินิวส์)
Kao Sod (ข่าวสด)
Krungthep Thurakit (กรุงเทพธุรกิจ)
The Nation
Matichon (มติชน)
Phujatkan (ผู้จัดการ)
Siam Rath (สยามรัฐ)
Thai Rath (ไทยรัฐ)
Thankanmuang (ฐานการเมือง)

Documents in Thai

'Action Plan' (nd), (Unpublished typescript). ('แผนปฏิบัติงาน' (ม.ป.ป.), เอกสารโรเนียว).

Assembly of Small Scale Farmers (2001) 'The Annual Report of the Assembly of Small Scale Farmers', (Unpublished typescript). (สมัชชาเกษตรกรรายย่อย (2544), 'สรุปการดำเนินงานสมัชชาเกษตรกรรายย่อย ประจำปี 2544', เอกสารโรเนียว).

Bamrung Kayotha (1994) Letter to Mongkhon Danthanin, 1 June. (บำรุง คะโยธา (2537) จดหมายถึงมงคล ด่านธานินทร์, 1 มิถุนายน).

Bamrung Kayotha, Verapon Sopa and Somkiat Pongpaiboon (1994) 'The Route of Thai Farmers', (Unpublished typescript). (บำรุง คะโยธา, วีรพล โสภา,และสมเกียรติ พงษ์ไพบูลย์ (2537), 'เส้นทางชาวนาไทย', เอกสารโรเนียว).

Cassava Farmers' Group (nd) 'Cassava' (Unpublished typescript). (ชมรมผู้ปลูก 1 (ม.ป.ป.), 'มันสำปะหลัง', เอกสารโรเนียว).

Chucheep Hansawat (2002) 'Order of the Ministry of Agriculture and Cooperatives, no. 110/2002', 22 February. (ชูชีพ หาญสวัสดิ์ (2545), 'คำสั่งกระทรวงเกษตรและสหกรณ์ ที่ 110/2545', 22 กุมภาพันธ์).

'Committee to Support the Formation of a Farmers' Group in Isan' (nd), (Unpublished typescript). ('คณะกรรมการสนับสนุนการรวมตัวของชาวนาในอีสาน' (ม.ป.ป.), เอกสารโรเนียว).

Executive Committee of the Small Scale Farmers' Assembly of Isan (1996) 'The Declaration of the SSFAI', (Unpublished typescript). (คณะกรรมการบริหารสมัชชา เกษตรกรรายย่อยภาคอีสาน (2536), 'คำประกาศสมัชชาเกษตรกรรายย่อยภาคอีสาน', เอกสารโรเนียว).

Farmers Rehabilitation Fund (nd) *The Farmers Rehabilitation Fund.* (np). (กองทุนฟื้นฟูและพัฒนาเกษตรกร (ม.ป.ป.), *กองทุนฟื้นฟูและพัฒนาเกษตรกร*, (ม.ป.ท.)).

'Meeting of Joint Committee between Government Representatives and the SSFAI (supplement 3)'. (1997), (Unpublished typescript). ('การประชุมคณะกรรมการร่วมระหว่างผู้แทนรัฐบาลและ สมัชชาเกษตรกรรายย่อยภาคอีสาน' (เอกสารประกอบ 3) (2540).

'Minutes of the National Committee on Farmers' Debt Management' (1994) (Unpublished typescript). ('บันทึกการประชุมคณะกรรมการจัดการปัญหาหนี้สินเกษตรกร แห่งชาติ' (2537), เอกสารโรเนียว).

Nakon Sriwipat (1995) 'Report on the Meeting of the Central Committee of the SSFAI', 7 November, (Unpublished typescript). (นคร ศรีวิพัฒน์ (2538), 'รายงานการประชุมคณะกรรมการกลาง สกย.อ.', 7 พฤศจิกายน 2538).

—— (1996a) 'Ideas for the Improvement of the SSFAI', Unpublished document submitted to the Central Committee of the SSFAI on 20 January. (นคร ศรีวิพัฒน์ (2539a), 'แนวคิดการปรับปรุงองค์กรสกย.อ.', เอกสารเสนอต่อคณะกรรมการกลางสกย.อ., 20 มกราคม).

—— (1996b) 'Report on the Meeting of the SSFAI Central Committee', 7 April. (Unpublished typescript). (นคร ศรีวิพัฒน์ (2539b), 'รายงานการประชุมคณะกรรมการกล างสกย.อ.', 7 เมษายน).

—— (1996c) 'The Debt Problem of Farmers', (Unpublished typescript). (นคร ศรีวิพัฒน์ (2539c), 'ปัญหาหนี้สินเกษตรกร', เอกสารโรเนียว).

—— (1997) Letter submitted to Agriculture and Cooperative Minister, 25 August. (นคร ศรีวิพัฒน์ (2540), จดหมายนเสนอต่อรัฐมนตรีว่าการกระทรวงเกษตรและสหกรณ์, 25 สิงหาคม).

—— (1998a) 'The Modern State', (Unpublished typescript). (นคร ศรีวิพัฒน์ (2541a), 'รัฐสมัยใหม่', เอกสารโรเนียว).

—— (1998b) 'The Rehabilitation of Small Scale Farmers', (Unpublished typescript). (นคร ศรีวิพัฒน์ (2541b), 'การฟื้นฟูชีวิตเกษตรกรรายย่อย', เอกสารโรเนียว).

Newin Chidchob (1999) 'The Announcement of the Ministry of Agriculture and

Cooperatives', 8 July. (เนวิน ชิดชอบ. (2542), 'ประกาศกระทรวงเกษตรและสหกรณ์', 8 กรกฎาคม).

Readjustment of Farming Structure and Production Office (1994) *The Readjustment of Farming Structure and Production Programme.* Bangkok: Agricultural Extension Department. (สำนักงานปรับโครงสร้างและระบบการผลิตการเกษตร (2537), โครงการปรับโครงสร้างและระบบการผลิตการเกษตร, กรุงเทพ: กรมส่งเสริมการเกษตร).

Small Scale Farmers' Assembly of Isan (1994a) 'The Small Scale Farmers'Assembly of Isan', (Unpublished typescript). (สมัชชาเกษตรกรรายย่อยภาคอีสาน (2537a), 'สมัชชาเกษตรกรรายย่อยภาคอีสาน', เอกสารโรเนียว).

—— (1994b) 'What is the Small Scale Farmers' Assembly of Isan?', (Unpublished typescript). (สมัชชาเกษตรกรรายย่อยภาคอีสาน (2537b), 'สมัชชาเกษตรกรรายย่อยภาคอีสานคืออะไร?', เอกสารโรเนียว).

—— (1994c) 'Meeting of the Central Committee of the SSFAI', 26 November, (Unpublished typescript). (สมัชชาเกษตรกรรายย่อยภาคอีสาน (2537c), 'การประชุมคณะกรรมการกลางสกยอ.', 26 พฤศจิกายน, เอกสารโรเนียว).

—— (1994d) 'Report of the Meeting of the Central Committee of the SSFAI', (Unpublished typescript). (สมัชชาเกษตรกรรายย่อยภาคอีสาน (2537d), 'สรุปรายงานการประชุมคณะกรรมการกลางสก.อ.', เอกสารโรเนียว).

—— (1994e) 'Summary Report of the Activities of the SSFAI', 30 October (Unpublished typescript). (สมัชชาเกษตรกรรายย่อยภาคอีสาน (2537e), 'สรุปรายงานการเคลื่อนไหวของสกอ.อ.', 30 ตุลาคม, เอกสารโรเนียว).

—— (1994f) 'Report of the Meeting of the Central Committee of the SSFAI', 14 August (Unpublished typescript). (สมัชชาเกษตรกรรายย่อยภาคอีสาน (2537f), 'สรุปรายงานการประชุมคณะกรรมการกลางสกย.อ.', 14 สิงหาคม, เอกสารโรเนียว).

—— (1995) 'The Proposal for Flexible Procedure for Access to Credit from the RFSPS projects', (Unpublished typescript). (สมัชชาเกษตรกรรายย่อยภาคอีสาน (2538), 'ข้อเสนอเพื่อการปฏิบัติที่ยืดหยุ่นเพื่อขอเงินกู้ปรุ', เอกสารโรเนียว).

—— (1996) 'Summary of the SSFAI activities in April 1996', (Unpublished typescript). (สมัชชาเกษตรกรรายย่อยภาคอีสาน (2539), 'สรุปความเคลื่อนไหวของสมัชชาเกษตรกรรายย่อยภาคอีสาน เดือนเมษายน 2539', เอกสารโรเนียว).

—— (1997) 'The Objectives of the SSFAI', (Unpublished typescript). (สมัชชาเกษตรกรรายย่อยภาคอีสาน (2540), 'วัตถุประสงค์ของสกย.อ.' เอกสารโรเนียว).

—— (nd) 'The Problem of Land-Forestry and the Long Term Solution', (Unpublished typescript). (สมัชชาเกษตรกรรายย่อยภาคอีสาน (ม.ป.ป.), 'ปัญหาป่าไม้ที่ดินและการแก้ปัญหาระยะยาว', เอกสารโรเนียว).

Terapon Arunakasikon, Patinun Santimatanedon, Satapon linmane, Paitun Nakcham, Suriyakan Chainet, and Nimon Ruangtue (eds) (2002) *The Farmers Rehabilitation Fund Act 1999*, Bangkok: Winyuchon. (ธีระพล อรุณะกสิกร, ปฏินันท์ สันติมทนีดล, สถาพร ลิมมณี, ไพรฑรุย์ นาคุจำ, สุริยกานต์ ชัยเนตร, และ นิมล เรื่องตื้อ (รวบรวม) (2545), พระราชบัญญัติกองทุนฟื้นฟูและพัฒนาเกษตรกร พ.ศ. ๒๕๔๒, กรุงเทพ: วิญญูชน).

Thai Volunteer Services Project (1984), The Concept of Development in Thai Society (Unpublished typescript). (โครงการอาสาสมัครเพื่อสังคม (2527), *แนวคิดการพัฒนาในสังคมไทย*, เอกสารโรเนียว).

Secondary Sources

Books and Articles in Thai

Anek Laothamatas (1995) *A Tale of Two Democracies*. Bangkok: Matichon. (อเนก เหล่าธรรมทัศน์ (2538), *สองนัคราประชาธิปไตย*. กรุงเทพ: มติชน)

Bamrung Boonpanya (nd) 'Look at Isan', (Unpublished typescript). (บำรุง บุญปัญญา (ม.ป.ป.), *มองอีสาน*, เอกสารโรเนียว).

—— (1991) 'Interview'. *Voice of Community*, Vol. 6, no. 7, pp. 15–18. (บำรุง บุญปัญญา (2534), สัมภาษณ์, *เสียงชุมชน* 6(7): 15–18).

Bamrung Kayotha (19931994) 'Interview: Asking for Participation in Policy Making Shocked the Government More Than Asking for PowerSharing'. *Thansetthakit Kanmuang*, 30 December–1 January, pp. 21–24. (บำรุง คะโยธา (2536-2537), 'สัมภาษณ์, 'ขอมีส่วนกำหนดนโยบาย: รัฐบาลช็อคกว่าขอแบ่งอำนาจ', *ฐานเศรษฐกิจการเมือง*, 30 ธันวาคม- 1 มกราคม, หน้า 21–24).

—— (1994) 'Interview'. *Phujatkan*, 8 June , p. 3. (บำรุง คะโยธา (2537), 'สัมภาษณ์', ผู้จัดการ, 8 มิถุนายน, หน้า 3).

——_ (1995b) 'Interview'. *Nation Sudsapda*, 27 January2 February, pp. 18–19. (บำรุง คะโยธา (2537b), 'สัมภาษณ์', *เนชั่นสุดสัปดาห์*, 27 มกราคม-2 กุมภาพันธ์, หน้า 18–19.

—— (1996) 'Interview'. *Arthit*, April 19–25, pp. 16–22. (บำรุง คะโยธา (2539), 'สัมภาษณ์', อาทิตย์, 19–25 เมษายน, หน้า 16–22).

Bonlers Siakim (1995) 'Bamrung Kayotha: General of Kao Wong and General Secretary of the SSFAI'. *Nation Sudsapda*, 10–16 February, pp. 33–34. (บุญเลิศ เซียคิม (2538), 'ขุนพลแห่งเขาวง: บำรุง คะโยธา เลขาธิการสกอ', *เนชั่นสุดสัปดาห์*, 10-16 กุมภาพันธ์: หน้า 33–34).

Bung-On Piyabhan. (1998) *The Lao in Early Bangkok. Bangkok: The Thailand Research Fund*. (บังอร ปิยะพันธุ์ (2541), *ลาวในกรุงรัตนโกสินทร์*, กรุงเทพ: สำนักงานสนับสนุนการวิจัย).

Chalermkiat Phiunual (1990) *Thai Democracy: The Political Thought of Thai Soldiers (1976–1986)*. Bangkok: Thai Studies Institute, Thammasat University. (เฉลิมเกียรติ ผิวนวล (2533), *ประชาธิปไตยแบบไทย: ความคิดทางการเมืองของทหารไทย* (2519–2529), กรุงเทพ: สถาบันไทยคดีศึกษา, มหาวิทยาลัยธรรมศาสตร์).

Fa Diew Kan (2004) January–March, p. 138. (ฟ้าเดียวกัน (๒๕๔๗) มกราคม-มีนาคม, หน้า ๑๓๘).

Isan NGOCORD (1997) *Isan NGOs: Alternatives, Sources of Strength, Changes*, Bangkok: Pimdee. (คณะกรรมการประสานงานองค์กรเอกชนพัฒนาชนบท (กป.อพช.) ภาคอีสาน (2540), *NGOอีสาน: ทางเลือกแห่งพลังการเปลี่ยนแปลง*,กรุงเทพ: พิมพ์ดี).

Jai Ungpakorn. (1998) 'Good Governance from Class Point of View'. In Pitaya Wongkul (ed.) *Good Governance: A Turning Point for Thailand?* Bangkok: Vision Project, (Globalization 6), pp. 163174. (ใจ อึ๊งภากรณ์ (2541), 'ธรรมรัฐในทัศนะชนชั้น', ใน พิทยา ว่องกุล (บก.), *ธรรมรัฐ: จุดเปลี่ยนประเทศไทย*, กรุงเทพ: โครงการวิถีทรรศน์, ชุดโลกาภิวัฒน์ 6, หน้า 163-174).

Jittima Sethasirivorakul (1996) 'Interest Group and Mobilization: A Case Study of the Assembly of Small Scale Farmers of the Northeast', unpublished MA Thesis, Department of Government Graduate School, Chulalongkorn University. (จิตติมา เศรษฐสิริวรกุล (2539) 'กลุ่มผลประโยชน์กับการรวมพลัง: กรณีศึกษาสมัชชาเกษตรกรรายย่อยภาคอีสาน', *วิทยานิพนธ์รัฐศาสตร์มหาบัณฑิต*, คณะบัณฑิตวิทยาลัย, จุฬาลงกรณ์มหาวิทยาลัย).

Kaen Sarika (1995) 'A Model Fighter?'. *Phujatkan*, 3 November, p. 8. (แคน สาริกา (2538), 'คือแบบอย่างนักต่อสู้', *ผู้จัดการ*, 3 พฤศจิกายน, หน้า 8).

Kuenpetch Ponrum (1994) 'Interview'. Kao Sod, 19 February, p. 6. (เขื่อนเพชร โพนรัมย์ (2537), 'สัมภาษณ์', *ข่าวสด*, 19 กุมภาพันธ์, หน้า 6).

'Manifesto of POI' (nd), (Unpublished manuscript). ('คำประกาศองค์กรประชาชนอีสาน' (ม.ป.ป.), (เอกสารโรเนียว).

Matichon Sudsapda (1998) 9–15 February, p. 12. (มติชนสุดสัปดาห์ (2541) 9–15 กุมภาพันธ์, หน้า12).

—— (1999) 2–8 February, p. 9 (*มติชนสุดสัปดาห์* (2542) 2–8 กุมภาพันธ์, หน้า9).

—— (1999) 9–15 February, p. 1 (*มติชนสุดสัปดาห์* (2542) 9–15 กุมภาพันธ์, หน้า1).

Naruemon Tabchumpon and Nitirat Sapsomboon (eds) (1999) *The Route of Thai Farmers: 25th Anniversary of the Farmers Federation of Thailand.* Bangkok: Kanghan. (นฤมล ทับจุมพลและนิติรัตน์ ทรัพย์สมบูรณ์ (บก.) (2542), *เส้นทางชาวนาไทย: รำลึก 25 ปี สหพันธ์ชาวนาชาวไร่แห่งประเทศไทย*, กรุงเทพ: กังหัน).

Plaeo Satjapa (1995a) 'Remembrance of Krong Chandawong: The 34 th Anniversary of His Execution on 31 May 1961'. *Phujatkan*, 29 May, p. 13. (เปลว สัจจาภา (2538a), 'ระลึกครอง จันดาวงศ์: ในโอกาสครบรอบ 34 ปีแห่งการถูกประหารเมื่อ 31 พฤษภาคม 2504', *ผู้จัดการ*, 29 พฤษภาคม, หน้า 13).

—— (1995b) 'Remembrance of Krong Chandawong: The 34 th Anniversary of His Execution on 31 May 1961'. *Phujatkan*, 31 May, p. 12. (เปลว สัจจาภา (2538b), 'ระลึกครอง จันดาวงศ์: ในโอกาสครบรอบ 34 ปีแห่งการถูกประหารเมื่อ 31 พฤษภาคม 2504', *ผู้จัดการ*, 31 พฤษภาคม, หน้า 12).

Prapas Pintongtang (1998) *Politics on the Street: 99 Days of the Assembly of the Poor. Bangkok: Krirk University.* (ประภาส ปิ่นตบแต่ง (2541), *การเมืองบนท้องถนน: 99 วันสมัชชาคนจน*, กรุงเทพ: มหาวิทยาลัยเกริก).

Prawase Wasi (1998) 'Interview'. In Chuchai Sobpawong and Uwadee Kadkarnkai (eds.), *Civil Society: Views from Thai Social Thinkers.* Bangkok: Matichon, pp. 1–36. (ประเวศ วะสี (2541), 'สัมภาษณ์' ใน ชูชัย ศุภวงศ์ และยุวดี คาดการณ์ไกล, *ประชาสังคม: ทัศนะนักคิดในสังคมไทย*, กรุงเทพ: มติชน, หน้า 1– 36).

Rangsan Tanapornpan (1987) *The Economics of the Rice Premium.* Bangkok: Thammasat University Press. (รังสรรค์ ธนะพรพันธุ์ (2530), *เศรษฐศาสตร์ว่าด้วยพรีเมี่ย*

มข้าว, กรุงเทพ: สำนักพิมพ์ธรรมศาสตร์).

Saneh Chamarik (1998) 'Good Governance and Thammarat'. *Phujatkan*, 21 May, p. 8. (เสนห์ จามริก (2541), 'Good Governance กับ ธรรมรัฐ', ผู้จัดการ, 21 พฤษภาคม, หน้า 8).

Siam Rat Sudsabda (1993) 25–31 October, p. 9 (สยามรัฐสุดสัปดาห์ (2536), 25–30 ตุลาคม, หน้า 9).

Somkiat Pongpaiboon (1995a) 'Bamrung Kayotha's Life: Holiday or Asylum in Japan'. *Krungthep Thurakij* [Isan Section], 17 October, p. 2 (สมเกียรติ พงษ์ไพบูลย์ (2538a) 'เส้นทางชีวิตบำรุง คะโยธา: พักร้อนหรือลี้ภัยในญี่ปุ่น', กรุงเทพธุรกิจ (อีสาน), 17 ตุลาคม, หน้า 2).

—— (1995b) 'The Isan Teacher's Movement'. *Krungthep Thurakij* [Isan Section], 30 March, p. 3. (สมเกียรติ พงษ์ไพบูลย์ (2538b), 'ขบวนการครูอีสาน', กรุงเทพธุรกิจ (อีสาน), 30 มีนาคม, หน้า 3).

—— (1995c) 'The Fourth Round of The SSFAI's Protest'. *Krungthep Thurakit* [Isan Section], 23 January, p. 3. (สมเกียรติ พงษ์ไพบูลย์ (2538c), 'การประท้วงยก 4 ของสกย.อ.', กรุงเทพธุรกิจ (อีสาน), 23 มกราคม, หน้า 3).

—— (1995d) 'The Historic Agreement'. *Krungthep Thurakit* [Isan Section], 6 February, p.3. (สมเกียรติ พงษ์ไพบูลย์ (2538d), 'ข้อตกลงประวัติศาสตร์', กรุงเทพธุรกิจ (อีสาน), 6 กุมภาพันธ์, หน้า 3).

—— (1995e) 'Forum of the Poor 1995'. *Krungthep Thurakit* [Isan section], 19 December, p. 8. (สมเกียรติ พงษ์ไพบูลย์ (2538e), 'สมัชชาคนจน ปี 2538', กรุงเทพธุรกิจ (อีสาน), 19 ธันวาคม, หน้า 8).

—— (2002) 'Power War in the Farmer Rehabilitation Fund'. *Nation Sudsubda*, 2026 May, p. 24. (สมเกียรติ พงษ์ไพบูลย์ (2545), 'สงครามอำนาจในกองทุนฟื้นฟูและพัฒนาเกษตรกร' เนชั่นสุดสัปดาห์, 20-26 พฤษภาคม, หน้า 24).

Sompan Techaartik (1990) 'Hot and Cool Situations in Development Work'. *Social Development* 3, pp. 107–109. (สมพันธ์ เตชะอธิก (2533), 'สถานการณ์ร้อน-เย็นในงานพัฒนา', สังคมพัฒนา 3, หน้า 107 – 109).

Somyong Kaewsupan (1997) 'Leaflets'. 1 May. (สมยงค์ แก้วสุพรรณ (2540), ใบปลิว, 1 พฤษภาคม).

Srisakara Vallibhotama (1990) *Isan Civilization Sites*. Bangkok: Matichon. (ศรีศักร วัลลิโภดม (2533), แอ่งอารยธรรมอีสาน, กรุงเทพ: มติชน).

Suthy Prasatset (1998) 'Eight Proposals about the Assembly of the Poor'. In The Assembly of the Poor (1998), *The Black Paper of the Assembly of the Poor: People's Handbook in the IMF Era*. Bangkok: Kanghan. (สุธี ประสาทน์เศรษฐ์ (2541), '8 ญัตติว่าด้วยสมัชชาคนจน' ใน สมัชชาคนจน (2541), สมุดปกดำสมัชชาคนจน: คู่มือประชาชนยุคไอเอ็มเอฟ,กรุงเทพ: กังหัน).

Thaveesilp Suebwattana (1988) 'The Perception of the Thai Rulers Towards Lao in the Rattanakhosin Period'. *Social Sciences Newsletter*, Vol. 11, no. 1, pp. 104–121. (ทวีศิลป์ สืบวัฒนะ (2541), 'ลาวในทัศนะของผู้ปกครองไทยในสมัยรัตนโกสินทร์', จดหมายข่าวสังคมศาสตร์, ปีที่ 11 ฉบับที่ 1, หน้า 104 – 121).

Thong Kasettakorn (1993a) 'From NGO to Assembly'. *Nation Sudsapda*, 12–18 September, pp. 22–23. (ธง เกษตรกร (2535a), 'จากเอ็นจีโอสู่สมัชชา', เนชั่นสุดสัปดาห์, 12–18 กันยายน, หน้า 22–23).

—— (1993b) 'Demands for Social Contract and the 'Leekpai' State'. *Nation Sudsapda*, 26 September–2 October, pp. 24–25. (ธง เกษตรกร (2535b), 'ข้อเรียกร้องสัญญาประชาคมกับรัฐหลีกภัย', เนชั่นสุดสัปดาห์, 26 กันยายน-2 ตุลาคม, หน้า 24–25).

Thongbai Thongpao (1974) *Ladyao Communism*. Bangkok: Konnum. (ทองใบ ทองเปาด์ (2517), *คอมมิวนิสต์ลาดยาว*, กรุงเทพ: คนหนุ่ม).

Udon Wongtabtim (1995) 'Four Generals of the Isan Free Thai Who Coordinated the Founding of the Lao Independence Movement'. *Phujatkan*, 19 July, p. 9. (อุดร หน้า 9).วงศ์ทับทิม (2538), '4 ขุนพลเสรีไทยผู้ประสานงานการก่อตั้งคณะลาวอิสระ', *ผู้จัดการ*, 19 กรกฎาคม,

Yukti Mukdawijit (1995) 'The Formation of the 'Community Culture' Movement in Thai Society (19771994)', Unpublished M. A. dissertation, Faculty of Sociology and Anthropology, Thammasat University. (ยุกติ มุกดาวิจิตร (2538), 'การก่อตัวของกระแส วัฒนธรรมชุมชนในสังคมไทย (2520 – 2537)', วิทยานิพนธ์ศิลปศาสตร์มหาบัณฑิต, คณะสังคมวิทยาและมานุษยวิทยา, มหาวิทยาลัยธรรมศาสตร์).

Voice of Community, October 1995, p.9. (เสียงชุมชน, ตุลาคม 2538, หน้า 9). 259

Thirayuth Boonmi (1998) 'Good Governance: the Strategy for Survival of Thailand'. Matichon Sutsapda. 27 January: 1213. (ธีรยุทธ บุญมี (2541), ธรรมรัฐ: ยุทธศาสตร์เพื่อการอยู่รอดของประเทศไทย, มติชนสุดสัปดาห์, 27 มกราคม, หน้า 12–13).

Yod Sukpattee (1998) 'The Political Philosophy on Good Governance of Thirayuth Boonmi'. In Pittaya Wongkul (ed.), *Good Governance: A Turning Point of Thailand?* Bangkok: Vision Project (Globalization 6), pp. 61–71. (ยอด สุขพัฒน์ธี (2541), 'ปรัชญาการเมืองเรื่องธรรมรัฐของธีรยุทธ บุญมี', ใน พิทยา ว่องกุล (บก.), *ธรรมรัฐ: จุดเปลี่ยนประเทศไทย,* กรุงเทพ: โครงการวิถีทรรศน์, ชุดโลกาภิวัฒน์ 6, หน้า 61-71).

Books and Articles in English

Althuser, Louis (1971) *Lenin and Philosophy and Other Essays.* London: New Left Books.

Alvarez, Sonia and Arturo Escobar (1992) 'Conclusion: Theoretical and Political Horizons of Change in Latin American Social Movements'. In Arturo Escobar and Sonia E. Alvarez (eds), *The Making of Social Movements in Latin America: Identity, Strategy, and Democracy.* Boulder: Westview Press, pp. 317–329.

Amara, Pongsapich and Nitaya Kataleeradahan (1994) *Philanthropy, NGO Activities and Corporate Funding in Thailand.* Bangkok: Chulalongkorn University Social Research Institute.

Ammar Siamwalla, Suthad Setboonsarng, and Direk Patamasiriwat (1993) 'Agriculture'. In Peter G. Warr (ed.), *The Thai Economy in Transition.* Cambridge: Cambridge University Press, pp. 81–117.

Amnesty International (2003) 'Thailand: Grave DevelopmentsKilling and Other Abuses' (http://web.amnesty.org/library/print/ENGASA390082003).

Anek Laothamatas (1992) *Business Associations and the New Political Economy of Thailand.* Boulder: Westview Press.

Asian Center for Human Rights (2004) 'In the line of fire: Human Rights Defenders in Thailand' 30 June (www.achrweb.org/Review/2004/2704.htm).

Bachrach, Peter and Aryeh Botwinick (1992) *Power and Empowerment: A Radical Theory of Participatory Democracy.* Philadelphia: Temple University Press.

Barber, Benjamin R. (1984) *Strong Democracy: Participatory Politics for a New Age.* Berkeley: University of California Press.

BBC News (2004) 'Thai Army Criticised Over Takbai' (http://news.bbc.co.uk/go/pr fr//2/hi/asiapacific/4512845.stm).

Beetham, David and Kevin Boyle (1995) *Introducing Democracy: 80 Questions and Answers.* Cambridge: Polity Press.

Barbalet, J. M. (1988) *Citizenship: Rights, Struggle, and Class Inequality.* Milton Keynes: Open University.

Barme, Scott (1993) *Luang Wichit Wathakan and the Creation of a Thai Identity.* Singapore: Institute of Southeast Asian Studies.

Bibic, Adolf (1994) 'Democracy and Civil Society'. In Adolf Bibic and Gigi Graziano (eds), *Civil Society, Political Society, Democracy.* Ljubljana: Slovenia Political Science Association, pp. 43–71.

Black, Antony (1984) *Guilds and Civil Society in European Political Thought from the Twelfth Century.* London: Methuen.

Bowie, Katherine A. (1997) *Rituals of National Loyalty.* New York: Columbia University Press.

Brass, Tom (1996) 'Popular Culture, Populist Fiction(s): The Agrarian Utopiates of A.V. Chayanov, Ignatius Donnelly and Frank Capra'. In Henry Bernstein and Tom Brass (eds), *Agrarian Questions: Essays in Appreciation of T.J. Byres.* London: Frank Cass, pp. 153–190.

Becker, Marvin B. (1994) *The Emergence of Civil Society in the Eighteenth Century.* Bloomington: Indiana University Press.

Brown, David (1994) *The State and Ethnic Politics in Southeast Asia.* London: Routledge.

Brown, McAlister and Joseph J. Zasloff (1986) *Apprentice Revolutionaries: The Communist Movement in Laos, 1930–1985.* Stanford, CA: Hoover Institution Press.

Bruun, Ole and Michael Jacobsen (2000) 'Introduction'. In Ole Bruun and Michael Jacobson (eds), *Human Rights and Asian Values: Contesting National Identities and Cultural Representations in Asia.* Copenhagen: Nordic Institute of Asian Studies.

Byres, T.J. (1995) 'Preface'. In Tom Brass (ed), *New Farmers' Movements in India*. Essex: Frank Cass, pp. 1–2.

Callahan, William (1998a) *Imagining Democracy: Reading the 'Events of May' in Thailand*. Singapore: Institute of Southeast Asian Studies.

—— (1998b) 'Challenging the Political Order: Social Movements'. In Richard Maidment, David Goldblatt and Jeramy Mitchell, *Governance in the Asia-Pacific*. London: Routledge, pp. 150–171.

—— (2000) *Pollwatching, Elections and Civil Society in Southeast Asia*. Hampshire: Asgate.

Canel, Eduardo (1992) 'New Social Movement Theory and Resource Mobilization: The Need for Integration'. In William K. Carroll (ed.), *Organizing Dissent: Contemporary Social Movements in Theory and Practice*. Ontario: Garamond Press, pp. 22–51.

Chai-Anan Samudavanija (1982) *The Thai Young Turks*. Singapore: Institute of Southeast Asian Studies.

—— (1989) 'Thailand: A Stable Semi-Democracy'. In Larry Diamond, Juan J. Linz and Seymour Martin Lipset (eds), *Democracy in Developing Countries, volume three: Asia*, Boulder, CO: Lynne Rienner, pp. 305–346.

Chatthip Nartsupha (1984) 'The Ideology of Holy Men Revolts in North East Thailand'. In Andrew Turton and Shigeharu Tanabe (eds), *History and Peasant Consciousness in South East Asia*. Senri Ethnological Studies, 13, pp. 111–134.

—— (1991) 'The Community Culture School of Thought'. In Manas Chitkasem and Andrew Turton (eds), *Thai Construction of Knowledge*. London: SOAS, pp. 118–141.

Clarke, Gerald (1998) *The Politics of NGOs in South-East Asia: Participation and Protest in The Philippines*. London: Routledge.

Cohen, E. (1991) *Thai Society in Comparative Perspective*. Bangkok: White Lotus.

Cohen, Jean and Andrew Arato (1994) *Civil Society and Political Theory*. Cambridge: MIT Press.

Demaine, Harvey (1986) 'Kanpatthana: Thai View of Development'. In Mark Hobart and Robert H. Taylor (eds), *Context, Meaning and Power in Southeast Asia*. Ithaca, NY: Southeast Asia Program, Cornell University Press, pp. 93–114.

Dickens, Peter (1996) *Reconstructing Nature: Alienation, Emancipation, and the Division of Labour*. London: Routledge.

Edwards, Michael and David Hulme (eds) (1995) *Non-Governmental Organisations: Performance and Accountability*. London: Earthscan.

Elliott, David (1978) *Thailand: Origins of Military Rule*. London: Zed Press.

Farington, John and David J. Lewis (eds) (1993) *Non-Governmental Organisations and the State in Asia*. London: Routledge.

Fowler, Alan and Rick James (1995) *The Role of Southern NGOs in Development Cooperation*. Oxford: Intrac.

Fox, Jonathan (1990) 'Editor's Introduction'. In Jonathan Fox (ed.), *The Challenge of Rural Democratisation: Perspectives from Latin America and the Philippines.* London: Cass, pp. 1–18.

Foweraker, Joe (1995) *Theorizing Social Movements.* Pluto Press: London.

Foweraker, Joe and Todd Landman (1997) *Citizenship Rights and Social Movements: A Comparative and Statistical Analysis.* Oxford: Oxford University Press.

Frolic, B. Michael (1997) 'State-Led Civil Society'. In Timothy Brook and B. Michael Frolic (eds), *Civil Society in China.* New York: M. E. Sharpe, pp. 46–67.

Gamson, William and David Meyer (1996) 'Framing Political Opportunity'. In Doug McAdam, John D. McCarthy and Mayer N. Zald (eds), *Comparative Perspectives on Social Movements: Political Opportunities, Mobilizing Structures, and Cultural Framings.* Cambridge: Cambridge University Press, pp. 273–290.

Giddens, Anthony (1999) *The Third Way: the Renewal of Social Democracy.* Malden: Polity Press.

Gill, Graeme (2000) *The Dynamics of Democratization: Elites, Civil Society and the Transition Process*, London: Macmillan.

Girling, John (1981) *Thailand: Society and Politics.* Ithaca, NY: Cornell University Press.

Grabowsky, Volker (ed) (1995) *Regions and National Integration in Thailand 1892– 1992.* Germany: Harrassowitz Verlag.

Grugel, Jean (2002) *Democratization: A Critical Introduction.* New York: Palgrave.

Hafner, J. (1990) 'Forces and Policy Issues Affecting Forrest Use In Northeast Thailand 1900–1985'. In Mark Poffenberger (ed), *Keepers of The Forest: Land Management Alternatives in Southeast Asia.* Manila: Antoneo De Manila University Press, pp. 69–94.

Harvey, Neil (1998) *The Chiapas Rebellion: The Struggle for Land and Rebellion.* Durham: Duke University.

Hellman, Judith A. (1992) 'The Study of New Social Movements in Latin America and the Question of Autonomy'. In Arturo Escobar and Sonia E. Alvarez (eds), *The Making of Social Movements in Latin America: Identity, Strategy, and Democracy.* Boulder: Westview Press, pp. 52–61.

Hewison, Kevin (1989) *Bankers and Bureaucrats: Capital and the Role of the State in Thailand.* New Haven: Yale University Southeast Asia Studies.

—— (1996) 'Political Opposition and Regime Change in Thailand'. In G. Rodan (ed), *Political Oppositions in Industrialising Asia.* London: Routledge, pp. 72–94.

Hirsh, Philip. (1993) *Political Economy of Environment in Thailand.* Manila: Journal of Contemporary Asia.

—— (1998) 'Dams, Resources and the Politics of Environment in Mainland Southeast Asia'. In Philip Hirsch and Carol Warren (eds), *The Politics of Environment in Southeast Asia*. London: Routledge, pp. 55–70.

Hobsbawm, Eric (1959) *Primitive Rebels*. Manchester: Manchester University Press.

Hunsaker, Bryan (1996) 'The Political Economy of Thai Deforestation'. In Bryan Hunsaker, T Mayer, B. Griffiths and Robert Dayley (eds), *Loggers, Monks, Students, and Entrepreneur: Four Essays on Thailand*. Illinois: Center for Southeast Asian Studies, Northern Illinois University, pp. 1–31.

Huntington, Samuel P. (1991) *The Third Wave: Democratization in the Late Twentieth Century*. Norman: University of Oklahoma Press.

Ichinohe, Yoshie (1999) 'Isan-based Peasant Movements and their Political Opportunities in Historical Perspective in Northeastern Thailand (1970s–1990s)', unpublished MA Thesis, The Hague: The Institute of Social Studies.

Ishii, Y. (1975) 'A Note on Buddhistic Millenarian Revolts in Northeastern Siam'. In Shinichi Ichimura (ed), *Southeast Asia: Nature, Society and Development*. Honolulu: The University Press of Hawaii, pp. 67–75.

Jarin Boonmathya (1995) 'Peasant Movement and Organisation: A Case Study of Esan Small Farmers Assembly (ESFA) in Northeastern Thailand', unpublished MA Thesis, The Hague: Institute of Social Studies.

Kamala Tiyavanich (1997) *Forest Recollections: Wandering Monks in Twentieth-century Thailand*. Chiang Mai: Silkworm Books.

Kamon Pragtong and D.E Thomas (1990) 'Evolving Management Systems in Thailand'. In Mark Poffenberger (ed), *Keepers of the Forest: Land Management Alternatives in Southeast Asia*. Manila: Ateneo De Manila University Press, pp. 167–186.

Kanokrat Lertchoosakul (2002) 'Conceptualising the Roles and Limitations of NGOs in the Anti-Pak Mon Dam Movement'. *Tai Culture*, June: 133–154.

Kanoksak Kaewtthep (1989) *The State and Agricultural Cooperatives in Japan and Thailand: A Comparative Interpretation*. Tokyo: Institute of Developing Economies.

Keane, John (1988) *Democracy and Civil Society*. London: Verso.

Kearney, Michael (1996) *Reconceptualizing the Peasantry*. Boulder: Westview Press.

Keyes, Charles F. (1967) *Isan: Regionalism in Northeast Thailand*. Ithaca, NY: Cornell University.

Kitahara, A. (1996) *The Thai Rural Community Reconsidered*. Bangkok: The Political Economy Center, Chulalongkorn University.

Kobkua Suwannathat-Pian (1995) *Thailand's Durable Premier: Phibun through Three Decades, 1932–1957*. Kuala Lumpur: Oxford University Press.

Kolakowski, Leszek (1981) *Main Currents of Marxism: The Founders*. Oxford: Oxford University Press.

Kriesi, Hanspeter (1996) 'The Organizational Structue of New Social Movement in a Political Context'. In Doug McAdam, John D. McCarthy and Mayer N. Zald (eds), *Comparative Perspectives on Social Movements: Political Opportunities, Mobilizing Structures, and Cultural Framing,* Cambridge: Cambridge University Press, pp. 152–184.

Kukathas, Chandran and David W. Lovell (1991) 'The Significance of Civil Society'. In Chandran Kukathas, David W. Lovell and William Maley (eds), *The Transition from Socialism: State and Civil Society in the USSR.* Melbourne: Longman Cheshire, pp. 18–40.

Lenin, Vladimir Il'ich (1969) *What is to Be Done?* New York: International Publishers.

Lindberg, S. (1992) 'Farmers' Agitation and the State in India'. In Lars Rudebeck (ed), *When Democracy Makes Sense.* Stockholm: AKUT, pp. 201–217.

Lindberg, Staffan (1995) 'New Farmers' Movements in India as Structural Response and Collective Identity Formation: The Cases of the Shetkari Sanghatana and the BKU'. In Tom Brass (ed), *New Farmers' Movements in India.* Essex: Frank Cass, pp. 95–125.

Linz, Juan L. and Alfred Stepan (1996) *Problems of Democratic Transition and Consolidation.* Baltimore: Johns Hopkins University Press.

Lohmann, Larry (1996) 'Freedom to Plant: Indonesia and Thailand in a Globalizing Pulp and Paper Industry'. In Michael J. Parnwell and Raymond L. Bryant (eds), *Environmental Change in South-East Asia*, London: Routledge, pp. 23–48.

London, Bruce (1980) *Metropolis and Nation in Thailand: The Political Economy of Uneven Development.* Boulder: Westview Press.

Lummis, C. Douglas (1996) *Radical Democracy.* Ithaca: Cornell University Press.

Luther, H.U. (1978) *Peasants and State in Contemporary Thailand: From Regional Revolt to National Revolution?*, Hamburg: Institute for Asian Studies.

McAdam, Doug (1996a) 'Conceptual Origins, Current Problems, Future Directions'. In Doug McAdam, John D. McCarthy and Mayer N. Zald (eds), *Comparative Perspectives on Social Movements: Political Opportunities, Mobilizing Structures, and Cultural Framings.* Cambridge: Cambridge University Press, pp. 23–40.

—— (1996b), 'The Framing Function of Movement Tactics: Strategic Dramaturgy in the American Civil Rights Movement'. In D. McAdam, J. McCarthy, and M. Zald (eds), *Comparative Perspectives on Social Movements: Political Opportunities, Mobilizing Structures, and Cultural Framings.* Cambridge: Cambridge University Press, pp. 338–355.

McAdam, Doug and David Snow (1997) 'Movements in Action: Strategies and Tactics'. In Dough McAdam and David Snow (eds), Social Movements: Readings on Their Emergence, Mobilization, and Dynamics. California: Roxbury, pp. 326– 327.

McAdam, Doug, John D. McCarthy and Mayer N. Zald (1996) 'Introduction: Opportunities, Mobilizing Structures, and Framing Processes – Towards a

Synthetic, Comparative Perspective on Social Movements'. In D. McAdam, J. McCarthy and M. Zald (eds), *Comparative Perspectives on Social Movements: Political Opportunities, Mobilizing Structures, and Cultural Framings.* Cambridge: Cambridge University Press, pp. 1–22.

McAdam, Doug and David Snow (1997) 'Movements in Action: Strategies and Tactics'. In Dough McAdam and David Snow (eds), *Social Movements: Readings on Their Emergence, Mobilization, and Dynamics.* California: Roxbury, pp. 326–327.

McCargo, Duncan (1997a) *Chamlong Srimuang and the New Thai Politics.* London: Hurst.

—— (1997b) 'Thailand's Political Parties: Real, Authentic, and Actual'. In K. Hewison (ed.), *Political Change in Thailand: Democracy and Participation.* London: Routledge, pp. 114–131.

—— (2000) *Politics and the Press in Thailand: Media Machinations.* London: Routledge.

—— (2002) 'Thailand's January 2001 General elections'. In Duncan McCargo (ed.), *Reforming Thai Politics.* Copenhagen: Nordic Institute of Asian Studies, pp. 247–260.

McCargo, Duncan and Ukrist Pathamanund (2005) The Thaksinization of Thailand. Denmark: NIAS.

Medhi Krongkeaw (1995) 'Contributions of Agriculture to Industrialization'. In Medhi Krongkeaw (ed.), *Thailand's Industrialization and Its Consequences.* London: Macmillan Press, pp. 33–65.

Migdal, Joel (1974) *Peasants, Politics and Revolution.* Princeton: Princeton University Press.

Missingham, Bruce (1999) 'The Assembly of the Poor in Thailand: From Local Struggles to National Social Movement', unpublished PhD. thesis, The Australian National University.

Moore, Barington (1967) *Social Origins of Dictatorship and Democracy.* London: Penguin.

Morell, David and Chai-Anan Samudavanija (1981) *Political Conflict in Thailand: Reform, Reaction, Revolution.* Cambridge: Oelschlager, Gunn & Hain.

Mullett, Michael A. (1987) *Popular Culture and Popular Protest in Late Medieval and Early Modern Europe.* London: Croom Helm.

O'Donnell, Guillermo and Philippe C. Schmitter (1986) *Transitions from Authoritarian Rule: Tentative Conclusions about Uncertain Democracies.* Baltimore: Johns Hopkins University Press.

O'Donnell, Guillermo, Philippe C. Schmitter and Laurence Whitehead (eds) (1986) *Transitions from Authoritarian Rule: Comparative Perspectives.* Baltimore: Johns Hopkins University Press.

Pasuk Phongpaichit (2004) *Thaksin: The Business of Politics in Thailand.* Denmark: NIAS.

Pasuk Phongpaichit and Chris Baker (1995) *Thailand: Economy and Politics.* Oxford: Oxford University Press.

Pasuk Phongpaichit, Sungsidh Piriyarangsanan and Nualnoi Treerat (1996) *Challenging Social Exclusion: Rights and Livelihood in Thailand.* Geneva: International Institute for Labour Studies.

Pateman, Carole (1970) *Participation and Democratic Theory.* Cambridge: Crambridge University Press.

Perez-Diaz, Victor (1993) *The Return of Civil Society.* London: Harvard University Press.

Piven, Frances Fox and Richard A. Cloward (1992) 'Normalizing Collective Protest'. In Aldon D. Morris and Carol McClurg Mueller (eds), *Frontiers in Social Movement Theory*, New Haven: Yale University Press, pp. 301–325.

Poulantzas, Nicos (1978) *State, Power, Socialism.* London: Verso.

Prizzia, R. (1986) *Thailand in Transition: The Role of Oppositional Forces.* Hawaii: University of Hawaii Press.

Prudhisan Jumbala (1992) *Nation-Building and Democratization in Thailand: A Political History.* Bangkok: Chulalongkorn University Press.

Przeworski, Adam (1986) 'Some Problems in the Study of the Transition to Democracy'. In Guilermo O'Donnell, Philippe C. Schmitter and Laurence Whitehead (eds) (1986) *Transitions from Authoritarian Rule: Comparative Perspectives.* Baltimore: Johns Hopkins University Press, pp. 47–63.

—— (1999) 'Minimalist Conception of Democracy: A Defense'. In Ian Shapiro and H-C Casiano (eds), *Democracy's Value.* Cambridge: Cambridge University Press, pp. 23–55.

Putnam, Robert (1993) *Making Democracy Work: Civic Traditions in Modern Italy.* Princeton, NJ: Princeton University Press.

Rigg, Jonathan (1995) 'Introduction'. In Jonathan Rigg (ed.), *Counting the Costs: Economic Growth and Environmental Change in Thailand.* Singapore: Institute of Southeast Asian Studies, pp. 3–26.

Riggs, Fred W. (1966) *Thailand: The Modernization of a Bureaucratic Polity.* Honolulu: East-West Press.

Robert, John (2004) 'Thaksin Stokes Further Conflict in Southern Thailand' (http://www.wsws.org/articles/2004/nov2004/thain26_prn.shtml).

Roberts, Kenneth M. (1998) *Deepening Democracy?: The Modern Left and Social Movements in Chile and Peru.* Stanford, CA: Stanford University Press.

Ross, H. and S. Thadaniti, (1995) 'The Environmental Costs of Industrialization'. In Medhi Krongkeaw (ed.), *Thailand's Industrialization and Its Consequences.* London: Macmillan Press, pp. 267–288.

Rueschemeyer, Dietrich, Evelyne Huber Stephens and John D. Stephens (eds) (1992) *Capitalist Development and Democracy*. Cambridge: Polity Press.

Schecter, Darrow (2000) *Sovereign States or Political Communities?: Civil Society and Contemporary Politics*. Manchester: Manchester University Press.

Scott, James C. (1976) *The Moral Economy of the Peasant*. New Haven: Yale University Press.

—— (1990) *Domination and the Arts of Resistance: Hidden Transcripts*. New Haven: Yale University Press.

Scott, James C. and Benedict J. Kerkvliet (1977) 'How Traditional Rural Patrons Lose Legitimacy: A Theory with Special Reference to Southeast Asia'. In Steffen W. Schmidt et al. (eds), *Friends, Followers, and Factions: A Reader in Political Clientelism*. Berkeley, CA: University of California Press, pp. 439–458.

Siffin, William (1966) *The Thai Bureaucracy: Institutional Change and Development*. Honolulu: East-West Center Press.

Simpson, Adam (2005) 'Green NGOs and Authoritarian Regimes: The Perils of Environmental Activism in Thaksin's Thailand', *Griffith Journal of the Environment*, June, pp. 134.

Skocpol, Theda (1995) *Social Revolutions in the Modern World*. Cambridge: Cambridge University Press.

Sombat Chantornvong (1998) 'The Political World of Sunthonphu'. In Amara Pongsapich (ed.), *Traditional and Changing Thai World View*. Bangkok: Chulalongkorn University Press, pp. 63–96.

Somboon Suksamran (1993) *Buddhism and Political Legitimacy*. Bangkok: Chulalongkorn University Press.

Srisuwan Kuankachorn (1995) 'Thai NGOs in an Industrializing Society: Past Experiences and Future Directions'. In Jaturong Boonyarattnasoontorn and Gawin Chutima (eds), *Thai NGOs: The Continuing Struggle for Democracy*. Bangkok: Thai NGOs Support Project, pp. 69–76.

Stran, Orin (1992) 'I Dreamed of Foxes and Hawks: Reflections on Peasant Protest, New Social Movements, and the Rondas Campesinas of Northern Peru'. In Arturo Escoba and Sonia E. Alvarez (eds), *The Making of Social Movements in Latin America*. Oxford: Westview Press, pp. 89–111.

Stowe, Judith A. (1991), *Siam Becomes Thailand*. Honolulu: University of Hawaii Press.

Surin Maisrikrod and Duncan McCargo (1997) 'Electoral Politics: Commercialisation and Exclusion'. In Kevin Hewison (ed.), *Political Change in Thailand: Democracy and Participation*. London: Routledge, pp. 132–148.

Suthy Prasartset (1995) 'The Rise of NGOs as Critical Social Movement in Thailand'. In Jaturong Boonyarattnasoontorn and Gawin Chutima (eds), *Thai NGOs: The Continuing Struggle for Democracy*. Bangkok: Thai NGOs Support Project, pp. 97–134.

Tandrup, Andres (1982) *Thailand: Internal Colonialism and Revolutionary War.* Copenhagen: University of Copenhagen Press.

Tarrow, Sidney (1994) *Power in Movement.* Cambridge: University of Cambridge Press.

Taylor, Charles (1994) 'The Politics of Recognition'. In A. Gutmann (ed.), *Multiculturalism: Examining the Politics of Recognition.* New Jersey: Princeton University Press.

Tej Bunnag (1977) *The Provincial Administration of Siam 1892–1915.* London: Oxford University Press.

Textor, R.B. (1961) *From Peasant to Pedicab Driver.* New Haven, CT: Yale University Press.

Thailand in Figures 1997–1998, Bangkok: Alpha Research.

Thak Chaloemtiarana (1979) *Thailand: The Politics of Despotic Paternalism.* Bangkok: Thammasat University.

Thaxton, Ralph A. (1997) *Salt of the Earth: The Political Origins of Peasant Protest and Communist Revolution in China*, Berkeley, CA: University of California Press.

Therborn, Goran (1978) *What Does the Ruling Class Do When it Rules?* London: New Left Books.

—— (1988) *The Ideology of Power and the Power of Ideology.* London: Verso.

Tsujii, H. (1975) 'Economic Analysis of the Rice Premium Policy of Thailand'. In Shimichi Ichimura (ed.), *South East Asia: Nature, Society and Development.* Honolulu: University Press of Hawaii, pp. 291–320.

Turton, Andrew (1978) 'The Current Situation in The Thai Countryside'. In Andrew Turton, Jonathan Fast and Malcolm Caldwell (eds), *Thailand: Roots of Conflict.* Nottingham: Spokesman, pp. 104–142.

—— (1987) *Production, Power, and Participation in Rural Thailand.* Geneva: United Nations Research Institute for Development.

Vella, Walter F. (1978) *Chaiyo: King Vajiravudh and the Development of Thai Nationalism.* Honolulu: University Press of Hawaii.

Weber, Max (1963) *The Sociology of Religion.* Boston: Beacon Press.

Wedel, Y. (1983) *The Thai Radicals and the Communist Party.* Singapore: Maruzen Asia.

Wedel, Y. and P. Wedel (1987) *Radical Thought, Thai Mind: The Development of Revolutionary Ideas in Thailand.* Bangkok: ABAC.

Wilson, D.A. (1960) 'Thailand and Marxism'. In Frank N. Trager (ed.), *Marxism in Southeast Asia: A Study of Four Countries.* Stanford, CA: Stanford University Press, pp. 58–101.

Wolf, Eric (1969) *The Peasant Wars of the Twentieth Century.* New York: Harper & Row.

Zald, Mayer N. (1996) 'Culture, Ideology, and Strategic Framing'. In Doug McAdam, John D. McCarthy and Mayer N. Zald (eds) *Comparative Perspectives on Social Movements: Political Opportunities, Mobilizing Structures, and Cultural Framings*. Cambridge: Cambridge University Press, pp. 261–274.

Zasloff, Joseph (1973) *The Pathet Lao: Leadership and Organization*. Massachusetts: Lexington Books.

Journal Articles

Apichai Puntasen, Somboon Siriprachai and Chaiyuth Punyasavatsut (1992) 'Political Economy of Eucalyptus: Business, Bureaucracy and the Thai Government'. *Journal of Contemporary Asia*, vol. 22, no. 2, pp. 187–206.

Arato, Andrew (1981) 'Civil Society Against the State: Poland 1980–81'. *Telos*, vol. 47, pp. 23–47.

Baker, Chris (2000) 'Thailand's Assembly of the Poor: Background, Drama, Reaction'. *South East Asia Research*, vol. 8, no. 1, March, pp. 5–29.

Bantorn Ondam and Boonthan Verawongse (1999) 'Assembly of the Poor: The Other Grassroots Movement Experiences from Thailand'. *Thai Development Newsletter*, July–December, pp. 48–50.

Blaney, David L. and Mustapha Kamal Pasha (1993) 'Civil Society and Democracy in the Third World: Ambiguities and Historical Possibilities'. *Studies in Comparative International Development*, vol. 28, no. 1, pp. 3–24.

Brysk, Alison (1996) 'Turning Weakness Into Strength: The Internationalization of Indian Rights'. *Latin American Perspectives*, vol. 23, no. 2, pp. 38–53.

Callahan, William A. and Duncan McCargo (1996) 'Vote-Buying in the Northeast: the Case of the July 1995 General Election'. *Asian Survey*, vol. 36, no. 4, pp. 376–392.

Cohen, Jean (1985) 'Strategy or Ideology: New Theoritical Paradigms and Contemporary Social Movements'. *Social Research*, 4, winter, pp. 663–716.

Crispin, Shawn (2000), 'Uncivil Society', *Far Eastern Economic Review*, 31 August, pp. 20–21.

Crispin, Shawn and Rodney Tasker (2001) 'On an Electoral Collision Course'. *Far Eastern Economic Review*, 11 January, pp. 22–23.

—— (2001) 'Thailand Incorporated'. *Far Eastern Economic Review*, 18 January, pp. 16–18.

Darling, Frank C. (1967) 'America and Thailand'. *Asian Survey*, vol. 7, no. 4, April, pp. 213–225.

de Almeida, Lucio Flavido and Felix Ruiz Sanchez (2000) 'The Landless Workers' Movement and Social Struggles Against Neoliberalism'. *Latin American Perspectives*, Vol. 27, No. 5, September, pp. 11–32.

de Beer, P. (1978) 'History and Policy of the Communist Party of Thailand'. *Journal of Contemporary Asia*, vol. 8, no. 1, pp. 143–157.

Fairclough, Gordon (1996) 'Vox Populi'. *Far Eastern Economic Review*, 19 December, p. 20.

Fowler, Alan (1991) 'The Role of NGOs in Changing State-Society Relations: Perspectives From Eastern and Southern Africa'. *Development Policy Review*, vol. 9, no. 1, pp. 53–84.

Fox, Jonathan (1994) 'The Difficult Transition From Clientelism to Citizenship: Lessons From Mexico'. *World Politics*, vol. 46, January, pp. 151–184.

Fraser, Nancy (2000) 'Rethinking Recognition', *New Left Review*, no. 3, May–June (www.newleftreview.net/NLR23707.shtml).

Giner, S. (1985) 'The Withering Away of Civil Society?' *Praxis International*, 5 (3),pp. 247–267.

Handley, Paul (1991a) 'The Land Wars'. *Far Eastern Economic Review*, 31 October, pp. 15–16.

—— (1991b) 'Sapping the Soil'. *Far Eastern Economic Review*, 31 October, p. 16.

Karl, Terry (1990) 'Dilemmas of Democratization in Latin America'. *Comparative Politics*, 23 (1), October, pp. 1–21.

King, Daniel and Jim LoGerfo (1996) 'Thailand: Toward Democratic Stability'. *Journal of Democracy*, vol. 7, no. 1, pp. 102–117.

Keyes, Charles F. (1964) 'Thailand, Laos, and The Thai Northeastern Problem'. *Australia's Neighbours* 4 (17), July–August, pp. 1–4.

—— (1966) 'Ethnic Identity and Loyalty of Villagers in Northeastern Thailand'. *Asian Survey*, vol. 6, no. 7, July, pp. 362–369.

—— (1977), 'Millennialism, Theravada Buddhism, and Thai Society', *Journal of Asian Studies*, vol. 36, no. 2, February, pp. 283–302.

Lohmann, Larry (1991) 'Peasants, Plantations, and Pulp: The Politics of Eucalyptus in Thailand'. *Bulletin of Concerned Asian Scholars*, vol. 24, no. 4, pp. 3–18.

Malalgoda, K. (1970) 'Millennialism in Relation to Buddhism'. *Comparative Studies in Society and History*, 12 October, pp. 424–441.

Mallet, M. (1978) 'Causes and Consequences of the October 76 Coup'. *Journal of Contemporary Asia*, vol. 8, no. 1, pp. 80–103.

Meszaros, George (2000) 'No Ordinary Revolution: Brazil's Landless Workers' Movement'. *Race and Class*, vol. 42, no. 2, pp. 1–18.

Neher, Clark D. (1995) 'Thailand's Politics as Usual'. *Current History*, December, pp. 435–439.

'NGOs and People's Movements: As Reflected by Themselves and Other'. *Thai Development Newsletter*, 29, 1995, p. 40.

Nopniwat Krailerg (2005) 'Police Vow to Nail Monk Killer Within Two Weeks' Chiangmai Mail, 25 June–1July (http://www.chiangmai.com/140/news.shtml).

Petras, James (1997) 'Latin America: The Resurgence of the Left'. *New Left Review*, May–June, pp. 17–47.

—— (1999) 'NGOs: In the Service of Imperialism'. *Journal of Contemporary Asia*, vol. 29, no. 4, pp. 429–440.

Pornpirom Iamtham (1987) 'The Student-Led Democratic Movement after the 14 October 1973 Incident and Its Relations with the Communist Party of Thailand'. *Asian Review*, 1, pp. 7–44.

Prudhisan Jumbala (1998) 'Thailand: Constitutional Reform Amidst Economic Crisis'. *Southeast Asian Affairs 1998*, Singapore: Institute of Southeast Asia Studies, pp. 265–291.

Shils, Edward (1991) 'The Virtue of Civil Society', *Government and Opposition*, vol. 26, no. 2, pp. 3–30.

Stewart, S. (1997) 'Happy Ever After in the Marketplace: Non-Government Organisations and Uncivil Society'. *Review of African Political Economy*, 71, pp. 11–34.

Tasker, Rodney (1990) 'Salt in the Wound'. *Far Eastern Economic Review*, 7 June, pp. 28–29.

Taylor, J. (1993) 'Social Activism and Resistance on the Thai Frontier: The Case of Phra Prajak Khuttajitto'. *Bulletin of Concerned Asian Scholars*, 25 (2), pp. 3–16.

Thai Development Newsletter, 29, 1995, p. 40.

The Friends of the People (1999) 'The Assembly of the Poor: the Power of the People'. *Thai Development Newsletter*, July–December, pp. 53–55.

Ubonrat Siriyuvasak (1991) 'The Environment and Popular Culture in Thailand'. *Southeast Asian Affairs*, Singapore: Institute of Southeast Asian Studies, pp. 298–310.

Vatikiotis, Michael and Gordon Fairclough (1996) 'Mission Impossible'. *Far Eastern Economic Review*, 28 November, pp.16–18.

Veltmeyer, Henry (1997) 'New Social Movements in Latin America: The Dynamics of Class and Identity'. *Journal of Peasant Studies*, vol. 25, no. 1, pp. 137–69.

Viksnins, G. (1973) 'United States Military Spending and the Economy of Thailand: 1967–1972'. *Asian Survey*, vol. 12, no. 5, May, pp. 441–457.

Wanida Tantiwittayapitak (1999) 'Interview: the AOP's Movement is Non-Violent'. *Thai Development Newsletter*, July–December, pp. 50–51.

Zimmerman, R. (1974) 'Student "Revolution" in Thailand: The End of the Thai Bureaucratic Polity?' *Asian Survey*, vol. 14, no. 6, June, pp. 509–529.

Conference and Working Papers

Albritton, R and Thawilwadee Bureekul 2003 'Conflict Resolution in the Decision to Build the TransThaiMalasian Pipeline', a report prepared by the Croft International Studies Oxford, Missippi, USA and King Prajhadipok's Institute Bangkok, Thailand.

Baker, Chris (1999) 'Assembly of the Poor: The New Drama of Village, City and State'. Paper presented at the 7th International Conference on Thai Studies, Amsterdam, 4–8 July.

Chaiwat SathaAnand (2004) 'Fostering 'Authoritarian Democracy' with Violence: The Effect of Violent Solutions to Southern Violence in Thailand', paper presented at the 5 th National Conference on Politics and Public Administration, Bangkok, 12 December.

Hewison, K (1999) 'Thailand's Capitalism: The Impact of the Economic Crisis', UNEAC Asia Papers, No.1, pp. 2149.

Kasian Tejapira (1996) 'Globalizers vs Communitarians: Post-May 1992 Debates among Thai Public Intellectuals'. Paper prepared for the Annual Meeting of the U.S. Association for Asian Studies, Honolulu.

Madsen, Stig Toft (1999) 'Contestation and Consensus in Contemporary Thailand'. Paper presented at the 7th International Conference on Thai Studies, Amsterdam, July 4–8.

Missingham, Bruce (1996) 'Internal Colonialism and Environmental Conflict: The Case of Northeast Thailand'. Proceedings of the 6th International Conference on Thai Studies, Chiang Mai, Thailand.

Pasuk Phongpaichit and Chris Baker (2002) 'The Only Good Populist is a Rich Populist: Thaksin Shinawatra and Thailand's Democracy'. Working Papers Series No. 36, Southeast Asia Research Centre, City University of Hong Kong.

Ratana Tosakul Boonmathya (1999) 'Prachakhom: Civil Society in Thailand: The Case of Khon Kaen Assembly (KKCA)'. Proceedings of the 7th International Conference on Thai Studies, Amsterdam, 4–8 July.

Newspaper Articles

Ampa Santimetaneedol (1997) 'Teaching Sukhavit a Thing about Politics'. *Bangkok Post*, 1 September (http://www.bangkokpost.com).

Atiya Achakulwisut (1991) 'The Hidden Cost of Building a Dam'. *Bangkok Post*, 17 August, p. 21.

—— (1992) 'Villagers Exploited by Their Own Advocates'. *Bangkok Post*, 11 September, p. 29.

Bamrung Kayotha (1995a) 'Interview'. *Bangkok Post*, 30 July, p. 19.

Chakrit Ridmontri (1997) 'Forum Demands Defy an Immediate Solution'. *Bangkok Post*, 2 April (http://www.bangkokpost.com).

Charoon Thongnual (1995) 'The Farmers' Army'. *The Nation*, 12 February, p. B4.

Kiatisak Vorathaveetamrong (1995) 'Raising Cain: Farm Protest Reaches a Boil'. *The Nation*, 5 February, p. B6.

Matichon Sutsapda, 2 February, 1999, p. 9.

Matichon Sutsapda, 9 February, 1999, p. 1.

Nantiya Tangwisuttijit and Pennapa Hongthong (1998) 'Infighting Weakens Farmers' Unity'. *The Nation*, 24 June, p. A4.

Naowarat Suksamran (1995) 'Krong: Fighter for the People'. *Bangkok Post*, 20 November, p. 4.

Naowarat Suksamran and Suphavadee Susanpoonthong (1995) 'Farmers Seek to Help Themselves'. *Bangkok Post*, 3 February, p. 5.

Onnucha Hutasingh (1999) 'Trespassers Use New Strategy'. *Bangkok Post*, 14 February (http:// www.bangkokpost.com).

Pravit Rojanaphruk (1993a) 'All Roads Lead to Bangkok'. *The Nation*, 10 November, pp. C1–2.

—— (1993b) 'Wrong Way to a Right Question'. *The Nation*, 1 April, p. C1.

Sanitsuda Ekachai (1992a) 'Victory for the Rural Poor'. *Bangkok Post*, 9 July, p. 4.

—— (1992b) 'Silence No Longer'. *Bangkok Post*, 17 August, pp. 29, 31.

—— (1994) 'Grassroots Activists in a Quandary'. *Bangkok Post*, 11 July, p. 33.

Siam Rat Sudsabda, 25–31 October 1993, p. 9.

Sirimas Chalanuchpong (1994) 'Education for Life'. *The Nation*, 19 February, p. C1.

Supara Janchitfah (1995) 'Trapped in Debt Cycle'. *Bangkok Post*, 3 September, p. 17.

—— (2003) 'Enemies of the State?' Bangkok Post, January (http://www.thaigo/ngo_info/book_032.htm).

Supawadee Susanpoolthong (1995a) 'Native of Northeast Emerges as the Voice of Battling Farmers'. *Bangkok Post*, 1 May, p. 4.

—— (1995b) 'Bamrung's Resignation to Test Mettle of Farmers Action Body'. *Bangkok Post*, 25 October, p. 4.

Suthichai Yoon (1998) 'Rich-Poor Gap: Rhetoric and Reality'. *The Nation*, 23 June, p. A4.

Suvit Suvit-Sawasdi (1995) 'Conspiracy Behind Activist's Murder?' *Bangkok Post*, 16 July, p. 19.

—— (1997) 'We will be Back if Promises are Broken'. *Bangkok Post*, 4 May (http:// www.bangkokpost.com).

Tunya Sukpanich (1994) 'Protesting a United Plight'. *Bangkok Post*, 13 February, p. 24.

Wasant Techawongtham (1993) 'NGO Movement: An Angel or a Devil?' *Bangkok Post*, 13 October, p. 20.

Wut Nontharit (1996) 'Farmers in Plea to have Debts Cleared'. *Bangkok Post*, 10 November (http://www.bangkokpost.com).

Yaowares Suthapinthu (1995) 'Bamrung Aiming to Strengthen the Underprivileged'. *The Nation*, 7 February, p. A2.

Interviews

Individual Interviews

Amnat Wisuttigo	Member of the 14 October Network (15 May 1998).
Asok Prasansorn	Chairman of the Thai Farmers' Foundation (7 December 1997; 10 May 1998).
Auychai Wata	Former chairman of the Small Scale Farmers' Assembly of Isan, Chairman of the Assembly of Isan Farmers (11 September 1997).
Baramee Chairat	Advisor of the Assembly of the Poor (6 October 1997).
Boontom Uthaipan	Former Mahasarakham secretary general of the Small Scale Farmers' Assembly of Isan (1 October 1997).
Boonyoung Bucha	Member of Khon Kaen provincial committee of the Small Scale Farmers' Assembly of Isan (10 January 1998).
Chaluen Chanasongkram	Advisor of the Small Scale Farmers' Assembly of Isan (1 October 1997, 5 October 1997).
Kamon Ruenjit	Chairman of the Silk Worm Breeding Group in Chaiyaphum, (23 May 1998).
Ken Fanglit	Member of the Central Committee of the Small Scale Farmers' Assembly of Isan (27 February 1998; 13 March 1998; 9 May 1998; 11 May 1998).
Kong Thawiworn	Founding Member of the Small Scale Farmers' Assembly of Isan (4 October 1997).
Nakon Sriwipat	Secretary General of the Small Scale Farmers' Assembly of Isan (11 July 1997; 1 August 1997; 2 August 1997; 14 December 1997; 15 January 1998; 26 January 1998; 15 April 1998; 8 June 1998; 21 July 1998; 20 August 2001; 5 October 2002).
Nares Yuwarat	*Matichon*'s veteran reporter in Nakon Ratchasima (22 February 1998).
Niramit Sujaree	Former member of the Executive Committee of the Small Scale Farmers' Assembly of Isan, Leader of the Small Scale Farmers' Assembly of Isan (1) (10 September 1997).

Nong Ya Plong   farmer 10 January 1998.

Pakpum Witranteerawat Advisor of the Assembly of the Poor, (6 October 1997).

Prachuab Klangnog   Khon Kaen Secretary General of the Small Scale Farmers' Assembly of Isan, (14 June 1998).

Ratsapa Namlaow   Advisor of the Small Scale Farmers' Assembly of Isan (1) (8 July 1997; 24 August 1997; 27 February 1998; 8 July 1998).

Ronachit Tummong   Member of the Central Committee of the Small Scale Farmers'Assembly of Isan (13 October 1997; 11 July 1998, 15 July 1998).

Santi Uthaipan   Official of Agriculture and Cooperatives Ministry.

Somdej Panmuang   Former NGO worker (4 February 1998).

Somsiri Wongwinai   Advisor of the Small Scale Farmers' Assembly of Isan (1 August 1997; 2 November 1997; 14 December 1997; 7 January 1998; 8 January 1998; 6 March 1998).

Son Roobsung   Advisor of the Small Scale Farmers' Assembly of Isan (19 August 1997; 10 June 1998; 10 July 1998).

Supot Agkrarapram   Leader of the Assembly of Isan Farmers (10 September 1997).

Term Kotsuno   *Pho khrua yai* of the Assembly of the Poor in Khon Kaen (9 January 1998).

Teepakon Kanwit   Former Zone 3 Secretary General of the Small Scale Farmers' Assembly of Isan (17 May 1998).

Thawan Phuthawan   Lecturer, Faculty of Social Science and Humanities, Mahasarakham University (24 May 2000).

Thaweesilp Suebwattana Lecturer, Faculty of Social Science and Humanities, Mahasarakham University (5 November 2002).

Uthai Potduang   Yasothorn Secretary General of the Small Scale Farmers' Assembly of Isan (25 February 1998).

Werapon Sopa   Advisor of the Assembly of the Poor (5 February 1998).

Yang Wongkraso   Member of the Central Committee of the Small Scale Farmers' Assembly of Isan (10 March 1998; 10 August 2005).

Group interviews

Dong Lan Committee of the Small Scale Farmers' Assembly of Isan (14 June 1998).

Former CPT members in Mukdahan (18 March 1998).

Former CPT members in Udonthanee (10 December 1997).

Isan Folk singers in Khon Kaen (25 December 1997).

Isan Folk singers in Ubon (4 January 1998).

Nong Bua Lamphu Provincial Committee of the Small Scale Farmers' Assembly of Isan (7 December 1997).

Yasothorn Provincial Committee of the Small Scale Farmers' Assembly of Isan, (1 July 1998).

Index